The Motor Racing Year No. 3

By the same author

The Racing Sports Car
Porsche
Ford Versus Ferrari

The Motor Racing Year No. 3

Anthony Pritchard

PELHAM BOOKS

First published in Great Britain by
PELHAM BOOKS LTD
52 Bedford Square
London, W.C.1
1972

7207 0577 0

Printed in Great Britain by
Tonbridge Printers Ltd,
Peach Hall Works, Tonbridge, Kent
in Monotype 10 on 11 Baskerville,
on paper supplied by P. F. Bingham Ltd
and bound by James Burn at Esher, Surrey

Contents

Illustrations

Author's Note

The present edition of *The Motor Racing Year* follows the pattern established by its predecessors, that is an attempt to give an entertaining and comprehensive account of the season's Formula 1 and Sports Car Championship racing, supplemented by briefer accounts and results of other important categories of racing. Each year slight changes have been made to the presentation of the book, mainly as a result of readers' suggestions, and I do indeed welcome hearing from readers who have suggestions that will improve either the contents of *The Motor Racing Year* or its layout.

I am once again deeply indebted to Keith Davey for his considerable help in the preparation of the book and I am also grateful to Nigel Snowdon for his continued co-operation in supplying illustrations.

Part One
The Grand Prix Year

1 The Cars and Teams

Despite ever-improving safety facilities, the death roll among drivers of both single-seaters and sports cars has continued in 1971 and motor racing lost two of its most skilful and best loved personalities; poor Pedro Rodriguez was killed in the Nuremberg 200 race at the wheel of a Ferrari 512M entered by Herbert Müller and it seemed all the more tragic that this great Mexican driver, at the height of his powers, driving magnificently at the wheel of BRM Grand Prix cars and Gulf-Porsche 917 sports cars, should lose his life in such a trivial, insignificent race. It was Rodriguez' love of racing, as opposed to a constant pre-occupation with the financial rewards that could be derived from it, that resulted in him driving in this Interserie race and when he died, he was doing what he enjoyed most of all. It seemed ironic that Jo Siffert should die at the race held in celebration of the Stewart and Tyrrell victories in the World Championships. This was the first fatality at the wheel of a BRM since the team began racing in 1950, but Siffert was the second of the team's drivers to die during the season and loss of these two top *pilotes* was a terrible blow for BRM to take.

1971 was a season of Stewart and Tyrrell domination, of the ever-increasing skill of young Ronnie Peterson and the ever-improving performance of the March Grand Prix cars. It was a year in which BRM increased in strength and speed to win two World Championship races, when the Ferrari team sank into a state of confusion and despondency and their flat-12 cars, potentially the fastest and most powerful of all, recorded failure after failure. For Lotus victory was always round the corner, but was never attained, Brabham, Matra and McLaren fortunes were in the doldrums, Team Surtees displayed early promise that was never fulfilled and Frank Williams with his unlucky private March driven by Henri Pescarolo staggered from trouble to trouble as the season progressed. But despite their failures all these teams are racing again in 1972, with new money, new hopes and, in some cases, new drivers.

At the Oulton Park Gold Cup race in August, 1970 the new Tyrrell-Cosworth Formula One car designed by Derek Gardner had made its debut. It was subsequently driven in the trans-Atlantic Grands Prix by Jackie Stewart and although it displayed a tremendous turn of speed, it retired in all three races. By 1971 Ken Tyrrell's team had the new car fully sorted and at the South African Grand Prix there appeared a second car for the team's number two driver Francois Cevert. This new car featured a four inch-longer monocoque, a wheelbase increased by 1.5 in., a thicker outer skinning to the monocoque and a simpler non-tubular front bulkhead. The front suspension had been modified and featured new cast, lower wishbones. Subsequently a similar car was completed for Jackie Stewart to drive. Once the specification of the Tyrrell had been settled, few changes were made during the season, but at the French race at the Paul Ricard circuit the car appeared with a streamlined nose. Here this nose was used only by Stewart, but by the British race it had also been adopted on Cevert's car. At the Italian race Stewart's car was fitted with an alloy spacer that increased the wheelbase by 4.3 in. and in private practice before this race the radiator was mounted at the extreme rear of the car.

By a combination of superb preparation of the cars (not matched by any other team), excellent team management and with the services of the World's finest driver at the present time, Elf Team Tyrrell achieved a domination during the early part of the season that was close to demoralising some of the other teams and by the Austrian race the Drivers' and Manufacturers' Championships were in the bag. There is no doubt, however that the team is going to find it much more difficult to stay on top in 1972.

Tyrrell

SPECIFICATION

Engine: Cosworth V-8. *Gearbox:* Hewland FG400 5-speed. *Chassis:* open bathtub-type monocoque constructed in 16-gauge NS4 aluminium alloy. *Front suspension:* double wishbones and combined coil spring/damper units. *Rear suspension:* twin parallel lower links, single top links, twin radius arms and combined coil spring/damper units. *Wheels:* centre-lock magnesium-alloy, 13-in. front and 15-in. rear. *Brakes:* Girling 10.5-in. ventilated discs, mounted inboard at the rear. *Wheelbase:* 7 ft 11.7 in. *Front track:* 5 ft 3 in. *Rear track:* 5 ft 2.9 in./5 ft 4.9 in. *Weight:* 1,120 lb.

For the 1971 season the BRM team continued its relationship with its sponsors, Yardley Perfumery, and while Pedro Rodriguez remained with the team, his Gulf team-mate Jo Siffert was signed to replace Jack Oliver who had cost the team rather a lot in 1970 with bills for blown-up engines. Canadian George Eaton who had paid his own way with the team dropped out of the picture and his place was taken by New Zealander Howden Ganley who was sponsored by Barry Newman. BRM also signed John Miles as test driver and he appeared in only two races for the team, the Race of Champions and the Jochen Rindt Gedächtnis-Rennen at Hockenheim. Later in the season when BRM had plenty of cars at their disposal they hired drives to a number of people including Helmut Marko. Vic Elford was given a drive in the German Grand Prix and after the death of Pedro Rodriguez, the empty seat in the team was filled by Peter Gethin who had left McLaren.

Although BRM introduced the new P160 car in time for the South African Grand Prix, Jo Siffert continued to drive a 1970 P153 car until a second P160 was completed for him and Ganley drove a P153 for most of the season. The new car was a development of the existing model, but it was lower and wider, the gearbox was more compact and the half-shafts were lighter. There were a whole host of minor changes and the P160 was an improved car in almost every respect. BRM had working on new cylinder heads for the V-12 with bifurcated ports and although these appeared on at least one car at most races during the season, they were not standardised. Nor was the new and long-awaited short-stroke version of the V-12 engine raced, although it did appear in practice. At Monaco a new 'shovel' nose style was first seen in practice and this was fitted regularly to the P160 cars from Zandvoort onwards. After the first two P160 cars had been completed, it was realised that the monocoques were too wide to comply with the regulations that would be in force in 1972 and cars subsequently built were much narrower.

The cars' chances were often ruined by silly, niggling faults, but the V-12 engines proved to be amongst the most reliable and most powerful racing. With wins by Siffert at the Osterreichring and by Gethin at Monza and second places by Rodriguez at Zandvoort and by Siffert at Watkins Glen, the season was fairly satisfactory for the Bourne team, but they have yet to again achieve the level of success which they enjoyed during the years of the old 1500 cc Grand Prix Formula. In 1972 the BRM team is being sponsored by Marlboro cigarettes and in addition to first-string cars driven by

Beltoise, Gethin and Ganley, a second string team is fielding entries for Marko and Alex Soler-Roig.

BRM P160

SPECIFICATION

Engine: 60-degree V-12 of 2998 cc (74.6 × 57.2 mm) developing 445 bhp at 11,000 rpm. *Gearbox:* BRM P161 5-speed. *Chassis:* open bathtub-type monocoque, constructed from 18-gauge L72 alloy sheeting. *Front suspension:* unequal-length double wishbones and coil spring/damper units. *Rear suspension:* top links, parallel radius rods, lower reversed wishbones and coil spring/damper units. *Wheels:* centre-lock 13-in. front, 13/15-in. rear. *Brakes:* Girling 10.5-in. discs, ventilated at the front only and mounted inboard at the rear. *Wheelbase:* 8 ft 0 in. *Front track:* 4 ft 10 in. *Rear track:* 4 ft 9 in. *Weight:* 1168 lb.

STP-March — *Colour: red*

During 1970 the new March team from Bicester had enjoyed mixed fortunes and the make's best performance had been a win in the Spanish Grand Prix by Jackie Stewart at the wheel of a Tyrrell-entered car. For 1971 a new car, the 711, was developed and perhaps its most striking features were the smooth lines of the body (which were the work of aerodynamicist Frank Costin) and the prominent nose-mounted aerofoil. Although the cars were usually powered by Cosworth engines, March had come to an arrangement with Autodelta that they would also enter a car powered by an Alfa Romeo V-8 engine. In addition Ronnie Peterson drove a works car proper with an Alfa Romeo engine in the *Daily Express* Trophy race, the Jochen Rindt Gedächtnis-Rennen and the French Grand Prix. After a failure of one of the shafts driving the inboard-mounted front brakes at the Race of Champions, these were abandoned and conventional outboard front brakes adopted and over-heating experienced at Kyalami resulted in the abandonment of the streamlined nacelles enclosing the side-mounted radiators.

Ronnie Peterson headed the works team and although he failed to win a single Grand Prix during the season, on the strength of second places at Monaco, Silverstone, Monza and Mosport Park he took second place in the Drivers' Championship. The Alfa Romeo-powered car was driven by either Andrea de Adamich or 'Nanni' Galli and in the early part of the season Spaniard Alex Soler-Roig paid his way with a Cosworth-powered works car. After Soler-Roig became dissatisfied with the team's persistent shortage of engines and broke off his relationship with March, the team entered a third car at most races for 'Nanni' Galli. In addition to the works cars, 711s were fielded by Frank Williams for Henri Pescarolo to drive and at some races by Clarke Mordaunt Racing with Alistair Guthrie for Mike Beuttler and by Gene Mason for Skip Barber. A number of the old 701 cars were raced during the season, but they were hopelessly uncompetitive.

March 711

SPECIFICATION

Engine: Cosworth V-8. *Gearbox:* Hewland FG400 5-speed. *Chassis:* full monocoque with 16-gauge outer skin and 18-gauge inner skin constructed from NS4 aluminium alloy. *Front suspension:* double wishbones and inboard-mounted coil spring/damper units. *Rear suspension:* upper trailing arms with short adjustable top links, lower wishbones, adjustable track rods and outboard coil spring/damper units. *Wheels:* centre-lock magnesium-alloy, 13-in. front, 15-in. rear. *Brakes:* Girling 10.5-in. ventilated discs, originally mounted inboard front and rear. *Wheelbase:* 8 ft 2 in. *Front and rear track:* 5 ft 0 in. *Weight:* 1190 lb.

S.p.a. Ferrari SEFAC *Colour: red*

At the beginning of the 1971 season Ferrari continued to race the 312B cars that had enjoyed such a run of success in the latter part of the previous season, but in practice before the South African Grand Prix there appeared a new version that was so extensively revised that it was to all intents and purposes a new model. This was the 312B/2 with an engine having roller main bearings throughout and revving up to 12,800 rpm, and with a new chassis that was very wedge-shaped. The frontal area was rather smaller and although the monocoque was still stiffened by tubing, there were less tubes. Although the geometry was different, the front suspension was in essence very similar to that of the 1970 cars, but at the rear there was a completely new layout. The coil spring/damper units were now mounted almost horizontally across the back of the car and actuated by bell-crank top wishbones and there were single top radius rods and wide-based lower wishbones. The rear brakes were mounted inboard (which was the real reason for adopting the unconventional suspension) and the aerofoil was split in two parts so that either side could be adjusted independently.

The season could hardly have started better for Ferrari, but there was a lot of luck in the team's successes. Andretti only won the South African race after Hulme's McLaren broke in the closing laps, Regazzoni's victory in the Race of Champions with the new 312B/2 and Andretti's win in the Questor Grand Prix were mainly because the team took the right gamble on tyres while others did not and after these races the team's organisation appeared to disintegrate. After a second place by Ickx at Barcelona and a win in the wet at Zandvoort, the team's fortunes went from bad to worse, the drivers seemed happier with the 1970 car than the latest model, they were unable to match the Tyrrell's lap times even on high-speed circuits and the cars became less and less reliable. All three drivers Ickx, Regazzoni and Andretti had a thoroughly miserable season, but Ferrari has always thrived on failure and come back the next season with renewed vigour. There is every reason to suppose that in 1972 the Ferrari team will have forgotten its disasters of the previous year and will be well organised, well co-ordinated and one of the most difficult teams to beat.

Ferrari Tipo 312B/2

SPECIFICATION

Engine: flat-12 of 2998.5 cc (79.0 × 52.6 mm) with twin overhead camshafts per bank of cylinders, Lucas fuel injection, Marelli transistorised ignition and a power output of 470 bhp at 12,800 rpm. *Gearbox:* Ferrari 5-speed. *Chassis:* monocoque constructed from 16-gauge alloy with tubular stiffening. *Front suspension:* upper rocking arms, wide-based lower wishbones and inboard-mounted coil spring/damper units. *Rear suspension:* bell-crank top wishbones, lower wishbones, single upper radius rods and inboard-mounted coil spring/damper units. *Wheels:* centre-lock, magnesium-alloy 15-in. *Brakes:* discs, mounted inboard at the rear. *Wheelbase:* 7 ft 8.76 in. *Front and rear track:* 4 ft 6.5 in.

Gold Leaf Team Lotus — *Colour: red, white, and gold*

The mainstay of Lotus efforts in 1971 was the 72 model which first appeared at the Spanish race in April, 1970. This advanced car with its 'shovel' nose, inboard front brakes, mid-mounted radiator and torsion bar suspension had brought Jochen Rindt four successive victories before his death at Monza and there followed another win in the United States race for Emerson Fittipaldi. The finalised 1970 car was known as the 72C, but at Monaco in 1971 there appeared the 72D version with more conventional rear suspension by parallel lower links and twin radius rods (but still retaining torsion bars) and this layout became standardised on the cars driven by both Emerson Fittipaldi and Reine Wisell. Although very little success came the team's way (the best performance was a second by Fittipaldi in the Austrian race), both drivers tried hard with machinery that was not the most competitive and it is sad that Wisell has been dropped from the team in 1972 in favour of Australian Dave Walker.

In addition Lotus also fielded their 56B gas-turbine car at two Championship races (Zandvoort and Monza) and several less important events during the year. Originally it had been hoped to race this car in 1969 when it would have been very competitive, but in 1971 it proved no match for the latest conventional Formula 1 machinery. The 56B was a development of the 1968 Lotus 56 which had run at Indianapolis. From this car, the 56B derived its four-wheel-drive, its wedge-shape and its double wishbones and inboard-mounted coil spring/damper units front and rear. However the monocoque (which was of the simple 'bathtub'-type) was constructed of lighter 18 and 20-gauge alloy (instead of the 16-gauge demanded at Indianapolis) and the Canadian-Built Pratt & Whitney gas-turbine was extensively modified. To comply with FIA equivalency formula for Formula 1 cars, one of the axial compressor stages was eliminated and the area of the high-pressure nozzle reduced. Total fuel capacity was 62 gallons in side tanks.

In 1972 Lotus is racing improved versions of the 72 known as 'John Player Specials', but it seems unlikely that much success will be achieved.

Lotus 72D

SPECIFICATION

Engine: Cosworth V-8. *Gearbox:* Hewland FG400 5-speed. *Chassis:* aluminium-alloy monocoque constructed from 18-gauge magnesium-alloy (outer panels) and 20-gauge (inner panels) with the front part of the frame reinforced by a steel sub-frame. *Front suspension:* torsion bars operated by a link system connected to the upper of the unequal-length double wishbones. *Rear suspension:* torsion bars, parallel lower rear links and twin radius rods. *Wheels:* light alloy 13-in. front, 15-in. rear. *Brakes:* 10.5-in. discs mounted inboard front and rear. *Wheelbase:* 8 ft 4 in. *Front and Rear track:* 4 ft 9 in. *Weight:* approx. 540 kg.

Bruce McLaren Motor Racing *Colour: orange*

Mainly because of the team's preoccupation with Can-Am racing and with their Indianapolis programme, Formula 1 racing took something of a back seat at Colnbrook in 1971. Although Hulme led the South African Grand Prix until shortly before the finish, the cars failed to repeat this form in later races and the new M19A model could at best be described as a qualified success. The work of Frank Bellamy an Australian who had previously worked three years for Brabham, the M19A was produced after a design by Jo Marquart (he left to start the Huron Prototype project) to succeed the existing M14A had been abandoned. Work on the new car did not start until November, 1970, but progressed so well that the first car was ready in time to compete in the South African Grand Prix in March.

The new car incorporated the wheels, hub carriers, suspension uprights and steering from the M14A, but there was a new, low, wide monocoque of the style pioneered by the 1969 Matra MS80 so that the fuel load remained near the centre of gravity throughout the race. However the truly novel feature of the design was the suspension which was designed to give progressive rate springing and ride height adjustment without altering spring travel. There is a triangulated wishbone at the front mounted between the two halves of the double steel bulkhead; this wishbone actuates a short pull-rod, actuating in turn a cast rocking arm with one end pivoted on the chassis and the other bolted to the upper spring eye. The spring deflection increases on bump, giving the variable rate. On the pull-rod there are screwed ends which allow speedy adjustments of ride height. Although the rear suspension is of fairly conventional appearance, the inboard-mounted coil spring/damper units are actuated by long adjustable push-rods running from the bottoms of the hub carriers and these operate cast rocking arms similar to those at the front. In this manner the ride height is easily adjustable.

Although the M19A showed tremendous promise in its first race and Hulme led at Kyalami until a few laps before the finish, the team's preoccupation with the Indianapolis cars and with its Can-Am programme resulted in the Grand Prix efforts being somewhat over-shadowed. Clearly the new suspension was not as successful as had been hoped and by the Austrian race one of the cars was fitted with conventional M14A suspension and by the Canadian race this had been adopted on both M19As. The loss of Gethin to BRM by the Austrian race, the decision to field only a single M14A for Jack Oliver at Monza and the sale of one of the M19As to Roger Penske in time for the Canadian race were all factors contributing to a season that seemed somewhat half-hearted and was certainly unsuccessful. Indeed Donohue's third place with the Penske car in the Canadian race was the best McLaren performance of the year. McLaren have now signed a three-year contract with Yardley and with Peter Revson joining Hulme in the Formula 1 team, there seems little doubt that McLaren's efforts in 1972 will be both more determined and more successful.

McLaren M19A

SPECIFICATION

Engine: Cosworth V-8. *Gearbox:* Hewland FG400 or DG300 5-speed. *Chassis:* full monocoque with Reynolds aluminium 16 swg double curvature side panels, 18-gauge forward upper portion and 20-gauge rear section and with steel bulkheads. *Front suspension:* tubular double wishbones (upper triangulated), pull-rods and rocking arms and inboard coil spring/damper units. *Rear suspension:* single transverse upper rods, lower reversed wishbones, double radius arms, push-rods and rocker arms and inboard coil spring/damper units. *Wheels:* centre-lock, cast magnesium-alloy, 13-in. front, 13/15-in. rear. *Brakes:* Lockheed 10.5-in. ventilated discs mounted outboard at the front, 10.4-in. ventilated discs mounted inboard at the rear. *Wheelbase:* 8 ft 4 in. *Front track:* 5 ft 3 in. *Rear track:* 5 ft 2 in. *Weight:* 1230 lb.

Équipe Matra — *Colour: blue*

For 1971 Matra lost their contract with the Elf oil company and signed up Chris Amon as joint number one driver with Jean-Pierre Beltoise (but did not re-engage Henri Pescarolo). Otherwise there were few changes at Vélizy and the team raced a slightly modified version of the 1970 MS120 known as the MS120B. A great deal of detailed development work was carried out on the V-12 engine which had first been raced in 1968 and this included new cam-shafts, modifications to the inlet porting, an improved exhaust system and improved lubrication. Even so, power output was never in excess of 450 bhp (and usually more like 430 bhp), the engines were supposed to rev. to 12,000 rpm (but this usually resulted in valve-spring trouble) and they were far from reliable. Apart from Amon's win in the non-Championship Argentine Grand Prix at the beginning of the year, no success came Matra's way and Beltoise missed several races because of the suspension of his licence. The team missed the Austrian race so as to concentrate on development work and although Amon then ran very well in the Italian Grand Prix, the team's next outing, the team was back to square one at the Canadian race. At the present time Matra (and their sponsors Chrysler-France) are spending a great deal of money on their Grand Prix programme and seeing very little return. Since the team entered Formula 1 in 1968 the best performances by the V-12-powered cars have been Beltoise's second place at Zandvoort in that year and Amon's win at Buenos Aires. It seems unlikely that Matra will pursue their Formula 1 programme for much longer unless substantial success comes their way soon.

Matra MS120B

SPECIFICATION

Engine: 60-degree V-12 of 2993 cc (79.7 × 50.1 mm) with four valves per cylinder, Lucas fuel injection and a power output of 430 bhp at 10,000 rpm. *Gearbox:* Hewland FG400 5-speed. *Chassis:* monocoque structure built in aluminium-alloy, formed by two main pontoons without partitions and engine acting as stressed member and locating rear suspension. *Front suspension:* double wishbones with combined coil spring/damper units. *Rear suspension:* parallel lower links, single top links, twin radius arms and combined coil spring/damper units. *Wheels:* 13-in. magnesium-alloy front and rear. *Brakes:* Girling 10.5-in. ventilated discs. *Wheelbase:* 8 ft 0 in. *Front and rear track:* 5 ft 3 in. *Weight:* 448 kg.

Team Surtees *Colours: white and dark blue*

In 1971 Team Surtees arranged sponsorship by Brooke Bond-Oxo and Rob Walker for the car driven by John Surtees, while a second car for German driver Rolf Stommelen was sponsored by the German magazine *Auto Motor und Sport* and the Eifelland Caravans concern. Although the 1970 TS7 model appeared under the works banner at a couple of races (and was also hired out), the team produced a new model known as the TS9. This was of basically similar specification, but the monocoque, while retaining the familiar Surtees razor-edge shape, was lower and flatter in appearance (the car was two inches lower at the scuttle), the wheelbase was three inches longer, the track an inch wider and the suspension pick-up points were changed.

Generally the season was very disappointing for the Surtees team. 'Big' John himself seemed unable to match the improved form he had shown with his McLaren and with the first Surtees TS7 in 1970 and Rolf Stommelen, one of the more temperamental of current Formula 1 drivers, seemed unhappy with his car, at loggerheads with Surtees and unable to match the performances he had turned in the previous season with the Brabham BT33. Apart from a fifth by Surtees at Zandvoort and fifth and sixth places by Stommelen and Surtees at Silverstone, the only successes to come the regular team's way during the 1971 season were Surtees' win in the poorly supported Oulton Park Gold Cup race and third places by the same driver in the Race of Champions and at Hockenheim. That the shortcomings were in the cockpit of the cars rather than in the cars themselves was made only too obvious in the latter part of the season when Mike Hailwood appeared for the team. In the Italian race he was up with the leaders all the way and finished fourth and he ran well at Watkins Glen until a deflating tyre caused him to spin off. In 1972 the team's regular drivers will be Mike Hailwood and Tim Schenken (Surtees himself has now retired from Grand Prix racing) and the chances of success for the Edenbridge concern are much enhanced.

Surtees TS9

SPECIFICATION

Engine: Cosworth V-8. *Gearbox:* Hewland DG400 5-speed. *Chassis:* monocoque structure with tubular frame at the front carrying the radiator and engine and gearbox forming the rear of the structure. *Front suspension:* fabricated upper links, tubular lower wishbones and inboard coil spring/damper units. *Rear suspension:* upper links, radius arms, lower links and outboard coil spring/damper units. *Wheels:* centre-lock, magnesium-alloy, 13-in. front, 15-in. rear. *Brakes:* Girling 10.5-in. ventilated discs, mounted inboard at the rear. *Wheelbase:* 8 ft 3.75 in. *Front track:* 5 ft 0 in. *Rear track:* 5 ft 1 in. *Weight:* 1340 lb.

Motor Racing Developments — *Colours: turquoise and yellow*

Although Graham Hill, Brabham's number one driver and his team-mate at the South African race only, Dave Charlton, both drove the 1970 BT33 cars at Kyalami, at the Race of Champions at Brands Hatch there appeared the new and very advanced BT34 model. The BT33 had been Brabham's first monocoque Formula 1 car and although the new model incorporated a considerable number of lessons learned from this, there were also substantial differences. After carrying out wind-tunnel tests, designer Ron Tauranac decided that it would be best to mount twin radiators at the front of the car and this system, apart from possessing excellent aerodynamics, made it possible to mount the front aerofoil between the radiator extensions (or 'lobster-claws' as they became known) in which position it was considered to be much more effective because conventional fins are affected at their tips by the disturbed air from the front tyres; an additional factor was that the air flow had lost much of its energy as it passed through the radiators before it encountered the front suspension and this reduced buffeting. In addition the car had a rather box-like shape (in complete contrast to the BT33 and earlier cars) because of the use of rectangular side fuel tanks which Tauranac believed to be much safer; these are less likely to deform and can be built up from a single sheet of metal with only one seam.

Hill drove the new car throughout the season, but he was never really happy with it, infinitely preferring the existing BT33, and his only worthwhile performances were on the car's debut at the Race of Champions (where he retired with engine trouble when in third place) and in the *Daily Express* Trophy race which he won. Schenken drove the BT33, fitted from the Nürburgring onwards with a full-width nose cowling. The Australian was almost inevitably faster in practice than his former World Champion teammate and usually better placed in the race before mechanical troubles intervened. It was Schenken, with a third place at the Österreichring, who turned in the marque's best Championship race performance of the season. By the Oulton Park Gold Cup race an ex-works BT33 had been acquired by Ecurie Evergreen for Chris Craft to drive, but this achieved no success, mainly because of Craft's inexperience in this class of racing.

Brabham BT34

SPECIFICATION

Engine: Cosworth V-8. *Gearbox:* Hewland FG400 5-speed. *Chassis:* monocoque structure with inner shell having sloping sides forming the cockpit and outer skin enclosing the fuel bag tanks. *Front suspension:* wide-based upper wishbones, tubular lower wishbones and outboard coil spring/damper units. *Rear suspension:* single transverse top links, lower reversed wishbones, twin radius arms and outboard coil spring/damper units. *Wheels:* centre-lock magnesium-alloy, 13-in. front, 15-in. rear. *Brakes:* Girling 10.5-in. ventilated discs. *Wheelbase:* 7 ft 11 in. *Front track:* 5 ft 2 in. *Rear track:* 5 ft 3 in.

Generally the 1971 season was one of rationalisation rather than revolution, with all the teams using the familiar Cosworth V-8 engine that appeared back in 1967 enjoying rather better reliability than in 1970 and the latest 11-series version of the engine proving a match for the 12-cylinder units that had threatened to topple it from power. One problem that was only too obvious during the year was the tremendous vibration trouble caused by the latest very wide, low profile tyres and despite the many and various anti-vibration devices used by the teams during the year, this was a problem that was never mastered.

2 The Drivers

Jackie (John) Stewart (World Champion, 62 points)

Born: Milton, Dunbartonshire, 1939. Drove Formula 1 BRM, 1965–7; Matra-Cosworth, 1968–9 (1969 World Champion); March and Tyrrell-Cosworth 1970; Tyrrell-Cosworth, 1971.

Throughout 1970 Stewart had struggled rather unhappily with his somewhat unwieldy and ill-handling Tyrrell-entered March and then at the last three Championship races of the season he had appeared with the new Tyrrell car designed by Gardner. With this very competitive car he led two of the races and held second place in the third until mechanical troubles brought his fast runs to a halt. It was the same story in 1971, but with the substantial difference that the Tyrrell was now fully sorted. Backed by Ken Tyrrell's meticulous and incomparable standards of preparation work, Jackie Stewart dominated the season's racing. His superb, fast, accurate and consistent drives at Barcelona and Monaco set the pattern that he was to maintain on faster circuits. Even on the high-speed Paul Ricard circuit, scene of the French Grand Prix, he had the legs of the theoretically faster Ferrari opposition and such was the superiority of this car/driver combination that the Ferrari team was morally defeated before it even arrived at the circuit – just the sort of situation that prevailed in 1954–5 when Fangio and the works Mercedes drove the Ferrari and Maserati opposition into the ground. At only one circuit did Stewart fail to maintain a true Champion's standards. His car at the Dutch Grand Prix at Zandvoort was not properly set up for wet-weather racing and his tyres proved, in these conditions, inferior to those of his rivals. Instead of fighting like a true champion Stewart trailed unhappily, not battling with the spirit that a Moss or a Fangio would have displayed under similar conditions. But despite this one lapse during an otherwise great season, Stewart is the fastest and most consistent Grand driver at the present time.

Ronnie Peterson (33 points)

Born: Sweden, 1944. Drove Antique Automobiles March, 1970; works March, 1971

Although Peterson drove a March entered by Colin Crabbe's Antique Automobiles concern in 1970, he was then in the first year of his three-year contract with March and at that time March designer and director Robin Herd predicted that Peterson would win the World Championship within three years. On the strength of his second Grand Prix season as March team-leader, Peterson is well on the way to fulfilling that prediction. His driving in 1971 was fast, courageous and very consistent and although he failed to win a single Grand Prix, his second places at Monaco, Silverstone, Monza and Mosport Park, coupled with a third place at Watkins Glen brought him second place in the Championship. In some ways his driving is, perhaps, still a little green, he was thoroughly out-foxed by Gethin at Monza and he still has a lot to learn about tactics and race strategy, but if the car provided by Herd for the 1972 season is good enough, that apparently rather reckless prediction could well be fulfilled. In addition to driving Formula 1 cars, Peterson won the 1971 European Formula 2 Championship with March 712 cars, he was co-winner with an Alfa Romeo in the Watkins Glen Six Hours race and in 1972 he is a member of the Ferrari Sports Car team.

Francois Cevert (26 points)

Born: Paris, 1944. Drove Tecno Formula 2 cars, 1969–71; Tyrrell-entered March-Cosworth, 1970; Tyrrell-Cosworth, 1971.

In 1971 Cevert proved beyond any shadow of doubt that he was more than just the pretty face that had attracted the attentions of Brigitte Bardot. Although finishing one place lower down in the Championship than Peterson, his overall successes were as great. Throughout 1970 and the early part of the 1971 season he had been learning all the time from team-leader Stewart, just as Moss learned from Fangio in 1955 and Collins from the Argentinian maestro in 1956. Just like Moss had in 1955, Cevert was instructed to follow in his leader's wheel-tracks and he was content to do so. He took second places to Stewart at both the Paul Ricard circuit and the Nürburgring, he finished third at Monza and rounded off a fine season with a victory in the United States race, the most lucrative of all Championship Formula 1 races. Quiet, unassuming and determined to do well, yet content with his role as number two to Stewart, Cevert is a great driver in the making and there is no doubt that many victories will come his way in the future.

Jackie (Jaques-Bernard) Ickx (19 points)

Born: Brussels, 1945. Drove Matra Formula 2 car entered by Tyrrell, 1967 (European Championship winner); Ferrari Formula 1 car, 1968; Brabham, 1969; Ferrari, 1970-1.

During the years 1967–70, Ickx' successes rose in a gradual crescendo. In 1967 he enjoyed a fine run of success in Formula 2 and appeared a couple of times at the wheel of works Formula 1 Cooper-Maseratis; in 1968 he joined the Ferrari team and scored a brilliant victory in the rain-soaked French Grand Prix at Rouen; the following year he switched to Brabham, won the German and Canadian races and took second place in the Championship – as well as winning at Le Mans with Jack Oliver at the wheel of a Wyer-entered Ford; for 1970 he reverted to Maranello and after a lot of bad luck early in the season while the new flat-12 Ferrari was still being sorted, he scored victories at the Österreichring, Mont Tremblant and Mexico City and took second place in the Championship. If any driver seemed destined to achieve World Championship honours in 1971, it was Ickx. But Andretti won for Ferrari at Kyalami and in the Questor race, Regazzoni was the victor at Brands Hatch and Stewart beat Ickx at both Barcelona and Monte Carlo. True, Ickx was the victor for Ferrari in the very wet Dutch race, but the challenge to his supremacy in the Ferrari team and the domination of Stewart and the Tyrrell seemed to strike at Ickx' confidence and rarely did he go effectively during the remainder of the season (even when the flat-12s were going well which was rare enough in itself). Only in Sports Car racing was the same, fast, confident Ickx to be seen and his performance in the opening laps of the Nürburgring 1000 Km race will be remembered for a long time. If Ickx is to repeat the great form he showed in 1969–70, he has a lot of lost ground to make up. Jackie stays with Ferrari in 1972 and it is to be hoped that both cars and driver are able to re-capture their former greatness and give the Cosworth-powered opposition a good run for their money.

Jo Siffert (19 points)

Born: Fribourg, Switzerland, 1937. Drove private and Rob Walker-entered Lotus, Brabham and Cooper cars, 1962–9; works March, 1970; works BRM, 1971.

Undoubtedly one of the two greatest Sports Car drivers of recent years, Siffert was a tower of strength in both the Gulf-Porsche and BRM teams (just as was his team-mate Pedro Rodriguez) and the deaths of these two fine drivers in one unhappy season was a terrible blow to the sport. Few drivers have given the spectators as much pleasure as did Siffert and Rodriguez, their ability to master the Porsche 917 was unmatched and their determination when the odds were against them was unequalled by any of their rivals. During 1968 Jo Siffert had also proved himself one of the fastest of Grand Prix drivers and had scored a well-deserved victory in the British race. The following year he was still well up with the leaders and took a third at Monaco and a second place at Zandvoort. There had followed a year of complete failure with March when in race after race he started with a poor engine and retired with engine trouble. For 1971 he switched to BRM and although it was Rodriguez who set the pace for the Bourne team in the early part of the season, 'Seppi' gradually came into his own; he scored a magnificent victory at the Osterreichring and he finished second at Watkins Glen. Siffert's fortunes were definitely improving, the BRM team was going from strength to strength and it seemed that he would enjoy a truly successful season in 1972. Then at the last race of the season, the Rothmans World Championship Victory Race at Brands Hatch, his car went out of control for no reason as yet satisfactorily explained, hit the bank and burst into flames. While the inferno blazed, motor racing lost one of its most colourful and popular personalities.

Emerson Fittipaldi (16 points)

Born: Brazil, 1947. Drove works Lotus-Cosworth cars, 1970–1.

Young Fittipaldi made his Formula 1 debut with an old Lotus 49C car in the 1970 British Grand Prix, but at Watkins Glen, following the death of Jochen Rindt in practice for the Italian race, he appeared as the Lotus number one driver and scored his first World Championship race victory. There was no hope of this fine driver continuing to achieve success at this level in 1971, for the Lotus 72D was no match for the latest Tyrrell and March opposition, but Fittipaldi is a driver who will undoubtedly enjoy considerable success in the future. He remains with the Lotus team in 1972.

Clay Regazzoni (13 points)

Born: Switzerland, 1940. Drove Formula 2 Tecno, 1968 and 1970; Formula 2 Ferrari, 1969; Formula 1 Ferrari, 1970–1.

Regazzoni achieved almost unmatched success for a driver in his first season of Grand Prix racing in 1970; he took fourth places in his first two Formula 1 races at Zandvoort and Brands, won the Italian race, was second at Mexico City and capped this magnificent season with victory in the European Formula 2 Championship. Like Ickx, Regazzoni has had to suffer Ferrari unreliability in 1971, that he is a fine driver remains undisputed, but he is a Ferrari man through and through and his future fortunes rest firmly in Maranello's hands.

Mario Andretti (12 points)

Born: Italy, 1940, emigrated to the United States, 1964; Indianapolis winner, 1969; drove Lotus-Cosworth Formula 1 cars in odd races in 1968–9; STP-March, 1970; works Ferrari, 1971.

Considered by Colin Chapman to be potentially one of the greatest Formula 1 drivers, little Mario Andretti has still driven in insufficient Formula 1 races to show his true potential and like Ickx and Regazzoni he suffered Ferrari unreliability in 1971. In addition to his USAC commitments which prevented him from running in the French, British, Austrian, Italian and United States races, he failed to qualify at Monaco because of mechanical trouble. Nevertheless his victories at Kyalami and in the Questor race revealed him to be a driver of both restraint and considerable skill. However, the words written in last year's edition of this book, 'However great his potential may be, it seems unlikely that it will be fulfilled unless he drives regularly in Formula 1 at the expense of his American racing commitments', still remain true.

Chris Amon (9 points)

Born: Bulls, New Zealand, 1943. Drove Formula 1 Lola and Lotus-BRM for Parnell team, 1963–5; Cooper, 1966; Ferrari, 1967–9; March, 1970; Matra, 1971.

No driver has worse luck, no driver has less chance to show his true ability than Chris Amon who has switched from team to team, each time moving on just as the team he is leaving is about to achieve success. So despairing of the shortcomings of his underpowered Matra was Amon in 1971 that he did not always seem to give of his best. Apart from his win in the non-Championship Argentine Grand Prix, 1971 was another completely wasted season for the talented New Zealander. One can only hope that Matra sort out their many problems for the 1972 season and Amon can at last achieve the substantial success that he so much deserves.

Peter Gethin (9 points)

Born: Epsom, 1941. Drove Formula 2 Brabham, 1968; Formula

5000 McLaren, 1969–70; Formula 1 McLaren, 1970; Formula 1 McLaren and BRM, 1971.

During the early part of the season while he was driving for the McLaren team, Gethin achieved little success, but after joining BRM to replace Pedro Rodriguez he scored a fine victory at Monza. Since Gethin entered Formula 1 in 1970, he has failed to show the same promise as others of the up-and-coming school of drivers and one feels that his true role is that of the steady, sober number two driver (the sort of driver which BRM's multi-car policy seems so happily to embrace) and that he will never achieve many outright wins.

Denis Hulme (9 points)

Born: Te Puke, New Zealand, 1936. Drove Formula 1 Brabhams, 1965–7 (1967 World Champion); Formula 1 McLarens, 1968–70.

Since Bruce McLaren's death in 1970, much of the zest seems to have gone from Dennie's driving (which is hardly surprising) and in 1971 with a car that was not the most competitive and with McLaren's heavy commitments at Indianapolis and in Can-Am racing little success came his way and it seemed that Formula 1 was playing a very secondary role in the life of both Hulme and the McLaren team as a whole. Now that the team has won a three-year sponsorship contract with Yardley this may all change and 1972 may well see Hulme fighting it out in front once more.

Pedro Rodriguez (9 points)

Born: Mexico, 1940. Drove Formula 1 Cooper-Maserati, 1967. BRM, 1968; Ferrari occasionally in 1969; BRM, 1970–1.

Until his death in the Nuremberg 200 Interserie race in July, Pedro Rodriguez was the mainstay of the BRM team. Always trying hard, usually doing fairly well and displaying his usual mastery in the wet. He was fourth at Barcelona, second in the wet at Zandvoort and lying second when forced to retire by coil failure at the Paul Ricard circuit. There is no doubt that Rodriguez would have won at least once race during the season, if his career had not been so horribly and abruptly terminated.

Reine Wisell (9 points)

Born: Sweden, 1943. Drove Chevron Formula 3 car, 1969; McLaren Formula 5000 and Lotus Formula 1 cars, 1970; Lotus Formula 1 car, 1971.

Some people regard Wisell's driving as displaying occasional brilliance but with rather disappointing lapses. This view is not shared by this writer who regards Wisell as a safe, consistent and thoroughly reliable driver. Unhappily he left the Lotus team at the end of the season. Wisell merits a Formula 1 drive with a competitive car and it is to be hoped that another team will soon offer him a place.

Tim Schenker (5 points)

Born: Australia, 1943. Drove de Tomaso Formula 1 car in certain races and Formula 2 Brabham, 1970.

As number two in the Brabham team and with the older and less competitive 1970 BT33 car, Schenken consistently outshone his team-leader Graham Hill; he is another driver of great determination, but considerable restraint. He may never achieve the greatness that seems destined for Peterson, Cevert and Fittipaldi, but he will be an asset to any team that engages him, reliable hard-working and ambitious. He has now left Brabham and is driving for Team Surtees in 1972.

Howden Ganley (5 points)

Born: New Zealand, 1942. Drove McLaren Formula 5000 car, 1970; Formula 1 BRM, 1971.

Ganley's place in the BRM team was privately sponsored by Barry Newman and the young New Zealander justified his sponsor's confidence by displaying the same qualities as Schenken. Throughout the season these two drivers were closely matched, with Schenken usually just having the upper hand in skill and speed, but a less reliable car. Ganley remains with BRM in 1972.

Mark Donohue (4 points)

Donohue's sole Formula 1 drive in 1971 was in the Canadian Grand Prix in which he appeared at the wheel of a McLaren M19A entered by Roger Penske. This very experienced American driver (but without Formula 1 experience) took a superb third place. He is undoubtedly a driver of considerable ability and if he were to persist with Formula 1 racing a lot of success would come his way.

Henri Pescarolo (4 points)

Born: France, 1942. Drove Matra Prototype, Formula 2 and Formula 1 cars, 1968–70; Frank Williams-entered March Formula 1 car, 1971.

Throughout 1971 Pescarolo struggled hard to do well with his private March, but the car was consistently in mechanical trouble and very little success was gained. Pescarolo will never be a great driver, but with a reliable car he is the sort of driver who will consistently finish in the first six.

Mike Hailwood (3 points)

Another driver whose Formula 1 appearances have been few and far between. In 1971 his only Grand Prix appearances were at Monza and Watkins Glen where he went well with a works Surtees TS9. He is leading the Surtees team in 1972 and can be expected to be well up with the leaders at most races.

Rolf Stommelen (3 points)

Born: Köln, Germany, 1943. Drove Porsche Sports Cars, 1964–9; Brabham Formula 1 car, 1970; Surtees Formula 1 car, 1971.

After a promising first Formula 1 season with Brabham in 1970, Stommelen's sponsored drive was switched to Team Surtees for 1971. Throughout the season he seemed unhappy with his car and unhappy with the team. No success worth speaking of came his way, although he has a fair amount of ability as his Sports Car drives for Alfa Romeo in 1971 have continued to show. He is again competing in Formula 1 in 1972, but with a special, modified March car.

John Surtees (3 points)

Born: Tatsfield, England, 1934. Drove Formula 1 Lotus, 1960; Lola, 1962; Ferrari, 1963–6 (1964 World Champion); Cooper, 1966; Honda, 1967–8; BRM, 1969; private McLaren and Surtees 1970; Surtees, 1971.

Just like team-mate Stommelen, Surtees was out of luck in 1971. Although the cars suffered a lot of mechanical trouble, it seemed that 'Big John's' business commitments prevented him from concentrating on his racing as much as he would have liked and he has now decided to retire from Formula 1. A very wise decision.

Graham Hill (2 points)

Born: London, 1929. Drove Formula 1 Lotus, 1958–9; Formula 1 BRM, 1960–6; works Formula 1 Lotus, 1967–8; Rob Walker-entered Lotus, 1970; works Brabham, 1971 (1962 and 1968 World Champion).

Now the oldest of the regular Grand Prix drivers and with the greatest experience in Formula 1 racing, Hill has been out of luck ever since he won his last World Championship. His last major

At Montjuich Park, one of the most picturesque circuits used in the World Championship series, Jackie Stewart and his Tyrrell head for the first of a long string of 1971 victories. (Nigel Snowdon)

1971 was an unsatisfactory season for Ferrari and his cars failed to match the speed and reliability of the Tyrrells. Here Andretti is seen in practice at Monaco where he failed to qualify as a starter because of mechanical trouble during the only dry practice session. (Nigel Snowdon)

One of the most brilliant drivers of the 1971 season was young Ronnie Peterson, seen here at Monaco where he took second place with his March 711. (Nigel Snowdon)

For much of the 1971 season the Brabham team-leader Graham Hill was plagued by misfortune and he was twice eliminated in accidents that were not his fault. Here he is seen at the wheel of the 'lobster-claw' BT34 car at Zandvoort. (Nigel Snowdon)

race victory was at Monaco in 1969, but he won the *Daily Express* Trophy race at Silverstone in 1971. For much of the season, however, he seemed thoroughly unhappy with the new Brabham BT34, he was, as mentioned, slower than team-mate Schenken, and at times it seemed that he just did not want to race. He is in fact leading the Brabham team again 1972 (but at the wheel of the BT33 car which he much prefers), but it does seem that his most sensible course would be to retire while his reputation stands high.

Jean-Pierre (*Maurice George*) *Beltoise* (1 point)

Born: Paris, 1937. Drove Matra Formula 2 cars, 1967–8 (1968 European Formula 2 Champion); Matra V-12 Formula One car, 1968; Tyrrell-entered Matra MS80 Formula 1 car, 1969; Matra MS 120 V-12 cars, 1970–1.

In a season ruined by the terrible accident in the Buenos Aires Sports car race that resulted in his licence being twice suspended, Beltoise's chances of success were further ruined by the unreliability of the V-12 Matra and no success came his way. Beltoise is a popular figure in racing circles and everyone wishes that his fortunes will much improve in 1972.

3 The World Championship Grands Prix

ROUND ONE

SOUTH AFRICAN GRAND PRIX

Kyalami (Circuit length: 2.55 miles) 6th March, 1971
Race length: 201.45 miles (79 laps) Weather: dry and hot

Since the 1970 race there had been no changes to the circuit, but, as usual, it was one of the most pleasant and well organised races of the season. The organisers had spent almost £100,000 on starting and appearance money – a substantial sum by any standards – but this was a race with many attractions besides mere money and warm sunshine and it is always popular with teams and drivers. As with the previous year when a total of seven new models appeared, there were several new cars running at Kyalami including the March 711s, the new McLaren M19A, one BRM P160 for Rodriguez and a new TS9 from Team Surtees. The week before the race another new car, the Ferrari 312B/2, had appeared at a testing session at the circuit, but this was almost written off when Regazzoni spun the car into an earth bank.

THE ENTRY

(As at many races in 1971 the No. 1 was left blank in the entry list as a tribute to Jochen Rindt, the posthumous World Champion).

Gold Leaf Team Lotus:

2. E. Fittipaldi (Lotus 72C-Cosworth, chassis no. R5)
3. R. Wisell (Lotus 72C-Cosworth, chassis no. R3)

S.p.a. Ferarri SEFAC:

4. J. Ickx (Ferrari 312B, chassis no. 001)
5. C. Regazzoni (Ferrari 312B, chassis no. 004)
6. M. Andretti (Ferrari 312B, chassis no. 002)

STP-March:

7. R. Peterson (March 711-Cosworth, chassis no. 02)
8. A. de Adamich (March 711-Alfa Romeo, chassis no. 01)
26. A. Soler-Roig (March 711-Cosworth, chassis no. 04)

Elf Team Tyrrell:

9. J. Stewart (Tyrrell-Cosworth, chassis no. 001)
10. F. Cevert (Tyrrell-Cosworth, chassis no. 002)

Since 1970 the name of the team had been changed to emphasise the Elf sponsorship – and the loss of it by Matra – and the cars were now painted a much darker shade of blue. At a tyre testing session at Kyalami in February Stewart had covered some 1400 miles and then crashed 001, but it had now been completely rebuilt. Cevert's car was a new model with a lengthened wheelbase and many other changes.

Bruce McLaren Motor Racing:

11. D. Hulme (McLaren M19A-Cosworth, chassis no. M19A/1)
12. P. Gethin (McLaren M14A-Cosworth, chassis no. M14A/1)

Motor Racing Developments:

14. G. Hill (Brabham BT33-Cosworth, chassis no. BT33/1)
15. D. Charlton (Brabham BT33-Cosworth, chassis no. BT33/3)

For the first time the team was running with thirteen-inch rear wheels. Although Hill's car bore the chassis number of a 1970 model, it had a completely new monocoque and was to all intents and purposes a new car. Dave Charlton, the South African Formula One Champion was included in the team for the one race and his car was finished in the colours of his sponsor, Lucky Strike Racing.

Yardley-BRM:

16. P. Rodriguez (BRM P160, chassis no. 01)
17. J. Siffert (BRM P153, chassis no. 06)
27. H. Ganley (BRM P153, chassis no. 03)

Rodriguez also had P153 car, chassis no. 07, as a spare.

Équipe Matra:

19. C. Amon (Matra-Simca MS120B, chassis no. 04)

Beltoise had been suspended as a result of the accident in the

Buenos Aires 1000 Km race and no attempt had been made to replace him for this race.

Team Surtees:

20. J. Surtees (Surtees TS9-Cosworth, chassis no. 001 sponsored by Brooke Bond-Oxo Racing with Rob Walker).
21. R. Stommelen (Surtees TS7-Cosworth, chassis no. 002 sponsored by *Auto Motor und Sport-Eifelland*).
28. B. Redman (Surtees TS7-Cosworth, chassis no. 001).

Frank Williams Racing Cars:

22. H. Pescarolo (March 701-Cosworth, chassis no. 06)

This team's new March 711 had not yet been tested, so Pescarolo was forced to drive the older, 1970 model.

Ecurie Bonnier:

23. J. Bonnier (McLaren M7C-Cosworth, chassis no. M7C/1)

This was the ex-works, ex-Surtees car that Bonnier had entered at certain 1970 races.

Team Gunston:

24. J. Love (March-Cosworth, chassis no. 10).
25. J. Pretorius (Brabham BT26A-Cosworth, chassis no. BT26/1)

The March was a car that had been supplied new to this local team in 1970 and the Brabham was the ex-works, ex-Frank Williams car.

PRACTICE

During the 1970 race Surtees and Brabham had shared a new lap record of 1 min 20.8 sec (113.61 mph), but in the meanwhile local driver Charlton had reduced this record to 1 min 20.2 sec and Stewart had turned in an unofficial 1 min 18.1 sec during his tyre testing sessions. At the first day's practice on the Wednesday, Stewart, running on the latest low-profile, Goodyear tyres, lapped in 1 min 17.8 sec and this remained unbeaten during the remaining sessions, as did Amon's second fastest time with the Matra on similar tyres in 1 min 18.4 sec. On the Thursday Stewart's engine blew up early in the session while he was practising with full tanks (i.e. he had no opportunity to improve on his earlier time with the car in 'sprint' trim) and Regazzoni was fastest in the session with a time of 1 min 18.7 sec.

There were no dramas on the Friday other than that both Soler-Roig and Fittipaldi suffered engine blow-ups. The only example of the 11-series Cosworth engine to appear at Kyalami arrived for Stewart and with this installed in his Tyrrell he lapped in 1 min 18.1 sec which was fastest of the session. During a half-hour untimed practice session on race morning, Cevert's engine blew up and the Tyrrell mechanics faced an incredible rush to get the car ready for the start. There was also trouble in the Matra pit because Amon's car had sprung a water leak and although this was cured, as a result of fuel mixture troubles the car was still not running properly at the start of the race.

THE GRID

J. Stewart (Tyrrell) 1 min 17.8 sec	C. Amon (Matra) 1 min 18.4 sec	C. Regazzoni (Ferrari) 1 min 18.7 sec
M. Andretti (Ferrari) 1 min 19.0 sec	E. Fittipaldi (Lotus) 1 min 19.1 sec	
J. Surtees (Surtees) 1 min 19.1 sec	D. Hulme (McLaren) 1 min 19.1 sec	J. Ickx (Ferrari) 1 min 19.2 sec
F. Cevert (Tyrrell) 1 min 19.2 sec	P. Rodriguez (BRM) 1 min 19.3 sec	
P. Gethin (McLaren) 1 min 19.6 sec	D. Charlton (Brabham) 1 min 19.8 sec	R. Peterson (March) 1 min 19.9 sec
R. Wisell (Lotus) 1 min 19.9 sec	R. Stommelen (Surtees) 1 min 20.1 sec	
J. Siffert (BRM) 1 min 20.2 sec	B. Redman (Surtees) 1 min 20.2 sec	H. Pescarolo (March) 1 min 20.2 sec
G. Hill (Brabham) 1 min 20.5 sec	J. Pretorius (Brabham) 1 min 21.7 sec	
J. Love (March) 1 min 21.9 sec	A. de Adamich (March) 1 min 22.2 sec	J. Bonnier (McLaren) 1 min 22.3 sec
H. Ganley (BRM) 1 min 23.7 sec	A. Soler-Roig (March) 1 min 25.8 sec	

With twenty-five cars on the grid, the race had one of the biggest fields seen for a long time and there were prospects of a close and exciting battle between the Tyrrell of Stewart and the very strong team of three Ferraris. When the one-minute signal was given, and the cars moved up from the dummy grid, Hill's Brabham refused to fire and he and Soler-Roig were the last away at the fall of the flag.

While both Stewart (very uncharacteristically) and Amon made poor starts – perhaps they were caught unawares by the speed with which the starter raised and lowered the flag – Regazzoni shrieked into the first corner followed by Fittipaldi, Ickx, Hulme and Rodriguez. The Swiss driver held his lead during the opening laps, gradually building up a small gap, with Fittipaldi in second place; by lap four Hulme had pushed the new McLaren by the Brazilian into second place and Fittipaldi fell back into the battling group formed by Rodriguez, Andretti, Stewart, Ickx, Surtees and Siffert. The first retirements came on lap five when Bonnier retired with suspension trouble and Soler-Roig was eliminated by engine failure. Two laps later Gethin retired his McLaren with a loose fuel line. Another driver in trouble early in the race was Jackie Ickx who deflated a tyre in a collision with a kerb and did several laps with a front tyre almost flat before coming in for a wheel-change.

Hulme closed right up on the race-leader and on lap seventeen passed Regazzoni under braking for the corner at the end of the pits straight. Behind these two the order was Surtees (who had just passed Rodriguez) and behind the BRM driver came Andretti, Stewart and Siffert. Five laps later local driver Pretorius retired his Brabham with a broken camshaft. The former World Champion with the new McLaren began to open up a good lead over the flat-12 Maranello car which was now being caught by Surtees and Rodriguez. All three BRMs, however, disappeared from the race in quick succession. On Siffert's car close slip-streaming had caused bad overheating and with all the water boiled away he pulled into the pits to retire on lap thirty-one. Two laps later Rodriguez was out of the race; the bodywork on the new P160 car had moved, causing the hot air from the radiator to enter the cockpit, and he came into the pits with oil all over the back of the car and with badly burnt feet. Ganley had been overcome by the heat – a state partly induced by his wearing an enclosed helmet – and after a pit stop, he rejoined the race, but he retired from exhaustion soon afterwards.

Because of a bad vibration from the front wheels Regazzoni was gradually falling back, at half-distance Hulme led by six seconds, Surtees had moved up into second place with the new TS9 and soon afterwards Andretti demoted his team-mate another place. Surtees' fast run now began to fade because a pipe to the gearbox oil cooler fractured and the gearbox was gradually sapped of all its lubricant. As gear-changing on the TS9 became more and more difficult, Andretti went by into second place and by the time of Surtees' retirement on lap fifty-eight he had fallen back to fifth spot. Another driver suffering from the heat was Francois Cevert; the combination of his fireproof balaclava hood and Bell Star helmet had caused him to perspire heavily, sweat was running down his face and on lap forty-seven when he blinked, he was temporarily blinded, lost control and crashed his seventh-place Tyrrell. Since the start Fittipaldi had gradually been falling back because of a sick engine and on lap fifty-eight, as he passed the pits in fifth place, the engine of his Lotus 72 blew up and he was out of the race.

Andretti was now really turning on the pressure in an effort to catch Hulme, Stewart was closing up on Regazzoni who hung on to third place until lap sixty-six and Wisell was a steady fifth with the surviving works Lotus. To keep the Ferrari at bay, Hulme speeded up, and although Andretti turned in fastest lap of the race on lap seventy-three it seemed unlikely that the New Zealander would be caught. But with only four laps to go to the chequered flag, Hulme felt the M19A lurch as he accelerated out of a corner, and the car started to weave badly. A bolt had dropped out of the right upper rear radius arm and Hulme staggered on slowly, hoping to finish, while Andretti disappeared into the distance with the race in his pocket. As the McLaren crawled past the pits, Hulme made frantic signs, but to the McLaren pit staff it was far from clear what the trouble was. At the flag Andretti was just over twenty seconds ahead of Stewart, Regazzoni was still in third place and Amon with a car that had been sick throughout the race had done well to finish fifth. Although it finished thirteenth and last, the March driven by de Adamich was the first car powered by the V-8 Alfa engine to finish a Grand Prix, enough in itself to give Chiti and the boys at Autodelta some encouragement.

Results:

1st, M. Andretti (Ferrari 312B), 1 hour 47 min 35.5 sec (112.36 mph)
2nd, J. Stewart (Tyrrell-Cosworth), 1 hour 47 min 56.4 sec
3rd, C. Regazzoni (Ferrari 312B), 1 hour 48 min 6.9 sec
4th, R. Wisell (Lotus 72C-Cosworth), 1 hour 48 min 44.9 sec
5th, C. Amon (Matra-Simca MS120B), 1 lap in arrears
6th, D. Hulme (McLaren M19A-Cosworth), 1 lap in arrears
7th, B. Redman (Surtees TS7-Cosworth), 1 lap in arrears

8th, J. Ickx (Ferrari 312B), 1 lap in arrears
9th, G. Hill (Brabham BT33-Cosworth), 2 laps in arrears
10th, R. Peterson (March 711-Cosworth), 2 laps in arrears
11th, H. Pescarolo (March 701-Cosworth), 2 laps in arrears
12th, R. Stommelen (Surtees TS7-Cosworth), 2 laps in arrears
13th, A. de Adamich (March 711-Alfa Romeo), 4 laps in arrears

Fastest lap: M. Andretti, 1 min 20.3 sec (114.32 mph)
Existing lap record: D. Charlton (Lotus 49C-Cosworth), 1 min 20.2 sec (114.464 mph – set in South African national race in 1970)
1970 winner: J. Brabham (Brabham BT33-Cosworth), 111.70 mph

Retirements: Lap 5: A. Soler-Roig (March), engine failure; J. Bonnier (McLaren), suspension trouble; lap 7: P. Gethin (McLaren), fuel leak; lap 22: J. Pretorious (Brabham), engine failure; lap 31: D. Charlton (Brabham), engine failure; J. Siffert (BRM), overheating; J. Love (March), gearbox failure; lap 33: P. Rodriguez (BRM), overheating; lap 42: H. Ganley (BRM), driver illness; lap 47: F. Cevert (Tyrrell), accident; lap 56: J. Surtees (Surtees), gearbox failure; lap 58: E. Fittipaldi (Lotus), engine failure.

ROUND TWO
SPANISH GRAND PRIX

Montjuich Park, Barcelona (Circuit length: 2.355 miles)
18th April, 1971
Race length: 176.62 miles (75 laps) Weather: warm and dry

For the Spanish race which alternates between the drab and rather uninteresting Jarama circuit near Madrid and Montjuich Park, it was Barcelona's turn in 1971. This circuit, set on a hillside overlooking the harbour has spacious, albeit make-shift paddock facilities on an avenue running parallel to the circuit and over-awed by an enormous, gloomy and derelict-looking football stadium. The track itself, flanked by the magnificent National Palace Museum, is lined throughout by Armco barriers which are installed specially for the race and removed afterwards. Certain sections have to be moved between practice sessions to permit the flow of normal traffic. It is a short circuit, but at the same time a true road circuit and one of the most interesting in Europe. The course is made up of a variety of gradients and corners, and perhaps the most interesting part is a fast downhill swoop, linking two hairpin bends, left-hand and right-hand respectively, with a nasty bump that gives the impression of hurling the cars at the Armco.

Although the BRM Ferrari, Matra and Tyrrell teams had all brought spare cars to the race, other teams were not in such a strong position and there was a shortage of engines among Cosworth users because of a bad batch of 10-series crankshafts.

THE ENTRY

Gold Leaf Team Lotus:

2. E. Fittipaldi (Lotus 72C-Cosworth, chassis no. R5)
3. R. Wisell (Lotus 72C-Cosworth, chassis no. R3)

Since the Race of the Champions the 72s had been fitted with rear oil cooler ducts to divert hot air from the exhausts away from the oil radiators. Larger oil tanks were fitted and the cars had the single tier, wider aerofoils seen at Oulton Park. Both cars were running with 10-series engines and the team had no spares.

S.p.a. Ferrari SEFAC:

4. J. Ickx (Ferrari 312B, chassis no. 003)
5. C. Regazzoni (Ferrari 312B, chassis no. 004)
6. M. Andretti (Ferrari 312B, chassis no. 002)

Bearing Regazzoni's number was the latest 312B/2 model, but this was purely a spare and not intended to be raced. This car had now been fitted with glass-fibre fairings for the oil cooler and a faired-in roll-over bar.

Motor Racing Developments:

7. G. Hill (Brabham BT34-Cosworth, chassis no. BT34/1)
8. T. Schenken (Brabham BT33-Cosworth, chassis no. BT33/1)

Bruce McLaren Motor Racing:

9. D. Hulme (McLaren M19A-Cosworth, chassis no. M19A/1)
10. P. Gethin (McLaren M14A-Cosworth, chassis no. M14A/1)

For the first two practice sessions the 11-series engine was removed from Gethin's car because he had never raced at the circuit before and it was anticipated that he would want to cover a great number of laps to familiarise himself. The team had also brought along M14A/2, minus engine, as a source of spares.

Elf Team Tyrrell:

11. J. Stewart (Tyrrell-Cosworth, chassis no. 003)
12. F. Cevert (Tyrrell-Cosworth, chassis no. 002)

Stewart was at the wheel of a brand new car that had just been completed; it had all the 1971 modifications incorporated in

Cevert's car which had been rebuilt since its Kyalami crash. The team also had the original car, no. 001, as a spare.

Yardley BRM:

14. P. Rodriguez (BRM P160, chassis no. 01)
15. J. Siffert (BRM P160, chassis no. 02)
16. H. Ganley (BRM P153, chassis no. 03)

The team had also brought along P153 car, chassis no. 07, as a spare. For the last practice session and the race Rodriguez' car was fitted with an engine having the Mk II cylinder heads.

STP-March:

17. A. de Adamich (March 711-Alfa Romeo, chassis no. 01)
18. R. Peterson (March 711-Cosworth, chassis no. 02)
19. A. Soler-Roig (March 711-Cosworth, chassis no. 04)

As a result of the over-heating that had plagued the cars at Kyalami, the 711s were still running without side radiator cowls or engine covers. Likewise, as investigation of the brake-shaft failure suffered on Peterson's car in the Race of Champions at Brands Hatch had revealed no fault in the material, the team was playing it safe and continuing to use the outboard front brake conversion. March were still using 10-series engines (one of which had been borrowed) and had two spares, but Max Mosley said that the team was hoping to receive at least one 11-series unit in time for the *Daily Express* Trophy race.

Équipe Matra:

20. C. Amon (Matra-Simca MS120B, chassis no. 04)
21. J-P. Beltoise (Matra-Simca MS120B, chassis no. 05)

After another bout of panic about the return of his racing licence, Beltoise was making a welcome come-back with a new version of the MS120B with re-shaped side panels housing larger fuel reservoirs – in 1970 the tanks had proved too small in the longer races and there had been several 'panic' refuelling stops. Since the Matras' last outing, a number of modifications had been made to the engines. Amon had as a spare car, chassis MS120/02

Team Surtees:

24. J. Surtees (Surtees TS9-Cosworth, chassis no. 001 sponsored by Brooke Bond-Oxo Racing with Rob Walker)
25. R. Stommelen (Surtees TS9-Cosworth, chassis no. 002 sponsored by *Auto Motor und Sport* – Eifelland)

Surtees was at the wheel of the car which he had driven at Kyalami, while Stommelen handled the car Surtees had driven at Oulton Park. It was widely thought that Surtees had obtained 11-series engines for both cars through sheer persistency rather than favourable treatment!

Frank Williams Racing Cars:

27. H. Pescarolo (March 711-Cosworth, chassis no. 03)

This private dark-blue March had now been worked over by Len Bailey who had advised the fitting of stronger lower front wishbones and a redesigned lower rear cross-member. This member had broken at Ontario, but Robin Herd had attributed the failure to Pescarolo's race collision. Bailey and Williams disagreed and their opinion was substantiated when one of the works cars cracked its chassis at the same place during the first practice session at Barcelona.

PRACTICE

At Barcelona there were three practice sessions held in the late afternoon of the Thursday, Friday and Saturday. The first session was held in fine, cool conditions and Stewart set the pace with a cracking lap in 1 min 26.9 sec, but two years previously when the race had last been held at Barcelona, Rindt with his Lotus 49B assisted by large front and rear wings had taken pole position on the grid with a time of 1 min 25.7 sec and this was not bettered throughout practice. Because of gearbox trouble Gethin did not get out at all during the first session, Hulme managed only eight laps with the M19A and Hill, looking far from happy with the Brabham BT34, spent a long time padding the cockpit with foam rubber before practising. Throughout the meeting the Surtees team was plagued by mechanical troubles and on the Thursday, Surtees' own car broke an engine quill-shaft and Stommelen was complaining about bad handling. Another driver complaining about his car was Amon, for the engine was off-song and the suspension had not been set up properly.

Friday's practice was dominated by the 12-cylinder cars. Ickx turned in a very effortless-looking lap in 1 min 25.9 sec which was to gain him pole position on the grid and Regazzoni was only a tenth-of-a-second slower. The Swiss Ferrari driver's time was matched by Amon whose car had been fitted with a new engine over-night and now had the suspension properly sorted. Amon had led this race before retiring in 1969 and he was expected to be very much in the hunt once again in 1971.

The final practice session was completely ruined by rain that started to fall during the Formula 3 race. Because of the terrible conditions most of the entry in this race went off the track or into the pits with water-logged electrics and the race seemed interminable. During this last session Gethin ran with the 11-series engine for the first time, and Rodriguez drove the latest BRM engine with the Mk II cylinder head first seen at Monza in 1970. Stewart was fastest of the session in 1 min 37.0 sec, running with Koni dampers at the rear.

THE GRID

C. Amon (Matra) 1 min 26.0 sec	C. Regazzoni (Ferrari) 1 min 26.0 sec	J. Ickx (Ferrari) 1 min 25.9 sec
P. Rodriguez (BRM) 1 min 26.5 sec	J. Stewart (Tyrrell) 1 min 26.2 sec	
M. Andretti (Ferrari) 1 min 26.9 sec	P. Gethin (McLaren) 1 min 26.8 sec	J-P. Beltoise (Matra) 1 min 26.6 sec
J. Siffert (BRM) 1 min 27.3 sec	D. Hulme (McLaren) 1 min 27.1 sec	
R. Peterson (March) 1 min 27.8 sec	F. Cevert (Tyrrell) 1 min 27.7 sec	H. Pescarolo (March) 1 min 27.5 sec
G. Hill (Brabham) 1 min 28.4 sec	E. Fittipaldi (Lotus) 1 min 27.9 sec	
A. de Adamich (March) 1 min 29.5 sec	H. Ganley (BRM) 1 min 28.6 sec	R. Wisell (Lotus) 1 min 28.6 sec
A. Soler-Roig (March) 1 min 29.8 sec	R. Stommelen (Surtees) 1 min 29.6 sec	
	J. Surtees (Surtees) 1 min 30.8 sec	T. Schenken (Brabham) 1 min 30.6 sec

THE RACE

Although Ickx had pole position on the grid, it was of very little advantage at Montjuich Park because on this anti-clockwise circuit, the first corner is a left-hander and yet for some reason that was far from clear, pole position was on the right-hand side of the front row of the grid. The low grid positions of the Surtees entries reflected the team's persistent mechanical troubles and more trouble followed on race morning when Surtees, already bothered by sticking fuel release valves, stopped out on the circuit during some additional practice and a Coca-Cola salesman tripped over the nose and bent the radiator stays.

Preceding the Grand Prix was a Formula 1430 race for locally built SEAT-powered cars, this started late and so the start of the main race was put back half-an-hour. Preceding the Grand Prix was a rather shambling display by a group of drum majorettes (not a patch on the Flamenco dancers who had entertained the press the previous evening!) and when the flag fell, the weather was warm, but with a cooling breeze.

At the start Ickx was away like a rocket, heading Regazzoni, Amon and Stewart, but the Scot had sneaked the Tyrrell through to second place by the first left-hand bend. As the cars lower down the grid reached the first hairpin, they almost came to a halt because of traffic congestion and in the scramble through the corner the cars of Siffert, Hill and Surtees all received thumps. By the end of the lap Ickx had pulled a lead of several cars' lengths over Stewart and Regazzoni, and the rest of the field were already dropping back. At the tail of the field were the Brabhams of Hill and Schenken, Wisell with the Lotus, the two Surtees TS9s and the March 711s of de Adamich and Soler-Roig.

Lap three saw Amon force his Matra into third place ahead of the Ferrari of Regazzoni and two laps later Stewart was ahead of Ickx and at once beginning to pull out a lead. At the end of that lap Hill's Brabham, which had been weaving badly, came into the pits, the trouble was traced to the steering rack which had been damaged in the first lap scramble and the car was retired. Siffert disappeared out on the circuit on lap five and later crawled in to retire with a broken front wing and damaged gear linkage. Stommelen's TS9 had dropped right to the end of the field and was sounding atrocious; the trouble was low fuel pressure caused by a sticking release valve. Although the car rejoined the race, it completed only another lap before retiring.

By the end of the tenth lap it was clear that Stewart had the legs of the pursuing Ferrari and had now opened the gap up to three seconds. Although Regazzoni was still in fourth place, his engine was running rough and he was gradually losing ground. When the Swiss driver came into the pits at the end of lap thirteen. Rodriguez moved up into fourth place and Andretti was now fifth, The Ferrari mechanics checked the plugs and then Regazzoni tried to re-start the car. The flat-12 engine refused to fire, a slave battery was linked up and as the engine started, so a broken fuel pump, which was the real cause of the trouble, ignited. The mechanics shouted to Regazzoni to get out of the car, but misunderstanding the situation, Clay accelerated down the pits road trailing slave battery and flames. He was stopped before he could rejoin the race and although the fire damage was slight, running the engine so long on a weak mixture had caused internal damage and the Ferrari was retired.

Andretti was now pressing Rodriguez hard, and Hulme was sixth ahead of Beltoise, Gethin, Cevert and Fittipaldi. On lap twenty-two Gethin's McLaren jumped out of gear and while he was trying to sort out a near-collision with the Armco, he was passed by both Cevert and Fittipaldi. Three laps later Peterson's March, which had not been running well since the start of the race, expired out on the circuit with ignition failure. Two other drivers in trouble were Pescarolo, whose engine was misfiring badly, and Wisell, whose car was jumping out of gear so that the driver had to restrict himself to the use of third and top ratios. At the end of lap thirty-one Fittipaldi, Wisell and Surtees (the latter a lap in arrears) all came into the pits. Fittipaldi's Lotus had braking trouble and although both he and Wisell rejoined the race, the Brazilian eventually retired after completing fifty-four laps because of a broken rear cross-member. Surtees rejoined the race without losing fourteenth place.

By half-distance Stewart had pulled out a lead of eight seconds, Ickx seemed to have lost all hope of regaining the lead and Amon had reconciled himself to finishing third. Behind Rodriguez, Andretti and Hulme were scrapping for fifth place, Beltoise was sixth, but being caught by Cevert, and Gethin was seventh. The remainder of the field had been lapped at least once. On laps thirty-nine and forty Andretti came round trailing flames from his 312B and he stopped at the pits at the end of lap forty-two. Once again the trouble was a broken fuel pump casting and fuel was being ignited by the pump's own electrical system. The pump was changed and Mario rejoined the race, but the stop had cost him eight laps. Next into the pits was Pescarolo with the dark-blue March who came in with a broken rear aerofoil. The mechanics quickly removed it, but 'Pepsi' found that the engine would not restart and the car was pushed away into retirement. Andretti's troubles were still not over and on his fiftieth lap he was cruising back to the pits to retire with loss of oil pressure when a loose union on the new fuel pump caused another fire. Andretti stopped the car by a fire marshall and the car eventually crawled back to the pits covered in extinguisher foam.

As the race entered its final stages, Ickx began to turn on the pressure and by lap sixty he was within five seconds of Stewart.

With ten laps to go the gap was reduced to three seconds, Cevert was signalled by his pit that Ickx was about to lap him – the message was clear that a little bit of baulking would not come amiss – but Ickx was past the dark-blue car before Cevert could do anything to help his team-leader. With six laps to go Ickx set a new lap record of 1 min 25.1 sec and closed within 2.3 seconds of Stewart, but next time round he nearly lost it at the left-hand bend after the pits, just managed to scrabble round the corner and staggered off down the hill with the engine popping and banging. Now he had lost all chance of catching Stewart and at the chequered flag he was still 3.4 seconds behind. As the local spectators, most of whom see only the one motor race during the year, wandered off to the football match and bullfight scheduled for later in the day, most of the experts were wondering whether Stewart would be able to repeat this brilliant victory at the equally tortuous Monaco circuit.

Results:

1st, J. Stewart (Tyrrell-Cosworth), 1 hour 49 min 3.4 sec (97.19 mph)
2nd, J. Ickx (Ferrari 312B), 1 hour 49 min 6.8 sec
3rd, C. Amon (Matra-Simca MS120B), 1 hour 50 min 1.5 sec
4th, P. Rodriguez (BRM P160), 1 hour 50 min 21.3 sec
5th, D. Hulme (McLaren M19A-Cosworth), 1 hour 50 min 30.4 sec
6th, J-P. Beltoise (Matra-Simca MS120B), 1 lap in arrears
7th, F. Cevert (Tyrrell-Cosworth), 1 lap in arrears
8th, P. Gethin (McLaren M14A-Cosworth), 2 laps in arrears
9th, T. Schenken (Brabham BT33-Cosworth), 3 laps in arrears
10th, H. Ganley (BRM P153), 4 laps in arrears
11th, J. Surtees (Surtees TS9-Cosworth), 8 laps in arrears
12th, R. Wisell (Lotus 72C-Cosworth), 17 laps in arrears

Fastest lap: J. Ickx (Ferrari 312B), 1 min 25.1 sec (99.64 mph – record).

Previous lap record: J. Rindt (Lotus 49-Cosworth), 1 min 28.3 sec (96.03 mph – set in 1969 race).

1970 winner (race held at Madrid): J. Stewart (March 701-Cosworth), 87.21 mph.

Retirements: Lap 6: G. Hill (Brabham), steering damage as result of collision; J. Siffert (BRM), damaged gear linkage; lap 10: R. Stommelen (Surtees), fuel pump trouble; lap 14: C. Regazzoni (Ferrari), engine damage; lap 25: R. Peterson (March), ignition; lap 27: A. de Adamich (March), crown wheel-and-pinion failure; lap 47: A. Soler-Roig (March), broken fuel line; lap 51: M.

Andretti (Ferrari), fuel pump, loss of oil pressure; lap 54: H. Pescarolo (March), failed to restart after pit stop caused by damaged bodywork; lap 55: E. Fittipaldi (Lotus), suspension trouble.

ROUND THREE

MONACO GRAND PRIX

Monte Carlo (Circuit length: 1.95 miles) 23rd May, 1971
Race length: 156.33 miles (80 laps) Weather: dry and cold

First held in 1929, the only surviving race to be held on a true round the houses circuit (albeit one lined throughout with Armco barriers), the Monaco race is one of the most popular events of the year and a total of 100,000 spectators flocked to the Principality to watch the 1971 race. Although the 'Geneva' agreement made between the organisers and the constructors stipulated that twenty cars should be allowed to start at each of the 1971 Championship races, this did not apply to Monaco for the Automobile Club de Monaco was not a signatory to the agreement. Here only the fastest eighteen of the twenty-three entries would start and this ruling was to have a very odd repercussion. Since the last race the circuit had been resurfaced, but at the exit of the Station hairpin the track was now narrower because of excavation work. It is through these little changes that do not seem to matter at the time that circuits gradually change character over the years. But one feature of Monaco never changes and that is the almost complete absence of any escape roads. This together with the kerbs and walls and the lack of a separate pits road are features that the Grand Prix Drivers' Association would have objected to strongly elsewhere, but for some reason – thank goodness – the Association leaves Monaco well alone and lets it carry on in the same 'dangerous' way as it has existed for the last forty years.

THE ENTRY

Gold Leaf Team Lotus:

1. E. Fittipaldi (Lotus 72D-Cosworth, chassis no. R5)
2. R. Wisell (Lotus 72C-Cosworth, chassis no. R3)

Although it was in fact the same chassis as he had driven at previous races, Fittipaldi's car had been up-rated to 'D' specification because it had new and much more conventional rear suspension featuring parallel lower links and twin radius rods (see 'The Cars and Teams', Page 18). Because downthrust was of prime importance on this difficult circuit, both cars were running with the 1970-style three-tier rear aerofoils.

S.p.a. Ferrari SEFAC:

4. J. Ickx (Ferrari 312B/2, chassis no. 006)
5. C. Regazzoni (Ferrari 312B/2, chassis no. 005)
6. M. Andretti (Ferrari 312B, chassis no. 002)

A second of the wedge-shaped 1971 312B/2 cars had now been completed and this was driven by Ickx, while Regazzoni had the prototype car with which he had won the Race of Champions. The third car for Andretti had not yet been completed and so he was entered with a 1970 model. Although it bore Ickx' racing numbers, the spare car, 312B chassis no. 003, was driven in practice by Andretti. For the first time the 1971 Ferraris were fitted with Lockheed brakes, previously seen only on McLaren cars.

Motor Racing Developments:

7. G. Hill (Brabham BT34-Cosworth, chassis no. BT34/1)
8. T. Schenken (Brabham BT33-Cosworth, chassis no. BT33/1)

Since its winning outing at Silverstone the BT34 had been modified in a number of minor aspects. Because of the confined conditions at Monaco the car was fitted with new pods for the divided front radiators which were cut back and bevelled off at the forward corners; there were now reinforced mounting plates for the rear radius rods and scoops were fitted to feed the rear inboard brakes with cool air.

Bruce McLaren Motor Racing:

9. D. Hulme (McLaren M19A-Cosworth, chassis no. M19A/1)
10. P. Gethin (McLaren M14A-Cosworth, chassis no. M14A/2)

At this race the team had M14A/1, the car raced by Gethin at Barcelona, without engine as a source of spares.

Elf Team Tyrrell:

11. J. Stewart (Tyrrell-Cosworth, chassis no. 003)
12. F. Cevert (Tyrrell-Cosworth, chassis no. 002)

Since Silverstone Stewart's car had been fitted with a new monocoque to replace that damaged in the crash and Stewart had the original car, 001, as a spare. In practice the team tried out on 002 some experimental Girling 'twin-disc' front brakes with thin discs 'floating' to a limited extent on the splines of the hub. The team had also brought along new-style radiator cowls.

Yardley-BRM:

14. J. Siffert (BRM P160, chassis no. 02)
15. P. Rodriguez (BRM P160, chassis no. 01)
16. H. Ganley (BRM P153, chassis no. 06)

Rodriguez had the latest Mk II bifurcated port cylinder heads as at Barcelona and for his car there was also available a new 'shovel-nose' radiator cowl. The Mexican had as a spare car P153, chassis no. 07, which was the car driven by Ganley at the *Daily Express* Trophy race and by Miles at the Race of Champions. Both of the P153 cars were fitted with a number of P160 modifications including the same oil tanks and ducted coolers. Ganley's car was fitted with Lockheed brakes which he preferred to the usual Girlings.

STP-March:

17. R. Peterson (March 711-Cosworth, chassis no. 02)
18. A. Soler-Roig (March 711-Cosworth, chassis no. 04)
19. N. Galli (March 711-Alfa Romeo, chassis no. 01)

Peterson's car was fitted with modified rear suspension incorporating a new rear cross-member, longer upper links and the dampers at a different angle. In practice he tried out some new ventilated front brake discs made of copper. Even the March team did not know why Alfa Romeo had deputed Galli to drive instead of de Adamich and he was at the wheel of the car crashed by Peterson at Silverstone, but this now had a new monocoque with a revised cockpit surround and was new in most other respects as well.

Équipe Matra:

20. C. Amon (Matra-Simca MS120B, chassis no. 04)
21. J-P. Beltoise (Matra-Simca MS120B, chassis no. 05)

In addition Amon had a brand new car as spare, chassis no. 06. For this race all three cars were fitted with shorter, narrower nose cowls to reduce the risk of accidental damage and both of the race cars had larger rear aerofoils that took the form of a tray covering the whole of the rear of the car and part of the engine. As an answer to the lubrication problems that had plagued the V-12 cars throughout their career and as a direct result of the engine troubles at Silverstone the MS120s now had external oil tanks mounted behind the Hewland transmission units (they were previously in the monocoques)

Team Surtees:

22. J. Surtees (Surtees TS9-Cosworth, chassis no. 001 sponsored by Brooke Bond-Oxo Racing with Rob Walker)

24. R. Stommelen (Surtees TS9-Cosworth, chassis no. 002 sponsored by *Auto Motor und Sport* – Eifelland)

This was the first appearance of Team Surtees with their own cars at Monaco. These were much as before, except that Surtees was another driver trying Lockheed brakes and both cars now had ventilated discs all round. The team had also brought the original TS7 car, chassis no. 001, last driven by Redman at Kyalami which was primarily intended for use as a camera car in the making of the Fangio film.

Frank Williams Racing Cars:

27. H. Pescarolo (March 711-Cosworth, chassis no. 03)

Now painted in the red colours of the Motul Oil Company who sponsored the team, this car had benefited further from the changes made by Len Bailey. A collector tank had been substituted for the seat bag tank and the battery had been repositioned at the front of the car.

Gene Mason Racing:

28. S. Barber (March 711-Cosworth, chassis no. 05)

This brand new March, red-painted like the works cars, was sponsored by a group of Philadelphia stockbrokers and was taking in Monaco, Zandvoort and Hockenheim before 'exporting' to the United States to compete in Formula A racing.

PRACTICE

The first practice session, on the Thursday afternoon, was completely ruined by torrential rain, most drivers completed only a few laps and Hulme, Siffert, Ganley, Cevert, Pescarolo and Soler-Roig failed to practice at all. Amon was fastest in this miserable session in 1 min 48.8 sec (twenty-five seconds slower than the lap record).

On the Friday practice was due to start at 7.30 am, after the Formula 3 cars had practised, but it was delayed an hour because the session for the smaller cars was lengthened to compensate for the cancellation of their session the previous day. It proved to be the only dry session and the weather was very cold. As was expected, Stewart proved fastest in 1 min 23.2 sec, equalling the record set by Rindt on the last lap of the 1970 race, and second fastest man, Ickx, was 1.2 sec slower which is quite substantial where the circuit is so short. Because this was the only dry session, mechanical troubles eliminated most of the non-qualifiers. Soler-Roig lost a wheel off his March because the part that failed had not been machined properly, Galli's Alfa-engined car had engine trouble throughout the session and the V-8 was constantly cutting out – this was later traced to fuel starvation – and Barber was unable to practice because his gear ratios had not been installed correctly and the gearbox had to be stripped. The real disappointment of the session was the troubles that afflicted Andretti. After only a couple of laps the Ferrari engine packed in at the Casino because of fuel injection trouble and he could not drive the spare car because this had been left in the garage. It seemed quite ludicrous that a driver lying second in the World Championship should be unable to race because mechanical trouble prevented him from qualifying, but Andretti accepted the situation philosophically. Howden Ganley was the other non-starter and his fastest lap in 1 min 28.8 sec was beaten by Schenken by half-a-second.

Despite the rain on the Saturday, Andretti tried desperately hard to qualify with both his own car and the spare, but without success. Galli, too, was trying hard and was sixth fastest in the wet in 1 min 34.6 sec (Siffert was fastest in 1 min 31.9 sec), but Barber did not even bother to turn out. Cevert took his Tyrrell out fitted with the Girling double-discs, but a disc cracked, probably because the driver was being too cautious and using the new brakes too much.

THE GRID

J. Ickx (Ferrari) 1 min 24.4 sec		J. Stewart (Tyrrell) 1 min 23.2 sec	
	C. Amon (Matra) 1 min 24.8 sec		J. Siffert (BRM) 1 min 24.8 sec
D. Hulme (McLaren) 1 min 25.3 sec		P. Rodriguez (BRM) 1 min 25.1 sec	
	R. Peterson (March) 1 min 25.8 sec		J-P. Beltoise (Matra) 1 min 25.6 sec
J. Surtees (Surtees) 1 min 26.0 sec		G. Hill (Brabham) 1 min 26.0 sec	
	R. Wisell (Lotus) 1 min 26.7 sec		C. Regazzoni (Ferrari) 1 min 26.1 sec
P. Gethin (McLaren) 1 min 26.9 sec		H. Pescarolo (March) 1 min 26.7 sec	

R. Stommelen
(Surtees)
1 min 27.2 sec

F. Cevert
(Tyrrell)
1 min 27.2 sec

T. Schenken
(Brabham)
1 min 28.3 sec

E. Fittipaldi
(Lotus)
1 min 27.7 sec

Failed to qualify:

H. Ganley (BRM)	1 min 28.8 sec
M. Andretti (Ferrari)	1 min 29.1 sec
N. Galli (March)	1 min 34.6 sec
A. Soler-Roig (March)	1 min 44.4 sec
S. Barber (March)	2 min 48.6 sec

THE RACE

Although rain threatened at the start of the race, with dark clouds hanging overhead, the circuit remained dry until the last lap. Before the warming-up lap there was a panic first of all because Regazzoni's fire extinguisher went off accidentally and he missed the lap while this was changed, and because of low fuel pressure Amon's Matra was difficult to start before the warming-up lap and then at the start proper it refused to fire at all. The Matra was pushed to the side of the track and Rodriguez nipped forward with his BRM to take the vacant place on the grid. Louis Chiron, who was starting the race to celebrate the anniversary of his victory at Monaco in 1931, waved furiously to Rodriguez to back up again, Fittipaldi and Schenken at the back of the grid mistook this for the starting signal, accelerated, braked hard when they realised their mistake and had just selected reverse when the flag fell for the start proper!

As the cars moved off, Siffert almost mowed down Chiron and Matra engineer Bruno Morin only escaped a similar fate by stepping between the wheels of Amon's Matra on which he was working. Stewart made a magnificent start and Siffert out-accelerated Ickx to hold second place. Amon's engine eventually fired and he screamed away in the forlorn hope of catching the rest of the field who were nearly a minute ahead. When the cars came past the pits at the end of the first lap the order was Stewart drawing away from Siffert who was worried by Ickx and then came Rodriguez, Peterson, Hulme, Beltoise and Hill. But five-times winner of the Monaco race Graham Hill did not stay in eighth place for long and on the second lap he clipped the Armco on the inside of Tabac corner and the impact shot the car across the road and into the wall. Two wheels were torn off the Brabham and the suspension and chassis were badly damaged.

Although Ickx was still harrying the second-place BRM of Siffert, his car was plagued by excessive wheelspin caused by a broken rear anti-roll bar. There was a tremendous battle going on between Rodriguez, Peterson, Hulme and Beltoise and every time they went into a corner, they looked as though they were going to have an enormous multi-car pile-up. On lap four Cevert's engine cut out completely in the middle of the Gasometer hairpin and to avoid him Schenken was forced to take to the pavement, bursting a rear tyre. While Schenken limped back to the pits for a wheel-change, Cevert succeeded in restarting his car, but two laps later he slid wide at the Station hairpin and buckled the left-hand rear suspension and burst a tyre.

By lap ten Stewart had extended his lead to five seconds, Siffert still led Ickx and Peterson was trying everything he knew to get past Rodriguez. When Peterson tried to overtake the Mexican on the inside at the Gasometer, he was so badly baulked that he was passed by Hulme, but on the next lap he was back in front of the New Zealander. On lap thirteen, Rodriguez, under pressure from Peterson, locked a wheel going into the Gasometer, rubbed a flat spot on the tyre and was forced to stop for a wheel-change. Rodriguez stopped again on the next lap to complain about the handling, but the mechanics could find nothing wrong and he was sent off to rejoin the race again. Another driver in trouble was poor Amon who lost more time when he stopped to change a wheel. Pescarolo was in trouble with a gearbox jumping out of gear and when it happened in the tunnel the revs shot up to 11,200 rpm and he was passed by Regazzoni, Stommelen, Fittipaldi and Surtees and carried on in twelfth place. Regazzoni was now right on Wisell's tail and on the next lap the Swedish driver missed a gear-change, Regazzoni swerved round the Lotus, but did not quite make it and the two cars collided. The Ferrari was pushed into the kerb and limped back to the pits with two smashed wheels on the right-hand side and Wisell crawled in to retire with the hub race of the right-hand rear wheel broken up. Gethin was eliminated on lap twenty-three when he hit the edge of the track and bent the right-hand front suspension and two laps later as Regazzoni accelerated out of the chicane, he clipped the wooden barrier; the car spun, an upper rear suspension link was broken and he limped back to the pits to retire.

Peterson, in fourth place, had now speeded up tremendously in an effort to catch the BRM and Ferrari immediately ahead of him. Ickx was still battling with Siffert to try to take second place, but Peterson caught them and passed them both on lap twenty-nine, sweeping past the second-place BRM under braking for the Gasometer hairpin. The Swedish March driver was now sixteen seconds behind Stewart and although the gap remained constant for several laps, Peterson seemed unable to maintain his fast pace and slowly began to lose ground. With forty of the eighty laps covered, the order was: 1st, Stewart; 2nd, Peterson; 3rd, Siffert; 4th, Ickx; 5th, Hulme; 6th, Beltoise; 7th, Fittipaldi; 8th, Stommelen; 9th, Surtees; 10th, Pescarolo. Pescarolo had lost a little ground, but no places when he stopped for a wheel-change on lap thirty-six – the mechanics had changed the wheel with a punctured tyre in a mere thirty seconds!

Beltoise lost sixth place to Fittipaldi when brake trouble forced him to take to the escape road at the chicane for the second time and shortly afterwards he was passed by Stommelen. Both Matras retired in quick succession with final drive failure, Amon with forty-five laps to his credit and Beltoise on lap forty-eight. As the race entered its closing stages Stewart with the Tyrrell increased his lead to twenty seconds and on lap fifty-seven reduced the lap record to 1 min 22.2 sec. Two laps later poor Jo Siffert, having turned in one of the finest Grand Prix drives of his career and with his right hand badly blistered by his efforts, coasted into retirement with complete loss of oil pressure – all the more unfortunate because the BRM V-12 engines had been proving so reliable in 1971. As he reeled off the final few laps, Stewart eased his pace and at the chequered flag he was twenty-five seconds ahead of Peterson, with Ickx third after a race that had disappointed him as well as his many supporters. But without doubt Peterson was the man of the race, fulfilling the promised potential that March designer Robin Herd had long claimed him to possess. For Ferrari and BRM the race was very disappointing, the former because the cars had simply failed to display the tremendous performance of which they were obviously capable and the latter because of Siffert's retirement after a great drive.

Results:

1st, J. Stewart (Tyrrell-Cosworth), 1 hour 52 min 21.3 sec (83.49 mph)
2nd, R. Peterson (March 711-Cosworth), 1 hour 52 min 46.9 sec
3rd, J. Ickx (Ferrari 312B), 1 hour 53 min 14.6 sec
4th, D. Hulme (McLaren M19A-Cosworth), 1 hour 53 min 28.0 sec
5th, E. Fittipaldi (Lotus 72D-Cosworth), 1 lap in arrears,
6th, R. Stommelen (Surtees TS9-Cosworth), 1 lap in arrears,
7th, J. Surtees (Surtees TS9-Cosworth), 1 lap in arrears
8th, H. Pescarolo (March 711-Cosworth), 3 laps in arrears
9th, P. Rodriguez (BRM P160), 4 laps in arrears
10th, T. Schenken (Brabham BT33-Cosworth), 4 laps in arrears

Fastest lap: J. Stewart, 1 min 22.2 sec (85.58 mph – record)
Previous lap record: J. Rindt (Lotus 49C-Cosworth), 1 min 23.2 sec (84.56 mph – set in 1970 race).
1970 winner: J. Rindt (Lotus 49C-Cosworth), 81.84 mph.

Retirements: Lap 2: G. Hill (Brabham), accident; lap 6: F. Cevert (Tyrrell), accident; lap 22: R. Wisell (Lotus), collapsed rear hub bearing; lap 23: P. Gethin (McLaren), accident; lap 25: C. Regazzoni (Ferrari), suspension; lap 46: C. Amon (Matra), crown wheel-and-pinion failure; lap 48: J-P. Beltoise (Matra), crown wheel-and-pinion failure; lap 59: J. Siffert (BRM P160), engine failure.

ROUND FOUR

DUTCH GRAND PRIX

Zandvoort (Circuit length: 2.61 miles) 20th June, 1971
Race length: 182.70 miles (70 laps) Weather: very wet and windy

Such is the changing face of motor racing that the post-war Zandvoort circuit, set in sand dunes, close to the North Sea, is now one of the oldest established circuits used in the World Championship series and only Monjuich Park, Monaco, the Nürburgring and Monza have existed longer. The first race was held at Zandvoort in 1948 and this event organised by the British Racing Drivers' Club was won by the Maserati of Prince Birabongse ('B. Bira') with Tony Rolt's Bi-motore Alfa, rebuilt with a single engine, in second place. The first Dutch Grand Prix took place two years later, but it was not a round in the Drivers' Championship until 1952 and in both that year and the following the 2-litre Tipo 500 Ferraris of Ascari and Farina took the first two places. Nowadays Zandvoort is regarded as one of the most pleasant of circuits, with good race organisation and a friendly atmosphere. It has an excellent safety record and the only driver to die there during a Championship race has been Piers Courage who crashed with his de Tomaso in the 1970 Dutch Grand Prix. A total of twenty-five entries were accepted for the 1971 race and all were to be allowed to start without the problem of having to qualify.

THE ENTRY

S.p.a. Ferrari SEFAC:

2. J. Ickx (Ferrari 312B/2, chassis no. 006)
3. C. Regazzoni (Ferrari 312B/2, chassis no. 005)
4. M. Andretti (Ferrari 312B/2, chassis no. 007)

A third 312B/2 had now been completed for Andretti and these cars were in the same trim as at Monaco apart from additional air scoops for the inboard rear brakes. Ickx' car only had the transverse vibration damper arrangement fitted to the cars at Monaco. In practice the team tried out very wide 17-in. rear rims, but the use of these proved disastrous! The team had also brought along two 1970 cars as spares, 004 running with Regazzoni's numbers and 003 with Andretti's, and after failure of one the new wide tyres had caused Andretti to crash in practice, he took over 003 and drove it in the race.

Elf Team Tyrrell:

5. J. Stewart (Tyrrell-Cosworth, chassis no. 003)
6. F. Cevert (Tyrrell-Cosworth, chassis no. 002)

Stewart also had car 001 as a spare. Both Tyrrells were fitted with the Girling twin-disc front brakes and were running with Koni dampers, following successful tests with these at Zandvoort after the Monaco race. The team also produced and tried out in practice a very aero-dynamic streamlined nose reminiscent in shape of the Porsche 908/3.

Yardley-BRM:

8. P. Rodriguez (BRM P160, chassis no. 01)
9. J. Siffert (BRM P160, chassis no. 02)
10. H. Ganley (BRM P153, chassis no. 06)

Rodriguez also had as a reserve car the third, narrower P160 car, chassis no. 03, first seen at Hockenheim. All three P160s had the shovel nose taken to Monaco and fairings at the rear covering the sides of the cars and the cylinder heads; the team had brought along a new streamlined nose which was tried out in practice.

Gold Leaf Team Lotus:

12. D. Charlton (Lotus 72D-Cosworth, chassis no. R5)
14. R. Wisell (Lotus 72D-Cosworth, chassis no. R3)
15. D. Walker (Lotus 56B-Pratt & Whitney, chassis no. 1)

Emerson Fittipaldi was out of the race because he had not yet recovered from a road accident and his place was taken by Formula 3 star Dave Walker. The gas-turbine Lotus was a possible non-starter as its engine had not yet been returned by the factory in Canada after the fire at the Jochen Rindt Gedächtnis-Rennen at Hockenheim. Both 72s were now to the latest specification. Charlton non-started after his car was crashed in practice by Walker.

STP-March:

16. R. Peterson (March 711-Cosworth, chassis no. 02)
18. N. Galli (March 711-Alfa Romeo, chassis no. 01)
19. A. Soler-Roig (March 711-Cosworth, chassis no. 04)

All three cars were fitted with the revised near suspension first seen at Monaco. Soler-Roig's car was fitted with an anti-vibration rear suspension arrangement. Peterson also had an Alfa Romeo-powered car, chassis no. 06, as it was not decided which he would drive until the team reached Zandvoort.

Équipe Matra:

20. C. Amon (Matra-Simca MS120B, chassis no. 04)
21. J-P. Beltoise (Matra-Simca MS120B, chassis no. 05)

Once again Amon had car 06 as a spare. The Matras had now reverted to the original wider, longer noses and the original location of the oil tanks in the monocoques. The team had also reverted to the smaller aerofoils.

Gene Mason Racing:

22. S. Barber (March 711-Cosworth, chassis no. 05)

Team Surtees:

23. J. Surtees (Surtees TS9-Cosworth, chassis no. 001 sponsored by Brooke Bond-Oxo Racing with Rob Walker)
29. R. Stommelen (Surtees TS9-Cosworth, chassis no. 002 sponsored *Auto Motor und Sport* – Eifelland)
30. G. van Lennep (Surtees TS7-Cosworth, chassis no. 001 sponsored by Stichting Autoraces Nederland)

Surtees' car was running with the new pressed magnesium wheels introduced by this team. The TS7, now largely brought up to TS9 specification, was owned by Surtees' subsidiary company, Speed Sport International, and painted red. It was intended to be hired out to various drivers and for this race it was taken by Le Mans winner Gijs van Lennep who was receiving sponsorship from a number of sources including Esso and Champion. He was the first Dutchman to compete in a Grand Prix since Carel Godin de Beaufort was killed in practice with his Porsche for the 1964 German Grand Prix.

Motor Racing Developments:

24. G. Hill (Brabham BT34-Cosworth, chassis no. BT34/1)
25. T. Schenken (Brabham BT33-Cosworth, chassis no. BT33/3)

Following Hill's crash with the BT34 at Monaco, there had been a frantic rush to get this car ready in time and in case they failed, the team also prepared the BT33. When he tried it, Schenken preferred this car and so drove it at Zandvoort instead of his usual car. It featured BT34 rear suspension and the lighter Hewland FG gearbox.

Bruce McLaren Motor Racing:

26. D. Hulme (McLaren M19A-Cosworth, chassis no. M19A/2)
28. P. Gethin (McLaren M19A-Cosworth, chassis no. M19A/1)

By dint of very hard work the McLaren team had succeeded in completing a second M19A which featured a higher monocoque behind the cockpit, the bracing tubes for the roll-over bar running forwards (instead of to the engine), a larger rear aerofoil and the lighter Hewland FG gearbox. The new car was taken by Hulme, and Gethin drove the older car.

Frank Williams Racing Cars:

31. H. Pescarolo (March 711-Cosworth, chassis no. 03)

This private March had been fitted with the latest rear suspension, and had a lighter, adjustable wing.

PRACTICE

Although the first of the practice sessions was on the Friday, there was an unofficial session on the Wednesday, attended by Ferrari, Lotus and March. On the Friday, Australian Dave Walker practised with the Lotus 72D, in case the engine for the gas-turbine car should not arrive. However, after only a couple of laps Walker spun off and wrecked the rear suspension. The team lacked the parts to repair the car and this meant that South African Champion, Dave Charlton, was definitely without a drive. Regazzoni had been fastest so far in 1 min 17.98 sec and was really going well when an oil pipe came undone and the engine ran its bearings. There was oil all the way round the back part of the circuit and practice was stopped for half-an-hour while the mess was cleared up.

When practice resumed, Regazzoni went out in the spare car, 1970 312/B chassis no. 004, running on the latest 17-in. rear rims; but a rear tyre came off the rim and the car spun into the protective fencing. Just before the end of practice slight rain began to fall; but before it had rained enough to affect the cars' handling, Andretti went into a violent spin in front of the pits and the car slid down the edge of the track, demolishing wooden posts and wire and coming to rest with both front and rear badly damaged. Once again the trouble had been caused by a deflating rear tyre and the Firestone technicians formed the view that despite the fitting of safety pegs the failures were caused by the tyres centrifuging off the rims. Although tyres of similar width had been used by Lotus without trouble, the Firestone boys advised Forghieri to stop using these wide rims at once. For the following day's practice and the race Andretti took over the spare car, 003.

The first practice session on the Saturday was marred by heavy rain. The Pratt & Whitney engine for the Lotus 56B was now ready as a result of all-night work by the Lotus mechanics and Walker turned in a large number of laps in an effort to learn the circuit. The engine of Stewart's Tyrrell blew up and he went out in the spare car – which meant that he had no chance to get his race car set up to suit wet-weather conditions. On the soaking wet track the only drivers to better 1 min 40 sec were Regazzoni (1 min 39.65 sec) and Rodriguez (1 min 39.96 sec). Over the lunch break the rain stopped and by the time practice had resumed the track had dried out and the weather was fine and warm. The wind was now blowing head-on down the main straight and so most drivers were forced to rely on Friday's times for their grid positions.

THE GRID

J. Stewart (Tyrrell) 1 min 17.64 sec		P. Rodriguez (BRM) 1 min 17.46 sec		J. Ickx (Ferrari) 1 min 17.42 sec
	C. Amon (Matra) 1 min 18.46 sec		C. Regazzoni (Ferrari) 1 min 17.98 sec	
J. Siffert (BRM) 1 min 18.91 sec		J. Surtees (Surtees) 1 min 18.71 sec		R. Wisell (Lotus) 1 min 18.70 sec
	R. Stommelen (Surtees) 1 min 19.11 sec		H. Ganley (BRM) 1 min 19.09 sec	
R. Peterson* (March) 1 min 19.73 sec		F. Cevert (Tyrrell) 1 min 19.54 sec		J-P. Beltoise (Matra) 1 min 19.16 sec
	H. Pescarolo (March) 1 min 20.01 sec		D. Hulme (McLaren) 1 min 19.74 sec	
M. Andretti (Ferrari) 1 min 20.32 sec		A. Soler-Roig (March) 1 min 20.26 sec		G. Hill (Brabham) 1 min. 20.07 sec

* Peterson set this time with the Alfa Romeo-powered March on the Friday.

N. Galli
(March)
1 min 20.61 sec

T. Schenken
(Brabham)
1 min 20.35 sec

P. Gethin
(McLaren)
1 min 22.07 sec

D. Walker
(Lotus)
1 min 21.83 sec

G. van Lennep
(Surtees)
1 min 20.79 sec

S. Barber
(March)
1 min 22.19 sec

THE RACE

Race day dawned dull, miserable, grey and very wet. All the cars were on wet-weather tyres with well waterproofed electrics and a host of improvisations to keep the water out of the cockpits. Because of the atrocious conditions there was an additional fifteen-minute untimed practice session. While the rest of the cars were assembling on the dummy grid, the Ferrari mechanics were working frantically on Andretti's car, changing the fuel pumps, because the fuel system had lost all its pressure. Although the start was delayed as long as possible, eventually the field was moved up to the grid proper and Andretti had to join the race late.

Because of the very slippery surface of the track, there was a perceptible delay between the fall of the flag and the cars moving off, and Ickx and Rodriguez pulled away from Stewart whose Goodyear tyres seemed to lack the grip of his Firestone-shod rivals. Siffert and Soler-Roig spun on the first lap, but both rejoined the race safely. On lap two, Amon, struggling to pass Stewart on the outside of Tarzan, slid over the edge of the corner and into the sand. Eventually he succeeded in getting the car back on to the track, but the radiator was split and he cruised round to the pits to retire.

Stewart was still in third place at the start of lap three, but as the Tyrrell went into Tarzan hairpin, it spun wildly and the Scot rejoined the race in eighth place. When the rest of the field was beginning its third lap, Andretti was joining the race. He rushed down the pits road on to the track and spun at Tarzan – having found out the hard way just how bad conditions were, he then proceeded at a much more modest pace! On lap five Pescarolo lost control of his March and collided with Schenken's Brabham; the 711's rather vulnerable front aerofoil was badly damaged and Pescarolo stopped at the pits for it to be removed.

Walker had been rushing through the field with the Lotus turbine and had risen to tenth place; then at Tarzan on lap six he left his braking much too late and went straight through the fence. The chassis of the Lotus was damaged and the engine sucked in vast quantities of sand. Out in front Ickx was still just managing to hold off a very determined Rodriguez, Regazzoni occupied a rather lonely third place, Surtees was fourth hotly pursued by Peterson and Wisell held fifth place with his Lotus. Wisell pulled of the track just past the pits on lap seven because a wheel was working loose; rather than complete a full lap with the car in such a condition, he decided to reverse back to the pits – and was promptly disqualified! On the following lap Francois Cevert and 'Nanni' Galli collided at Tarzan and the cars, locked together, spun off into the sand. The March was rather battered and out of the race, but Cevert rejoined the race; twenty laps later the suspension broke as a result of this incident and the Tyrrell spun again – and this time Cevert was definitely out. Andretti completed only three laps before returning to the pits to retire with a recurrence of the fuel pump trouble.

Rodriguez slipped by Ickx to take the lead at Tarzan on lap nine, but the Belgian Ferrari driver kept up the pressure and was never more than a second behind the British V-12. Peterson took fourth place from Surtees, Beltoise was sixth and Stommelen seventh – for once the TS9s seemed to be going really well. Siffert had climbed back to seventh place after his first-lap spin, Ganley was eighth and Stewart, who seemed to have given up trying altogether, a rather hopeless ninth. On lap nineteen Stommelen spun off and was disqualified for receiving a push-start.

As the race progressed, so the track began to dry out a little and Ickx tried harder to get in front again. On lap twenty-nine the two cars were alongside each other as they roared out of the Hunserug bend and then the Ferrari went ahead again. Rodriguez fought back, went in front of the Maranello car on the next lap when they were both baulked by Schenken and Pescarolo. Ickx repassed the BRM at the same point on the following lap and began to draw away from the Mexican. While these two were battling for the lead, they lapped both Peterson and Surtees. Siffert was now sixth, Ganley seventh, van Lennep had brought the 'old' red TS7 through to eighth place, Beltoise was ninth and Hill tenth.

On lap forty-nine Ickx turned in a time of 1 min 34.95 sec which proved to be fastest of the race and had soon pulled out a lead of five seconds. Surtees was still worrying Peterson every inch of the way, but nothing that he did could fluster the cool Swedish driver who was turning in a performance to match his fine drive at Monaco. After pit stops to sort out a damaged spoiler, deranged throttle linkage and to remove the rear anti-roll bar, poor Tim Schenken at last gave up the struggle and retired his Brabham BT33. The final retirement came on lap fifty-eight when Soler-

Roig, right at the tail of the field, retired his March, the engine smothered in oil and laying a thick smoke trail.

As the race drew to a close, it became more and more obvious that Rodriguez' BRM was running far from well and at the two slow hairpin bends he was having to drop to first gear to keep the revs up and stop the engine from misfiring, while his Maranello rival was pulling smoothly away from these corners in third gear. Only five laps from the finish Regazzoni, after a smooth and trouble-free race joined the long list of drivers who had gone off the road at Tarzan. Despite a badly battered nose, the result of his collision with the protective fence, the Ferrari rejoined the race; during this incident he was lapped by both Ickx and Rodriguez and soon after he had restarted, the Ferrari shed its nose altogether. On the following lap Surtees clipped the guard-rail at the Hunserug with his right-hand front wheel and carried on to finish with the suspension on that side sadly awry.

When the flag fell, Ickx was just under eight seconds ahead of the Mexican BRM driver. These two drivers had turned in performances that were truly memorable, both Peterson and Surtees had acquitted themselves well in conditions that were really atrocious, but some of the distinguished drivers who had finished at the tail of the field had very little to be proud about.

Results:
1st, J. Ickx (Ferrari 312B), 1 hour 56 min 20.09 sec (94.06 mph)
2nd, P. Rodriguez (BRM P160), 1 hour 56 min 28.08 sec
3rd, C. Regazzoni (Ferrari 312B), 1 lap in arrears
4th, R. Peterson (March 711-Cosworth), 2 laps in arrears
5th, J. Surtees (Surtees TS9-Cosworth), 2 laps in arrears
6th, J. Siffert (BRM P160), 2 laps in arrears
7th, H. Ganley (BRM P153), 4 laps in arrears
8th, G. van Lennep (Surtees TS7-Cosworth), 5 laps in arrears
9th, J-P. Beltoise (Matra-Simca MS120B), 5 laps in arrears
10th, G. Hill (Brabham BT34-Cosworth), 5 laps in arrears
11th, J. Stewart (Tyrrell-Cosworth), 5 laps in arrears
12th, D. Hulme (McLaren M19A-Cosworth), 7 laps in arrears
13th, H. Pescarolo (March 711-Cosworth), 8 laps in arrears
14th, S. Barber (March 711-Cosworth), 10 laps in arrears
15th, P. Gethin (McLaren M19A-Cosworth), 10 laps in arrears

Fastest lap: J. Ickx, 1 min 34.95 sec (98.78 mph)
Existing lap record: J. Ickx (Ferrari 312B), 1 min 19.23 sec (118.38 mph – set in 1970 race).
1970 winner: J. Rindt (Lotus 72-Cosworth), 112.95 mph

Retirements: Lap 2: C. Amon (Matra), radiator damaged after spin; lap 4: M. Andretti (Ferrari), fuel pump and engine trouble; lap 6: D. Walker (Lotus), accident; lap 8: N. Galli (March), accident; lap 17: R. Wisell (Lotus), disqualified for reversing into pits; lap 19: R. Stommelen (Surtees), disqualified for receiving push-start; lap 28: F. Cevert (Tyrrell), suspension damaged after accident; lap 39: T. Schenken (Brabham), suspension damage after accident; lap 58: A. Soler-Roig (March), engine trouble.

ROUND FIVE

FRENCH GRAND PRIX

Paul Ricard (Circuit length: 3.604 miles) 4th July, 1971
Race length: 198.22 miles (55 laps) Weather: hot and dry

After two successful races held on the attractive and interesting Circuit de Charade at Clermont-Ferrand, the 1971 race was transferred to the new Paul Ricard circuit situated between Marseilles and Toulon. Although this was a conveniently located circuit for many of the teams and spectators from Southern Europe, it meant a long drive for the British press and the few British spectators, as well as those from Belgium and the more Northern countries. In place of the difficult curves and high-speed descents of Clermont, the new circuit offered little to compensate; it is flat, characterless and uninteresting, but undoubtedly very safe, and with the most splendid and spacious pit and paddock facilities. A total of twenty-three entries arrived at the circuit and all were to be allowed to start without qualifying problems.

THE ENTRY

Gold Leaf Team Lotus:

1. E. Fittipaldi (Lotus 72D-Cosworth, chassis no. R5)
2. R. Wisell (Lotus 72D-Cosworth, chassis no. R3)

Since the cars' last appearance no changes had been made and Emerson Fittipaldi had now fully recovered from his road accident.

S.p.a. Ferrari SEFAC:

4. J. Ickx (Ferrari 312B/2, chassis no. 006)
5. C. Regazzoni (Ferrari 312B/2, chassis no. 005)

At this race Mario Andretti was not in the team because of a USAC commitment. His 312B/2, chassis no. 007, had, however, been brought along as a spare. All three cars were fitted with the rear suspension anti-vibration damper arrangement and Regazzoni's

Entering the tunnel at Monaco is Reine Wisell with his Lotus 72. He retired with hub failure. The Lotus team was out of luck in 1971. (Nigel Snowdon)

With never enough power to be competitive, the Matra team achieved little success in 1971. One of the best performances was at Barcelona where Chris Amon, seen here leading Fittipaldi's Lotus, took third place. (Nigel Snowdon)

The other user of a V-12 engine, BRM, only came up to expectations in the latter part of the season. The late Jo Siffert took sixth place with this P160 car at Zandvoort. (Nigel Snowdon)

car had an additional damper device fitted ahead of the rear suspension uprights. The circuit was one at which power was at a premium and before the start of practice the Ferraris were clear favourites for victory.

Motor Racing Developments:

7. G. Hill (Brabham BT34-Cosworth, chassis no. BT34/1)
8. T. Schenken (Brabham BT33-Cosworth, chassis no. BT33/3)

Hill's car had revised oil piping, and both cars featured slight suspension modifications, high ram-type air boxes and single oil coolers.

Bruce McLaren Motor Racing:

9. D. Hulme (McLaren M19A-Cosworth, chassis no. M19A/2)
10. P. Gethin (McLaren M19A-Cosworth, chassis no. M19A/1)

No changes had been made to the McLarens apart from the fitting of a high air-box on Hulme's car. The team had the misfortune to suffer a major breakdown with their transporter on the way to the circuit and the drivers missed Friday's practice.

Elf Team Tyrrell:

11. J. Stewart (Tyrrell-Cosworth, chassis no. 003)
12. F. Cevert (Tyrrell-Cosworth, chassis no. 002)

Both of the Tyrrells had slightly modified rear wings and both of Stewart's cars were fitted with the Girling twin-disc front brakes. As usual the first car, 001, had been brought along for Stewart as a spare. Stewart's car only was raced with the streamlined nose.

Yardley-BRM:

14. J. Siffert (BRM P160, chassis no. 02)
15. P. Rodriguez (BRM P160, chassis no. 01)
16. H. Ganley (BRM P153, chassis no. 06)

Once again Rodriguez had P160, chassis no. 03, as a spare and only his car was fitted with the Mk II cylinder heads. All three cars had modified aerofoils with adjustable leading and trailing edges. As before the P160s had the shovel noses.

STP-March:

17. R. Peterson (March 711-Alfa Romeo, chassis no. 06)
18. A. Soler-Roig (March 711-Cosworth, chassis no. 04)
19. A. de Adamich (March 711-Alfa Romeo, chassis no. 01)

Apart from a new high air-box on Peterson's car, the 711s were unchanged from Zandvoort. As a result of the series of blown-up engines suffered at the circuit, the team was desperately short of engines. It had been hoped to field a fourth car for 'Nanni' Galli, but engine problems made this impossible, although the car was present.

Equipe Matra:

20. C. Amon (Matra-Simca MS120B, chassis no. 04)
21. J-P. Beltoise (Matra-Simca MS120B, chassis no. 05)

Amon also had chassis no. 06 as a spare and decided to drive it in the race. As a result of air losses experienced with the previous style of front wheel, the Matras now had a new type of wheel at the front.

Team Surtees:

22. J. Surtees (Surtees TS9-Cosworth, chassis no. 001 sponsored by Brooke Bond-Oxo Racing with Rob Walker).
24. R. Stommelen (Surtees TS9-Cosworth, chassis no. 002 sponsored by *Auto Motor und Sport* – Eifelland)

An almost completed new car, chassis no. 004, had also been brought along and was run in practice on the Saturday. As before Surtees was running with Lockheed brakes and Stommelen with Girlings. Surtees had wanted to use the new lightweight wheels produced by Magnesium Electron Ltd., but one of the rims was damaged during tyre fitting and so it was decided to leave them unused for the time being.

Frank Williams Racing Cars:

27. H. Pescarolo (March 711-Cosworth, chassis no. 03)
28. J. Max (March 701-Cosworth, chassis no. 06)

At the behest of the Motul Oil Company, Williams had brought along the old 1970 March, an ex-works car, that Pescarolo had driven at the beginning of the season, for local driver Jean Max. Since Zandvoort, the team's 711 had been almost completely rebuilt and most of the suspension parts were new.

Jo Siffert Automobiles:

34. F. Mazet (March 701-Cosworth, chassis no. 07)

With sponsorship from Shell-France this ex-Tyrrell 1970 car had been entered for Francois Mazet. Like all the other March entries in the race, it was painted red.

PRACTICE

Most of the teams had already visited the Paul Ricard circuit for testing and the seven-and-a-half hours of practice available on the Friday and Saturday seemed rather over-generous. Throughout practice Matra, hoping so very hard that they would do well on home territory, were plagued by the valve spring breakages that had disrupted a recent testing session on the Bugatti circuit at Le Mans and eventually the drivers were forced to limit themselves to 11,500 rpm (the latest V-12 engine was supposed to peak at 12,000 rpm). On the Friday Stewart was fastest in 1 min 52.72 sec and Regazzoni turned in second fastest lap in 1 min 53.46 sec. Clearly the Ferraris (and the BRMs) had more power at their disposal than the Cosworth-powered Tyrrells, but equally clearly all was not right with the Maranello flat-12s and what was wrong neither Forghieri nor the drivers knew.

It was much the same story on the Saturday morning when Stewart was fastest in an improved 1 min 51.70 sec, Ickx was next quickest in 1 min 52.15 sec and Regazzoni, who spent much of the time complaining about lack of adhesion, was third fastest with both his race car and the team's spare. With his own car he turned in 1 min 52.43 sec and with the spare he was .06 of a second slower. Rodriguez was fourth fastest for BRM with a lap in 1 min 52.66 sec. Matra had set up an electronic timing device at the end of the main straight and this revealed Stewart to be attaining 295 kph, the Ferraris around 288 kph and the Matras 280 kph. But just how much of this extra Tyrrell speed was due to the new streamlined nose that Stewart was using and how much to the extra 'horses' of the special Cosworth engines that were supposed to be supplied to the Tyrrell team nobody knew. During the afternoon Regazzoni gritted his teeth and turned in fastest lap so far in 1 min 51.53 sec, but it was to no avail for Stewart replied with 1 min 50.71 sec. And the Ferrari team felt like packing their bags and going home . . . In contrast the Brabham team was very happy, for Hill, through bad temper as much as anything else, had for the first time in 1971 achieved a respectable practice time and Schenken had won his personal battle with Ganley.

THE GRID

J. Ickx (Ferrari) 1 min 51.88 sec	C. Regazzoni (Ferrari) 1 min 51.53 sec	J. Stewart (Tyrrell) 1 min 50.71 sec
P. Rodriguez (BRM) 1 min 52.46 sec	G. Hill (Brabham) 1 min 52.32 sec	

J-P. Beltoise (Matra) 1 min 52.92 sec	F. Cevert (Tyrrell) 1 min 52.69 sec	J. Siffert (BRM) 1 min 52.50 sec
R. Stommelen (Surtees) 1 min 53.10 sec	C. Amon (Matra) 1 min 52.94 sec	
J. Surtees (Surtees) 1 min 53.57 sec	R. Peterson (March) 1 min 53.36 sec	D. Hulme (McLaren) 1 min 53.24 sec
R. Wisell (Lotus) 1 min 53.75 sec	T. Schenken (Brabham) 1 min 53.58 sec	
H. Pescarolo (March) 1 min 54.27 sec	E. Fittipaldi (Lotus) 1 min 54.22 sec	H. Ganley (BRM) 1 min 53.77 sec
A. de Adamich (March) 1 min 56.17 sec	P. Gethin (McLaren) 1 min 54.90 sec	
F. Mazet (March) 2 min 00.51 sec	J. Max (March) 1 min 59.79 sec	A. Soler-Roig (March) 1 min 57.07 sec

THE RACE

Although a very elaborate electronic starting board, sponsored by the Marlboro cigarette concern, had been installed at the circuit, this gave trouble at the start of the Formula 3 race because of a time-lag and so a flag start was used for the Grand Prix. Stewart, Regazzoni and Ickx moved off together at the fall of the flag, but at the chicane shortly after the start there was a tremendous traffic jam, Ickx' Ferrari was crowded out, thumped about and fell right back. At the end of the first lap the order was Stewart, well clear of Regazzoni, Rodriguez, Beltoise, Amon, Cevert, Siffert and then Ickx. Right at the tail of the field were the two slow and hopelessly uncompetitive March 701 cars.

That Stewart and the Tyrrell – in contrast to their weak performance at Zandvoort – were complete masters of the race soon became apparent and after only three laps they had pulled out a lead of nearly six seconds. Rodriguez, in third place, was chasing Regazzoni hard and both of the Matras were running smoothly and impressively. On only lap four of this fifty-five lap race Soler-Roig retired his March out on the circuit because of a sticking fuel pressure release valve and on the following lap Ickx was out because of a suspected broken crankshaft. Rodriguez locked his wheels at the chicane and while he bounced across the kerbs, Beltoise slipped by into third place. The Mexican soon made up for his mistake, however, and re-took third place from the Frenchman. With eight laps under his Goodyears, Stewart was all of ten seconds ahead of Regazzoni and the race as such was over. It was only a question of whether the Tyrrell chassis and Cosworth engine would hold together for the remaining forty-five laps.

Cevert was going well with the second Tyrrell and now slipped by into fourth place ahead of Beltoise. Right from the start Hulme's McLaren had been running badly and on lap sixteen he retired with ignition failure. Another driver in trouble was Wisell whose Lotus was running slowly and sounding very sick, but Fittipaldi with the other Gold Leaf entry had been picking up places after a poor start and was now in ninth place behind Siffert, Amon and Hill. Next to go was Peterson whose Alfa engine had been down on power since the start and on lap twenty it blew up, spreading oil all over the track. When Regazzoni hit the oil, the Ferrari skidded into the Armco, damaging the right-hand rear suspension and wheel. Rodriguez and Cevert skated by into second and third places without trouble, but Hill, battling hard with the 'lobster-claw' Brabham, spun on the oil and clanged into the Armco. The BT34 crawled back to the pits with a damaged front wheel and steering and although Hill eventually rejoined the race, he later retired with loss of oil pressure, caused by a leak which sprayed oil all over the back tyres and resulted in a nasty spin at the chicane.

So the order behind Stewart was now Rodriguez – Cevert (driving one of the finest races of his career to date) – Siffert – Fittipaldi – Amon – Beltoise – Schenken – Surtees – Wisell – Pescarolo – Stommelen. On lap twenty-eight, by when Stewart had a lead of almost thirty seconds, Rodriguez' BRM rolled to a halt out on the circuit. The trouble was failure of a Marelli coil – a silly, niggling fault and after the race a mechanic was able to drive the car back to the paddock. Cevert now inherited second place and the race was completely Tyrrell-dominated. Siffert was third for BRM and then came Fittipaldi, Amon, Schenken and Beltoise. On lap thirty-two, de Adamich, who had spent the whole race trailing at the tail of the field retired with a blown-up engine. As the race progressed, so Siffert and Fittipaldi closed up on Cevert, and Schenken got to grips with Amon's Matra. Pescarolo's limited slip differential was not working and as a result of this he spun and retired on lap forty-five. Fittipaldi had now forced his way into third place ahead of Siffert, but then Siffert went ahead again for four laps, only to be repassed by the determined Brazilian. On lap forty-two Schenken, a constantly improving driver, snatched fourth place from Amon and a little later an exhaust pipe broke on the right-hand side at the manifold on Cevert's second-place Tyrrell. Despite an unpleasant change in the engine note of the Tyrrell, its performance was unaffected and the car kept going steadily. Only six laps from the finish Schenken's fine drive came to an end when his Cosworth engine lost all its oil pressure and the car ground to a halt near the finishing line – under the regulations he was not allowed to push it across when the flag fell.

After an hour and three-quarters of Tyrrell domination, Stewart crossed the finishing line twenty-eight seconds ahead of his team-mate and this brilliant display by the British team brought back memories of the 1969 French race at Clermont-Ferrand when the Tyrrell-entered Matra MS80s finished first and second. Then the second-place driver was Jean-Pierre Beltoise, Cevert's brother-in-law, but now, while the younger man was on the crest of success with one of the fastest and best prepared of all Grand Prix cars, poor Beltoise was struggling with the recalcitrant V-12 Matra; the fifth and seventh places by Amon and Beltoise were certainly no reflection on the drivers' ability, but an indictment of the failure of the technicians at Vélizy, for after four years' development work the Matra V-12 engine was still no match for its V-8 Cosworth rival and the roadholding of the chassis fell short of the standards set in 1969 by the old MS80. Although the Lotus 72s were never in a position to challenge for the lead, Fittipaldi's third place and Wisell's sixth spot were enough to give Colin Chapman some encouragement, for they were the best places achieved in a season that had so far been fraught with trouble.

Results:

1st, J. Stewart (Tyrrell-Cosworth), 1 hour 46 min 41.68 sec (111.66 mph)
2nd, F. Cevert (Tyrrell-Cosworth), 1 hour 47 min 9.80 sec
3rd, E. Fittipaldi (Lotus 72D-Cosworth), 1 hour 47 min 15.75 sec
4th, J. Siffert (BRM P160), 1 hour 47 min 18.85 sec
5th, C. Amon (Matra-Simca MS120B), 1 hour 47 min 22.76 sec
6th, R. Wisell (Lotus 72D-Cosworth), 1 hour 47 min 57.66 sec
7th, J-P. Beltoise (Matra-Simca MS120B), 1 hour 47 min 58.61 sec
8th, J. Surtees (Surtees TS9-Cosworth), 1 hour 48 min 6.59 sec
9th, P. Gethin (McLaren M19A-Cosworth), 1 lap in arrears
10th, H. Ganley (BRM P153), 1 lap in arrears
11th, R. Stommelen (Surtees TS9-Cosworth), 2 laps in arrears
12th, T. Schenken (Brabham BT33-Cosworth), 5 laps in arrears – classified, but not running at the finish
13th, F. Mazet (March 701-Cosworth), 5 laps in arrears
14th, J. Max (March 701-Cosworth), 9 laps in arrears

Fastest lap: J. Stewart, 1 min 54.09 sec (113.91 mph – new lap record)

Previous lap record: F. Cevert (Tecno-Cosworth Formula 2 car), 2 min 1.4 sec (107.06 mph – set in Formula 2 race the previous year).

1970 winner (race at Clermont-Ferrand): J. Rindt (Lotus 72-Cosworth), 98.42 mph.

Retirements: Lap 4: A. Soler-Roig (March), fuel pump trouble; lap 5: J. Ickx (Ferrari), engine failure; lap 16: D. Hulme (McLaren), ignition trouble; lap 20: R. Peterson (March), blown-up engine; lap 21: C. Regazzoni (Ferrari), damaged rear wheel and suspension after accident; lap 28: P. Rodriguez (BRM), coil failure; lap 32: A. de Adamich (March), engine failure; lap 35: G. Hill (Brabham), loss of oil pressure; lap 45: H. Pescarolo (March), transmission failure; lap 50: T. Schenken (Brabham), loss of oil pressure and seized engine.

ROUND SIX

BRITISH GRAND PRIX

Silverstone (Circuit length: 2.927 miles) 17th July, 1971
Race length: 199.04 miles (68 laps) Weather: hot and dry

Now the oldest of British motor racing circuits, Silverstone, a former military airfield, was despised when it was first opened for its flat, characterless landscape and was regarded as a poor substitute for the true Continental road circuits such as Bremgarten (heavily wooded and picturesque setting of the Swiss Grand Prix), Reims (at that time running through the streets of the village of Gueux) and Barcelona (the Pedralbes circuit through the outskirts of that magnificent city). But now Silverstone is the epitome of the simple, safe, uninteresting motor racing circuit, very similar in concept to the Paul Ricard circuit, but with the distinct advantage that its twenty-three years of history have given it a degree of character and atmosphere. In the first British Grand Prix, the 1948 race, the Scuderia Ambrosiana Maseratis of silver-haired 'Gigi' Villoresi and the plump Ascari took the first two places; two years later the race was won by the great Nino Farina with his Alfa Romeo 158; and the 1951 race saw the first 100 mph lap of Silverstone set in practice by Froilan Gonzalez and the first defeat of the all-conquering 'Alfettas' by this same Argentinian driver. By 1958 Peter Collins and his V-6 Ferrari had pushed the race-winning average up to 102.05 mph and eleven years later race winner Jackie Stewart averaged 127.25 mph and set a new lap record in 1 min 21.3 sec (129.61 mph). The 1970 race had been held at Brands Hatch and so Stewart's record stood until the 1971 *Daily Express* Trophy race when Stewart himself turned in a lap of 1 min 20.5 sec.

THE ENTRY

Gold Leaf Team Lotus:

1. E. Fittipaldi (Lotus 72D-Cosworth, chassis no. R5)
2. D. Charlton (Lotus 72D-Cosworth, chassis no. R3)
3. R. Wisell (Lotus 56B-Pratt & Whitney, chassis no. 1)

To compensate for his failure to get a drive at Zandvoort Charlton had been included in the team and this meant that Wisell had to drive the gas-turbine car, a state of affairs with which he was none too happy. The 72s were now fitted with ram air-boxes over the induction trumpets and flaps on the rear aerofoils.

S.p.a. Ferrari SEFAC:

4. J. Ickx (Ferrari 312B/2, chassis no. 006)
5. C. Regazzoni (Ferrari 312B/2, chassis no. 005)

The Maranello team had originally entered a third car for Andretti, but because of a USAC commitment the following day, there had never been any hope of him starting. Once again his car was brought along as a spare. In practice Ferrari tried out streamlined noses, consisting of angled vertical members attached to the front wings and although these were retained for the race, the team abandoned the air-boxes that they had also tried in practice.

Motor Racing Developments:

7. G. Hill (Brabham BT34-Cosworth, chassis no. BT34/1)
8. T. Schenken (Brabham BT33-Cosworth, chassis no. BT33/3)

Since their last appearance both Brabhams had been fitted with new drive-shafts. The BT34 now had shafts with constant velocity joints (instead of roller splines) and the BT33 was fitted with Hewland's own shafts incorporating Hooke-type joints and roller splines. The RAC. Scrutineers are notoriously strict and to ensure that they would be quite satisfied with the BT34, the exhaust pipes had been raised slightly and this had necessitated repositioning the oil coolers. Hill's car was fitted in practice with Girling twin-disc brakes.

Bruce McLaren Motor Racing:

9. D. Hulme (McLaren M19A-Cosworth, chassis no. M19A/2)
10. P. Gethin (McLaren M19A-Cosworth, chassis no. M19A/1)

11. J. Oliver (McLaren M14A-Cosworth, chassis no. M14A/2)

There were no changes to the two M19As. Oliver was making a return to Grand Prix racing after being dropped by the BRM team at the end of the 1970 season.

Elf Team Tyrrell:

12. J. Stewart (Tyrrell-Cosworth, chassis no. 003)
14. F. Cevert (Tyrrell-Cosworth, chassis no. 002)

Streamlined noses were now fitted to both cars. The team had also brought along 001 as a spare, but it was not used at all in practice. The twin-disc brakes had been abandoned.

Yardley-BRM:

16. J. Siffert (BRM P160, chassis no. 02)
17. H. Ganley (BRM P153, chassis no. 06)

The team's number one driver Pedro Rodriguez had been killed at the Norisring the previous weekend and an aura of despondency hung over BRM. The cars were as before, except that Siffert's was fitted with the Mk II cylinder heads intended for use by Pedro and Siffert had the 'slim-line' P160, chassis no. 03, as a spare.

STP-March:

18. R. Peterson (March 711-Cosworth, chassis no. 06)
19. A. de Adamich (March 711-Alfa Romeo, chassis no. 01)
20. N. Galli (March 711-Cosworth, chassis no. 04)

Peterson drove the same car as at the French race. but now fitted with a Cosworth engine. Alex Soler-Roig had left the team because he felt he was not getting much consideration as far as engines were concerned and so the team had fielded Galli without sponsorship because they had a very high opinion of his potential.

Équipe Matra:

21. C. Amon (Matra-Simca MS120B, chassis no. 06)
22. J-P. Beltoise (Matra-Simca MS120B, chassis no. 05)

Because of transporter difficulties the team had been unable to bring along a spare car. Since the team's last outing apparently nothing had been done to overcome these cars' only too obvious shortcomings.

Team Surtees:

23. J. Surtees (Surtees TS9-Cosworth, chassis no. 001 sponsored by Brooke Bond-Oxo Racing with Rob Walker).

24. R. Stommelen (Surtees TS9-Cosworth, chassis no. 002 sponsored by *Auto Motor und Sport* – Eifelland)

25. D. Bell (Surtees TS9-Cosworth, chassis no. 004)

Bell had originally been entered with the 1970 TS7 car, chassis no. 001, with sponsorship which he had raised privately. However Surtees decided to let Bell drive the latest TS9 car in the race.

Frank Williams Racing Cars:

26. H. Pescarolo (March 711-Cosworth, chassis no. 03)

Clarke Mordaunt Racing with Alistair Guthrie:

35. M. Beuttler (March 711-Cosworth, chassis no. 02)

This car was the ex-works 711 that Peterson had driven into second place at Monaco, now fitted with a number of bits and pieces from this team's old March 701. Although the car practised bearing the number 35, it raced as number 6.

PRACTICE

Largely as expected, Stewart dominated the first practice session on the Thursday morning with a time of 1 min 19.4 sec and Fittipaldi with the Lotus 72 was a fifth of a second slower. At this stage the Ferraris had not been properly sorted to suit the circuit, but even so Regazzoni was third fastest in 1 min 20.2 sec. During this session Siffert tried out his P160 fitted with the wheel-width nose and a ram air scoop, but neither of these devices was persevered with. The same three drivers were fastest during the afternoon session and although both Stewart and Fittipaldi improved on their times, Regazzoni seemed stuck at the 1 min 20.2 sec mark. Hulme tried out his M19A with a 'shovel'-type nose and the high air-box seen at the Paul Ricard circuit, but it was decided to run the car without either 'extra'.

Fittipaldi set the pace on the Friday morning with a lap in 1 min 18.3 sec and Stewart replied with a lap that was a tenth of a second faster. But when Regazzoni went out and recorded a lap in 1 min 18.1 sec, the Scot was unable to match it. Because of handling problems and a slipping clutch Ickx was unable to turn in any fast laps and another driver in trouble was Hill whose BT34, just fitted with an 11-series engine, managed to suck in a stone and damage a cylinder after only a couple of laps. Ickx was still in trouble during the afternoon session; his flat-12 engine holed a piston and was wheeled away for an engine change. Stewart trying his hardest, just managed to equal Regazzoni's time, but his efforts were hampered by a strong wind and but for this he would probably have been faster.

THE GRID

J. Siffert (BRM) 1 min 18.2 sec		J. Stewart (Tyrrell) 1 min 18.1 sec		C. Regazzoni (Ferrari) 1 min 18.1 sec
	R. Peterson (March) 1 min 19.0 sec		E. Fittipaldi (Lotus) 1 min 18.3 sec	
D. Hulme (McLaren) 1 min 19.6 sec		T. Schenken (Brabham) 1 min 19.5 sec		J. Ickx (Ferrari) 1 min 19.5 sec
	F. Cevert (Tyrrell) 1 min 19.8 sec		C. Amon (Matra) 1 min 19.7 sec	
D. Charlton (Lotus) 1 min 20.05 sec		R. Stommelen (Surtees) 1 min 19.88 sec		H. Ganley (BRM) 1 min 19.84 sec
	J-P. Beltoise (Matra) 1 min 20.2 sec		P. Gethin (McLaren) 1 min 20.1 sec	
J. Surtees (Surtees) 1 min 20.6 sec		H. Pescarolo (March) 1 min 20.5 sec		G. Hill (Brabham) 1 min 20.3 sec
	M. Beuttler (March) 1 min 20.7 sec		R. Wisell (Lotus) 1 min 20.66 sec	
D. Bell (Surtees) 1 min 22.3 sec		J. Oliver (McLaren) 1 min 21.0 sec		N. Galli (Brabham) 1 min 20.9 sec
			A. de Adamich (March) 1 min 23.2 sec	

THE RACE

On race morning, which was beautifully warm and sunny, there was forty-five minutes of untimed practice, but several drivers did not even bother to turn out for this. Ickx, however, took the session very seriously and was putting in some very quick laps towards the end. Afterwards Ickx commented that the new engine fitted to his car was the best he had ever tried and that even with full tanks it would pull 12,600 rpm in top gear. So at least he had this consolation to make up for the troubles suffered in practice.

On his warming-up lap Charlton's engine burnt a piston and the Lotus 72 arrived on the dummy grid wreathed in smoke and covered with oil. There seemed little alternative but for the car to start the race and when the field was moved up to the grid proper, Charlton went with them. When starter Dean Delamont raised the flag, Regazzoni anticipated the start, accelerated forwards and then stopped again. Several other cars moved forward and as if disciplining a pack of unruly children, Delamont hesitated before dropping the flag. By the time the flag had fallen, several cars were out of their proper place, Oliver at the back of the grid moved forward, stopped and was then shoved into the back of Hill's Brabham and both cars were out of the race. Ron Tauranac lodged a protest that Oliver had jumped the start and this was upheld by the stewards. Oliver was fined £50 and most people felt very sorry for Jack that such an unfortunate incident should happen on his return to Formula 1 racing. It was difficult to have much sympathy for Hill whose driving had been hopelessly slow for much of the season and if he had not been so uncompetitive at Silverstone, he would not have been so far back on the grid and thus not in a position in which Oliver could hit him.

Regazzoni was away first and Ickx accelerated hard to come through from the third row to hold second spot behind his team-mate; Stewart was third ahead of Siffert and Schenken. Charlton with the smoking Lotus 72 completed a single, slow lap before coming into the pits to retire. Although the two Ferraris still led at the end of lap one, Stewart was almost alongside Ickx as they swung into Copse, the first right-hander after the pits. By Stowe, on the far side of the circuit, Stewart was through to second place and Siffert followed through on Stewart's tail so that Ickx was pushed back to fourth spot. Peterson was now in fifth place ahead of Schenken. On lap four Stewart took the lead from Regazzoni under braking for Stowe and at once began to pull away from the flat-12 car. On the following lap Siffert swept by the Ferrari to take second place.

By lap ten Stewart had pulled out a lead of 3.5 seconds over Siffert and the Swiss driver was two seconds ahead of his compatriot. Behind Regazzoni and Ickx came Peterson, Schenken, Fittipaldi and Hulme. Then, after quite an interval, Ganley led Gethin, Cevert, Fittipaldi, Stommelen and Amon. Three laps later Schenken lost a place to the Lotus of Fittipaldi, and the Brazilian now began to worry Peterson. Despite Ickx' satisfaction with his new engine on the morning of the race, it was now beginning to cut out on corners and the next in trouble was poor Siffert who had been driving an inspired race; because of tyre vibration the BRM's rear aerofoil had worked loose and was lying at a flatter angle than intended. The result was a pronounced oversteer and while 'Seppi' was endeavouring to cope with this, Regazzoni slipped back into second place. By lap twenty Stewart had increased his lead to fourteen seconds and he was dominating the race as easily as he had at the Paul Ricard circuit.

On lap eighteen Gethin pulled into the pits to complain about the steering; the trouble was traced to a deflating tyre and he rejoined the race a lap in arrears. Next in trouble was Cevert, in tenth place, who stopped on lap twenty, soaked in petrol from the broken pressure gauge. Two laps were lost while the trouble was sorted out and by the time the young Frenchman had rejoined the race, he had lost all hope of repeating his performance in the French race. On lap twenty-two Beuttler retired his March with fluctuating oil pressure and two laps later Derek Bell with the new TS9 was out because of a sheared radius rod bracket. It was on this lap that Peterson lost fifth place to Fittipaldi and it was now Ickx who was struggling to hold off the Brazilian's attacks.

By half-distance, lap thirty-four, Stewart had extended his lead to eighteen seconds and Regazzoni was having a rough time holding off Siffert's BRM. The Swiss driver had now accustomed himself to the changed handling of the Bourne car and was giving the Ferrari driver no quarter. Still the retirements continued, Hulme had pulled off the road at Becketts on lap thirty-two with smoke pouring out of his Cosworth engine and three laps later Amon coasted into the pits to retire his Matra with burnt-out inlet valves. Now Ickx was in trouble, his front left-hand tyre had started to blister and at the end of lap thirty-eight he stuck up his hand and headed for the pits. By the time the wheel had been changed and the car had rejoined the race, Ickx was at the back of the field in thirteenth place.

Peterson was now in fourth place behind Regazzoni and Siffert, whose engine was beginning to sound very rough. When the BRM pulled into the pits at the end of lap forty-two, the red March moved up another place. The trouble with the BRM was traced to loose brackets attaching the coil to the roll-over bar stay and Siffert rejoined the race in fourteenth place. Six laps later Peterson had moved up another place for Regazzoni was in the pits with a blistered front tyre and the engine low on oil. Extra oil cannot be added during a race and the flat-12 car was pushed away into retirement. Behind Peterson came Schenken, driving the best race of his short Formula 1 career, and Fittipaldi whose car was jumping out of fourth gear. Then came Pescarolo, Stommelen and Surtees, all dicing merrily, but at no particularly high speed. At the end of lap fifty-one Ickx, still well down the field, pulled out of the race with a very rough engine. Wisell was in and out of the pits with the Lotus turbine which was not revving properly and Gethin retired with a blown-up engine on lap fifty-four. Schenken and Fittipaldi closed up again on Peterson, but the battle evaporated when Schenken's Brabham began to jam in fourth and fifth gears and he retired at Abbey Curve with a seized-up gearbox on lap sixty-three. On the last lap Galli ceded tenth place to Cevert when his car lost all its fuel pressure.

At the chequered flag Stewart led by over thirty-five seconds from Peterson who had driven a magnificently steady and persistent race. For Lotus, Fittipaldi did well to take third place despite a gearbox that had given persistent trouble. It was much the same story with the Williams-entered March and Pescarolo had strived hard for his fourth place, for his car had kept jumping out of gear and as a result he had over-revved the engine on several occasions.

Results:

1st, J. Stewart (Tyrrell-Cosworth), 1 hour 31 min 31.5 sec (130.48 mph)
2nd, R. Peterson (March 711-Cosworth), 1 hour 32 min 7.6 sec
3rd, E. Fittipaldi (Lotus 72D-Cosworth), 1 hour 32 min 22.0 sec
4th, H. Pescarolo (March 711-Cosworth), 1 lap in arrears
5th, R. Stommelen (Surtees TS9-Cosworth), 1 lap in arrears
6th, J. Surtees (Surtees TS9-Cosworth), 1 lap in arrears
7th, J-P. Beltoise (Matra-Simca MS120B), 2 laps in arrears
8th, H. Ganley (BRM P153), 2 laps in arrears
9th, J. Siffert (BRM P160), 2 laps in arrears
10th, F. Cevert (Tyrrell-Cosworth), 3 laps in arrears
11th, N. Galli (March 711-Cosworth), 3 laps in arrears
12th, T. Schenken (Brabham BT33-Cosworth), 5 laps in arrears – classified but not running at finish.
— R. Wisell (Lotus T56B – Pratt & Whitney), 11 laps in arrears – still running but not classified as a finisher
— A. de Adamich (March 711-Alfa Romeo), 12 laps in arrears – still running but not classified as a finisher

Fastest lap: J. Stewart, 1 min 19.90 sec (131.88 mph – record).
Previous lap record: J. Stewart (Tyrrell-Cosworth), 1 min 20.5 sec (130.90 mph – set in the *Daily Express* Trophy race earlier in the year).
1970 winner (race at Brands Hatch): J. Rindt (Lotus 72-Cosworth), 108.69 mph).

Retirements: Lap 1: G. Hill (Brabham), accident on starting line; J. Oliver (McLaren), accident on starting line; lap 2: D. Charlton (Lotus), engine trouble; lap 22: M. Beuttler (March), fluctuating oil pressure; lap 24: D. Bell (Surtees), rear suspension failure; lap 32: D. Hulme (McLaren), engine trouble; lap 36: C. Amon (Matra), engine trouble; lap 49: C. Regazzoni (Ferrari), loss of oil pressure; lap 52: J. Ickx (Ferrari), engine trouble; lap 54: P. Gethin (McLaren), loss of oil pressure; lap 63: T. Schenken (Brabham), gearbox failure.

ROUND SEVEN

GERMAN GRAND PRIX

Nürburgring (Circuit length: 14.19 miles) 1st August, 1971
Race length: 170.27 miles (12 laps) Weather: warm and dry

In 1970 the German Grand Prix had been held at the Hockenheim Motordrom near Stuttgart because modifications to the Nürburgring requested by the Grand Prix Drivers' Association had not been completed and the Association had voted not to race at the circuit in its existing form. The Nürburgring is, with Spa-Francorchamps, one of the two finest road circuits in the world and the organisers of the German Grand Prix realised that it was better to run their National race on a rather 'tame' version of the existing circuit than to see it permanently debased by being run on a dull, lifeless, artificial circuit. Some alterations to the circuit had been completed by the 1000 Kilometres race in May and some since. Although the general layout of the circuit remained unchanged, some corners had been re-shaped so that they were now left-hand corners instead of right-hand and some were right-hand instead of left and several drivers were thoroughly confused and had to start learning the circuit all over again. And relearning was not helped by the complete disappearance of the many familiar 'signs', such as clumps of trees, that had vanished altogether. All the spectacular 'jumps' (or 'yumps' if you prefer it) had been ironed out, thousands of trees had been felled to provide sanded run-off areas and mile upon mile of Armco barrier had been installed (and the manufacturers of this must now be very wealthy men). Despite all these changes the Nürburgring remains a magnificent circuit and one of the most difficult to master. Because of these changes the times set in practice and the race in 1969 had to be completely disregarded and the nearest guide-line to a good time was something better than the new lap record of 7 min 40.8 sec set by Ickx with the flat-12 Ferrari 312P Prototype in the 1971 Nürburgring 1000 Kilometres race.

Elf Team Tyrrell:

2. J. Stewart (Tyrrell-Cosworth, chassis no. 003)
3. F. Cevert (Tyrrell-Cosworth, chassis no. 002)

The cars were fitted with the streamlined noses and were unchanged from Silverstone. As usual the team had brought along the original car, 001, as a spare.

S.p.a. Ferrari SEFAC:

4. J. Ickx (Ferrari 312B/2, chassis no. 006)
5. M. Andretti (Ferrari 312B/2, chassis no. 007)
6. C. Regazzoni (Ferrari 312B/2, chassis no. 005)

As a spare car Ferrari had brought along the 1970 312B car, chassis no. 004. Apart from the lack of the wheel-width noses the cars were unchanged from Silverstone.

Team Surtees:

7. J. Surtees (Surtees TS9-Cosworth, chassis no. 001 sponsored by Brooke Bond-Oxo Racing with Rob Walker)
12. R. Stommelen (Surtees TS9-Cosworth, chassis no. 002 sponsored by *Auto Motor und Sport* – Eifelland)

The team had also brought along the TS7 'hire car' for Dieter Questor, but this did not run as the driver had been unable to raise the necessary sponsorship. Both of the TS9s were fitted with new ram air-boxes, but were otherwise unchanged.

Gold Leaf Team Lotus:

8. E. Fittipaldi (Lotus 72D-Cosworth, chassis no. R5)
9. R. Wisell (Lotus 72D-Cosworth, chassis no. R6)

Wisell was at the wheel of a brand new car and both were to Silverstone specification apart from ventilated brake discs front and rear.

Équipe Matra:

10. C. Amon (Matra-Simca MS120B, chassis no. 06)

Once again Beltoise's licence had been suspended because of the Argentine incident at the beginning of the year and Matra had made no attempt to replace him. Amon had chassis no. 04 as a spare. The cars were unchanged from Silverstone.

Frank Williams Racing Cars:

14. H. Pescarolo (March 711-Cosworth, chassis no. 03)

This March was now running with an air-box and Bilstein gas-filled dampers.

STP-March:

15. R. Peterson (March 711-Cosworth, chassis no. 06)
16. A. de Adamich (March 711-Alfa Romeo, chassis no. 01)
17. N. Galli (March 711-Alfa Romeo, chassis no. 04)

Of the two Alfa Romeo-powered cars, only that of de Adamich was works-backed. All three 711s had new and stronger rear suspension uprights and Peterson's car had an air-box, cowls over its side radiators and Bilstein gas-filled dampers.

Bruce McLaren Motor Racing:

18. D. Hulme (McLaren M19A-Cosworth, chassis no. M19A/2)
20. P. Gethin (McLaren M19A-Cosworth, chassis no. M19A/1)

There were no changes from Silverstone except that Hulme's car was fitted with Hewland drive-shafts and drilled front brake discs. A third entry for Oliver had been scratched because of a shortage of Cosworth engines.

Yardley-BRM:

21. J. Siffert (BRM P160, chassis no. 02)
22. V. Elford (BRM P160, chassis no. 01)
23. H. Ganley (BRM P153, chassis no. 06)

The team had also brought along P160, chassis no. 03, as a spare for Siffert. The presence of Vic Elford in the team was not because of the death of Rodriguez, for Louis Stanley had promised him a drive before this had occurred. This was Elford's first Grand Prix since he had crashed with Colin Crabbe's McLaren in the 1969 German race. Both Siffert's race and spare car were fitted with the Mk II cylinder heads. The only changes made to the BRMs since Silverstone were strengthened stays for the rear aerofoils.

Motor Racing Developments:

24. G. Hill (Brabham BT34-Cosworth, chassis no. BT34/1)
25. T. Schenken (Brabham BT33-Cosworth, chassis no. BT33/3)

Schenken's car had reverted to the original type of drive-shaft and in practice it ran with a very ugly full-width nose. As an insurance against the trouble suffered at Silverstone the team had brought along its own transmission technician.

Ecurie Bonnier:
27. J. Bonnier (McLaren M7C-Cosworth, chassis no. M7C/1)

Since its last appearance at Kyalami, Bonnier's ageing McLaren had been rebuilt with a new monocoque and suspension. It was the only car to appear with the supposedly compulsory rear red light!

Clarke Mordaunt Racing with Alistair Guthrie:
28. M. Beuttler (March 711-Cosworth, chassis no. 02)

PRACTICE

Those Formula 1 drivers who did not compete in either Sports Car racing or Formula 2 had a lot of learning to do and two drivers had virtually no knowledge of the Nürburgring in its original form. Gethin had arrived early, hoping to put in some laps on the Monday before the race with his Porsche 911E, but was thwarted by the work still in progress – he had not raced there since 1963 when he drove a Diva. Howden Ganley had never raced at the Nürburgring and he went round on foot (in four hours twenty minutes!) to familiarise himself. BRM, Ferrari and March were all able to get in some unofficial practice on the Wednesday. On the Thursday the Tyrrell team arrived to find the circuit closed, so Stewart took his car out on the Sudschleife, the short and as yet unchanged South Circuit.

The first official practice, starting at midday on the Friday, took place in warm sunshine. The session was dominated by Stewart who turned in a sizzling 7 min 21.9 sec, while *Ringmeister* Ickx, the lap record holder of both the old and new circuits, was puffing round with a smoking engine and could manage only fifth fastest in 7 min 35.8 sec. It was during this session that Pescarolo arrived at the pits with ripples in the monocoque of the Williams March which had buckled under the stresses of the circuit. March had to content themselves with the excuse that this car had the older and lighter 18-gauge monocoque, the heavier 16-gauge being used on all the later cars!

During the afternoon session Stewart brought his time down to 7 min 19.0 sec and Ickx was second fastest in 7 min 22.3 sec. Regazzoni had a nasty moment went he took off with full tanks at the Pflanzgarten (one of the few points on the circuits where all four wheels still take off the ground), landed badly and crashed the flat-12. Fortunately he was uninjured and the damage was limited to battered bodywork. Both Schenken and Stewart, now at the wheel of his spare car, had engine blow-ups. Although not quite able to match Stewart's time, Ickx joined the exclusive under-twenty club on the Saturday with a lap in 7 min 19.2 sec. It was during Saturday's session that for the third time in 1971 the Williams March, the monocoque now braced with tubing, broke a rear suspension upright. Pescarolo spun off and came to rest without incident. But it was a very uneasy Frank Williams who accepted a pair of the later and stronger March rear uprights from the works team and he declared that the car would not be raced again until it had been fitted with the very much heftier Can-Am components.

THE GRID

	J. Ickx (Ferrari) 7 min 19.2 sec		J. Stewart (Tyrrell) 7 min 19.0 sec
C. Regazzoni (Ferrari) 7 min 22.7 sec		J. Siffert (BRM) 7 min 22.4 sec	
	D. Hulme (McLaren) 7 min 26.0 sec		F. Cevert (Tyrrell) 7 min 23.4 sec
E. Fittipaldi (Lotus) 7 min 27.5 sec		R. Peterson (March) 7 min 26.5 sec	
	H. Pescarolo (March) 7 min 30.3 sec		T. Schenken (Brabham) 7 min 29.8 sec
R. Stommelen (Surtees) 7 min 34.7 sec		M. Andretti (Ferrari) 7 min 31.7 sec	
	H. Ganley (BRM) 7 min 36.6 sec		G. Hill (Brabham) 7 min 36.1 sec
C. Amon (Matra) 7 min 37.3 sec		J. Surtees (Surtees) 7 min 36.7 sec	
	V. Elford (BRM) 7 min 39.98 sec		R. Wisell (Lotus) 7 min 39.96 sec
A. de Adamich (March) 7 min 41.7 sec		P. Gethin (McLaren) 7 min 41.4 sec	
	M. Beuttler (March) 7 min 52.6 sec		N. Galli (March) 7 min 47.5 sec

Failed to qualify:

J. Bonnier (McLaren) 8 min 17.0 sec

It was pleasant and rather surprising after dry practice sessions (apart from the latter part of the Saturday session) that race day should dawn fine and conditions were perfect for racing. Before the start there was a warming-up lap round the pits loop and then the cars assembled on the dummy grid. When Hill's car was started up in the paddock, the fuel pressure was found to be very low and it only just made the grid after a frantic rush by the mechanics to sort out the trouble. While the cars were lined up on the grid proper, Hill found that his throttle linkage had become deranged and Wisell's Lotus had developed a fuel vapour lock. As the rest of the field roared away these two cars were left on the grid. Wisell went off about thirty seconds late after the mechanics had squirted fuel down the inlet trumpets, but in Hill's case a vital nut had been left off in the rush to get the car ready and the Brabham had lost half-a-lap before it joined the race.

Stewart and Ickx moved off side by side at the fall of the flag, but the Scot passed the Belgian under braking for the North Curve and assumed a lead that he never lost throughout the twelve laps of the race. By the end of lap one Stewart had already pulled out a lead of three seconds over Ickx and then came Regazzoni, Siffert, Peterson, Hulme, Andretti and Cevert. De Adamich had stopped out on the circuit because of fuel injection trouble and came into the pits long after the rest of the field had gone by to start their third lap. He rejoined the race, but retired after only another lap.

On the second lap of the race Ickx lost control and spun at Wipperman and a collision with the Armco barrier tore off the electrics at the rear of the car and put him out of the race. Regazzoni had his own little excursion into the in-field while avoiding his team-mate and was passed by Siffert. A leaking fuel bag had soaked Hulme with petrol and he fell back behind Andretti and Cevert and at the end of the lap Amon came past the pits with his V-12 engine misfiring badly. As he started lap three, Stewart had already pulled out a lead of sixteen seconds and behind him the order was now Siffert, Regazzoni, Peterson, Andretti and Cevert, with the latter pair running side-by-side. As he accelerated along the stretch behind the pits on lap three, Ganley switched off and retired with oil pouring into the cockpit and at the end of the lap a petrol-soaked Hulme pulled into the pits to retire. Next to go was Beuttler who punctured a tyre shortly after starting his fourth lap and instead of completing a full lap, he took the short cut through the pits loop and was disqualified.

On lap three Cevert had snatched fourth place from Peterson and on the next lap Stewart set a new official record of 7 min 27.2 sec.

Siffert's engine had now developed a bad misfire and on lap five he fell back to fourth place behind Regazzoni and Cevert. On that lap Stewart reduced the record to 7 min 25.5 sec and increased his lead to thirty-three seconds. Pescarolo retired his March with collapsed suspension and now Regazzoni's Ferrari was beginning to sound very rough. Stewart, still increasing his average, reduced the record to 7 min 23.6 sec on lap six, and after starting the next lap Siffert cut through the loop road to return to the pits. As a coil had ceased to function and the right-hand lower front wishbone was detaching itself from the chassis he was not grieved at disqualification. Gethin had gone off the road on lap six at Metzgefeld and abandoned his McLaren, and Amon collided with the Armco on the same lap, but crawled back to the pits to retire.

Cevert passed Regazzoni and Schenken went ahead of Fittipaldi, but then the Brazilian stopped at his pit at the end of lap seven to have a broken rear anti-roll bar cut away. At the end of the following lap Peterson stopped at the pits to have a battered glass-fibre radiator cowl removed and Fittipaldi brought the Lotus 72 in with oil all over the engine and the car was retired. Galli had already stopped to have the collapsed rear aerofoil removed and now he stopped with collapsed engine mountings, but eventually staggered away in the hope of finishing the race. On that lap Stewart set a new record of 7 min 22.9 sec and behind him the order was Cevert, Regazzoni, Andretti, Peterson and Schenken. Regazzoni's engine was now sounding better and on lap nine he made a determined effort to catch Cevert, but it was to no avail for the Frenchman turned in a really inspired lap ten in 7 min 20.1 sec, a time which even Stewart failed to match. Throughout the race Elford's BRM had been running badly and at the end of lap ten he stopped at the pits for a new coil to be fitted. He rejoined the race to finish last but for Galli's very sick March-Alfa.

As the race drew to a close Stewart eased his pace and at the chequered flag Cevert was just under thirty seconds behind his team-leader. For the Tyrrell team the results could hardly have been more pleasing. Cevert had improved enormously since he first drove for Tyrrell at the 1970 Dutch Grand Prix and it seemed that it would not be long before he won his first World Championship race. With third and fourth places by Regazzoni and Andretti, Ferrari fortunes had improved a shade over their recent performances, but the team was still falling far short of the standards it had set in 1970. Tim Schenken gained sixth place and a well deserved Championship point after atrocious luck in his two previous races. Here was another driver who was improving beyond recognition and his fine drives with a car that was not the most competitive were putting his elder and more experienced team-leader to shame.

Results:

1st, J. Stewart (Tyrrell-Cosworth), 1 hour 29 min 15.7 sec (114.46 mph)
2nd, F. Cevert (Tyrrell-Cosworth), 1 hour 29 min 45.8 sec
3rd, C. Regazzoni (Ferrari 312B), 1 hour 29 min 52.8 sec
4th, M. Andretti (Ferrari 312B), 1 hour 31 min 20.7 sec
5th, R. Peterson (March 711-Cosworth), 1 hour 31 min 44.8 sec
6th, T. Schenken (Brabham BT33-Cosworth), 1 hour 32 min 14.3 sec
7th, J. Surtees (Surtees TS9-Cosworth), 1 hour 32 min 34.7 sec
8th, R. Wisell (Lotus 72D-Cosworth), 1 hour 35 min 47.4 sec
9th, G. Hill (Brabham BT34-Cosworth), 1 hour 35 min 52.7 sec
10th, R. Stommelen (Surtees TS9-Cosworth), 1 lap in arrears
11th, V. Elford (BRM P160), 1 lap in arrears
12th, N. Galli (March 711-Alfa Romeo), 2 laps in arrears

Fastest lap: F. Cevert, 7 min 20.1 sec (116.07 mph – record).
Previous Formula 1 lap record: J. Ickx (Brabham BT26-Cosworth), 7 min 43.8 sec (110.13 mph – set in 1969 race). Note: Ickx with the Ferrari 312P Prototype lapped in 7 min 40.8 sec in the 1971 Nürburgring 1000 Kilometres race.
1970 winner (race held at Hockenheim): J. Rindt (Lotus 72-Cosworth), 123.90 mph.

Retirements: Lap 2: J. Ickx (Ferrari), damaged electrics and rear suspension after accident; lap 3: H. Ganley (BRM), engine trouble; A. de Adamich (March), fuel injection trouble; lap 4: M. Beuttler (March), disqualified for wrong entry into pit after puncture; D. Hulme (McLaren), leaking fuel bag; lap 6: H. Pescarolo (March), suspension failure; P. Gethin (McLaren), damaged rear suspension after accident; lap 7: J. Siffert (BRM), coil failure and suspension damage; C. Amon (Matra), damaged suspension after accident; lap 9: E. Fittipaldi (Lotus), loss of oil pressure.

ROUND EIGHT

AUSTRIAN GRAND PRIX

Osterreichring (Circuit length: 3.763 miles) 15th August, 1971
Race length: 198.34 miles (54 laps) Weather: warm and dry

The Austrian Grand Prix had first been held at the artificial Osterreichring near Zeltweg in 1970. Although the circuit was built purely for racing, it had been conceived with such skill and careful thought that it blended perfectly with the contours of the hillsides and its combination of fast curves, many of them completely blind, succeeded in creating the illusion that it was a natural road circuit. The first Formula 1 race at the new circuit had represented the turning point in Maranello fortunes and Jacky Ickx had scored a fine victory with the 312B flat-12 car and Stommelen had finished second ahead of Stommelen's Brabham. After four further major victories and two minor wins, the Ferrari onslaught had disintegrated in the face of Jackie Stewart and the Tyrrell and, now, after five victories by the dark-blue British car and its Scottish driver and a sole win by Ickx and his Ferrari at the rain-swept Zandvoort circuit, every enthusiast was wondering whether Maranello would regain its form on the Austrian circuit to which its cars were so well suited and which was much liked by the Ferrari drivers.

THE ENTRY

Gold Leaf Team Lotus:

2. E. Fittipaldi (Lotus 72D-Cosworth, chassis no. R5)
3. R. Wisell (Lotus 72D-Cosworth, chassis no. R6)

The only changes made to the red and gold cars were modifications to the drive-shaft universal joints which, it was hoped, would cure the rear tyre vibration problems.

S.p.a. Ferrari SEFAC:

4. J. Ickx (Ferrari 312B/2, chassis no. 006)
5. C. Regazzoni (Ferrari 312B/2, chassis no. 005)

Once again Andretti was out of the team because of a USAC commitment (at Milwaukee) and his car, 007, had been brought along as a spare. The cars were in exactly the same trim as at the Nürburgring.

Motor Racing Developments:

7. G. Hill (Brabham BT34-Cosworth, chassis no. BT34/1)
8. T. Schenken (Brabham BT33-Cosworth, chassis no. BT33/3)

Since the Nürburgring the Brabhams had been modified in detail. The suspension, specially raised for that circuit, had been lowered and both cars featured new streamlined oil tanks. Schenken's car ran with the full-width nose tried in practice at the Nürburgring.

Bruce McLaren Motor Racing:

9. D. Hulme (McLaren M19A-Cosworth, chassis no. M19A/2)
10. J. Oliver (McLaren M19A-Cosworth, chassis no. M19A/1)

Hulme's car was unchanged, but as an experiment the team's

second car was fitted out with M14A rear suspension. Gethin had now been released from his contract (which in any case expired after the Italian Grand Prix) to drive for BRM and his place had been taken by Jack Oliver.

Elf Team Tyrrell:

11. J. Stewart (Tyrrell-Cosworth, chassis no. 003)
12. F. Cevert (Tyrrell-Cosworth, chassis no. 002)

The team had as usual brought along car 001 as a spare. At the first and second practice sessions Stewart's car appeared with a large alloy spacer between the engine and gearbox and the effect of this was to increase the wheel base by 4.3 in. To give effect to this modification it was necessary to use different radius rods, gearbox spigot shaft and exhaust system. It was an interesting experiment at relatively low cost for the increased wheelbase altered the weight distribution and the polar moments of inertia, thereby altering the handling characteristics. The car was modified to standard specification in time for the final practice session. Both Tyrrells ran with streamlined noses.

Yardley-BRM:

14. J. Siffert (BRM P160, chassis no. 03)
15. H. Ganley (BRM P160, chassis no. 04)
16. H. Marko (BRM P153, chassis no. 07)
23. P. Gethin (BRM P160, chassis no. 01)

Gethin had now moved to the BRM team to replace the late Pedro Rodriguez, and his car was fitted with the Mk II cylinder heads. The car on which Siffert was entered, 03, was the so-called 'slim-line' car that had first appeared in practice at Hockenheim and it ran in practice with the latest short-stroke engine. For the final practice session and the race Siffert switched to his spare car, 02, with Mk II cylinder heads and this was the car he usually raced. Ganley was at the wheel of a brand new P160. Marko's car was a 'hire-drive' entry sponsored by Mobiloil, Dinitrol and Arden for Men (!).

STP-March:

17. R. Peterson (March 711-Cosworth, chassis no. 06)
19. N. Galli (March 711-Alfa Romeo, chassis no. 04)
26. N. Lauda (March 711-Cosworth, chassis no. 01)

There were no changes to the 711s, but Niki Lauda's car was a 'hire-drive' entry sponsored by Levi's Jeans.

Team Surtees:

22. J. Surtees (Surtees TS9-Cosworth, chassis no. 004 sponsored by Brooke Bond-Oxo Racing with Rob Walker)
24. R. Stommelen (Surtees TS9-Cosworth, chassis no. 001 sponsored by *Auto Motor und Sport* – Eifelland)

At the Nürburgring Stommelen had complained about the handling of his car, but Surtees tried it and found nothing wrong. To settle the matter he gave the German driver his own car for the Austrian race and drove the latest car, while Stommelen's car was brought along as a spare.

Frank Williams Racing Cars:

25. H. Pescarolo (March 711-Cosworth, chassis no. 03)

Since its last appearance the Williams March had been rebuilt with a completely new monocoque constructed by Maurice Gomm, and at a price much lower than that quoted by the Bicester factory. Because of a transporter breakdown the car did not arrive at the circuit until the Saturday and so Pescarolo missed two of the practice sessions.

Clarke Mordaunt Racing with Alistair Guthrie:

27. M. Beuttler (March 711-Cosworth, chassis no. 02)

Since the Nürburgring the monocoque of this car had been reinforced and the suspension strengthened.

Ecurie Bonnier:

28. J. Bonnier (McLaren M7C-Cosworth, chassis no. M7C/1)

Matra missed this race to concentrate on some much-needed development work.

PRACTICE

There was a three-hour session on each of the three practice days. Although the Formula 1 lap record stood to Ickx with a time of 1 min 40.4 sec set in the 1970 race, this had been bettered twice. In practice in 1970 Jochen Rindt with the Lotus 72 had recorded 1 min 39.2 sec and in the Austrian 1000 Km race earlier in 1971 the late Pedro Rodriguez at the wheel of a Porsche 917 had reduced the record to 1 min 39.35 sec. It was anticipated that these times would be easily beaten and it came as no surprise when Stewart turned in a lap of 1 min 37.65 sec during the Thursday session. Both Ickx and Regazzoni were credited with a time of 1 min 38.27 sec. Although Lauda had been driving carefully within the 9,000 rpm limit prescribed by March (in view of his inexperience with Formula 1 machinery), the engine blew up towards the end of the session and, as March were suffering from their usual chronic shortage of engines, there was nothing that could be done about it until a new engine arrived by van from England.

After only half-an-hour of Friday's practice Stommelen's engine blew up and deposited oil all round the track. It remained slippery for the rest of the session and brought an end to most drivers' hopes of turning in a good time. More trouble followed for March when Peterson's engine blew up and the new engine fitted to Galli's Alfa (that from the Tipo 33/TT/3 Sports Prototype which he had crashed in practice at Watkins Glen) had to be taken out again because of crossed threads on an oil pipe. Fastest of the session was Fittipaldi in 1 min 38.41 sec and Stewart was second fastest in 1 min 38.50 sec.

It was not until the Saturday morning that Oliver's McLaren arrived – like the Williams March it had been delayed by a transporter breakdown. At the start of the session Oliver was eager to get cracking at once, but after only half a dozen laps he was in the pits to report low oil pressure. He was told to carry on, but he failed to complete the next lap; at the downhill corner known as Bosch Curve the McLaren's brakes failed completely and Oliver had no alternative but to put into the Armco. The front of the car and the rear suspension were damaged and although the car was repaired in time to run in the race, it meant that Oliver had to start from right at the back of the grid. Siffert dominated this session at the wheel of his training car and took pole position on the grid with a time of 1 min 37.44 sec. The Swiss driver was completely happy with his car and full of confidence and when practice came to an end he gave the mechanics strict instructions to change absolutely nothing! And it was indicative of BRM's new-found reliabilty that not a single engine change was needed at the Austrian race.

THE GRID

	J. Siffert (BRM) 1 min 37.44 sec		J. Stewart (Tyrrell) 1 min 37.65 sec
F. Cevert (Tyrrell) 1 min 37.86 sec		C. Regazzoni (Ferrari) 1 min 37.90 sec	
	E. Fittipaldi (Lotus) 1 min 37.90 sec		J. Ickx (Ferrari) 1 min 38.27 sec

T. Schenken
(Brabham)
1 min 38.64 sec

G. Hill
(Brabham)
1 min 38.70 sec

D. Hulme
(McLaren)
1 min 38.80 sec

R. Wisell
(Lotus)
1 min 38.95 sec

R. Peterson
(March)
1 min 39.01 sec

R. Stommelen
(Surtees)
1 min 39.08 sec

H. Pescarolo
(March)
1 min 39.09 sec

H. Ganley
(BRM)
1 min 39.46 sec

N. Galli
(March)
1 min 39.54 sec

P. Gethin
(BRM)
1 min 39.67 sec

H. Marko
(BRM)
1 min 39.80 sec

J. Surtees
(Surtees)
1 min 40.37 sec

M. Beuttler
(March)
1 min 41.46 sec

J. Bonnier*
(McLaren)
1 min 41.66 sec

N. Lauda
(March)
1 min 43.68 sec

J. Oliver
(McLaren)
1 min 44.22 sec

* Bonnier failed to start because of a fuel leak on his McLaren.

THE RACE

No sooner had the cars moved up from the dummy grid to the grid proper than the flag was dropped and Siffert was screaming up the hill slightly ahead of Stewart. At the end of the first lap it was still BRM leading Tyrrell and then came Regazzoni, Cevert, Ickx, Schenken, Fittipaldi, Wisell and Hill. At the start Beuttler's engine had refused to fire and he eventually joined the race two laps in arrears. At the end of lap two Ganley came into the pits with the engine of his BRM sounding very rough and although the mixture was adjusted, it sounded very little better when he rejoined the race. On the third lap Siffert and Stewart began to draw away from the rest of the field, but already it was apparent that all was not well with the Tyrrell; the car was handling badly and Stewart was having to lift off for some of the corners far more than he had done in practice. On lap four Schenken passed Ickx on the straight, it was obvious that the Belgian's Ferrari was down on power, and on the next lap Ickx was passed by Fittipaldi. Hulme's McLaren retired out on the circuit with a hole in the crankcase and after calling at the pits five times in six laps Ganley retired his BRM.

Now Regazzoni was losing ground and Cevert passed him to take third place. Clay fought back, the Ferrari slipped ahead again and then the battle was over with the Ferrari out of the race on lap nine with a blown-up engine and Regazzoni walking back to the pits. Ickx had fallen right out of the picture as he struggled with his ailing car and once again the Ferrari challenge had completely disintegrated. By the end of lap ten Siffert had pulled out a lead of almost three seconds and Stewart was being caught by team-mate Cevert. Schenken and Fittipaldi were still scrapping furiously for fourth place and Wisell had dropped way behind them. On lap thirteen another car joined the retirement list when Surtees' engine blew up. Two laps later Siffert had increased his lead to five seconds, Cevert was close behind Stewart and Graham Hill with the badly oversteering Brabham had got ahead of Wisell's Lotus.

On lap twenty-two Siffert set a new lap record of 1 min 38.47 sec and Cevert was now in front of Stewart, but with precious little chance of catching the race-leader. By lap thirty-two Fittipaldi was clearly ahead of Schenken and now started to chase after the two Tyrrells. After a pit stop in a fruitless effort to sort out his engine problems, Ickx decided to retire his very sick Ferrari. Wisell was now well clear of Hill again and Fittipaldi was right on Stewart's tail; but before the Brazilian could get to grips with the Tyrrell, the car was out of the race. On lap thirty-six, at the double left-hand bend behind the pits the left-hand rear drive-shaft broke and the dark-blue car shed a wheel. The Tyrrell spun down the road and came to a halt after cannoning into the bank. Stewart was completely unhurt and, once he had returned to the pits, delighted to hear the news that with Ickx' retirement he was unassailable in the Drivers' Championship. Around lap forty Cevert's Tyrrell started to develop gear-selector trouble, in the space of a couple of laps he lost a tremendous amount of ground to Siffert and was re-passed by Marko whom he had just lapped. On lap forty-three the inevitable happened, a gear failed to engage as he passed the pits, the revs soared and the young Frenchman was out of the race in a great cloud of smoke with a broken engine.

With only ten laps to go to the finish Siffert led Fittipaldi by twenty-four seconds, but Siffert was only too obviously slowing and the Brazilian was reducing the deficit at the rate of four seconds a lap. As Fittipaldi drew closer and closer to the BRM, so the staff in the Bourne pits became more and more anxious. When the

V-12 started its final lap it led by seven seconds and Siffert was still four seconds ahead of the Lotus when the flag fell. Only then was the cause of the trouble appreciated – a rear tyre had punctured and 'Seppi' had covered the last few laps of the race with the tyre almost flat. For BRM the win was a magnificent triumph and their first World Championship victory since Rodriguez' win at Spa in 1970. Supporters of the marque were hoping that it was the starting point of a long string of victories as it had been for Ferrari the previous year. But celebrations were not limited to the BRM team, for Stewart and the Tyrrell organisation, despite their two retirements, were celebrating that with fifty-one points to the nineteen of second-place man Ickx, the Scot was confirmed as 1971 Drivers' Champion.

Results:

1st, J. Siffert (BRM P160), 1 hour 30 min 23.91 sec (132.30 mph)
2nd, E. Fittipaldi (Lotus 72D-Cosworth), 1 hour 30 min 28.03 sec
3rd, T. Schenken (Brabham BT33-Cosworth), 1 hour 30 min 43.68 sec
4th, R. Wisell (Lotus 72D-Cosworth), 1 hour 30 min 55.78 sec
5th, G. Hill (Brabham BT34-Cosworth), 1 hour 31 min 12.34 sec
6th, H. Pescarolo (March 711-Cosworth), 1 hour 31 min 48.42 sec
7th, R. Stommelen (Surtees TS9-Cosworth), 1 hour 32 min 1.33 sec
8th, R. Peterson (March 711-Cosworth), 1 lap in arrears
9th, J. Oliver (McLaren M19A-Cosworth), 1 lap in arrears
10th, P. Gethin (BRM P160), 2 laps in arrears
11th, H. Marko (BRM P153), 2 laps in arrears
12th, N. Galli (March 711-Alfa Romeo), 3 laps in arrears
—, M. Beuttler, (March 711-Cosworth), 10 laps in arrears – still running but not classified as a finisher.

Fastest lap: J. Siffert, 1 min 38.47 (134.39 mph – record).
Previous lap record: P. Rodriguez (Porsche 917), 1 min 39.35 sec (132.90 mph – set in Austrian 1000 Km race earlier in the year).
Previous Formula One record: J. Ickx and C. Regazzoni (Ferrari 312B), 1 min 40.4 sec (131.70 mph – set in 1970 race).

Retirements: Lap 6: D. Hulme (McLaren), engine failure; H. Ganley (BRM), electrical failure; lap 9: C. Regazzoni (Ferrari), engine trouble; lap 13: J. Surtees (Surtees), engine trouble; lap 21: N. Lauda (March), handling problems; lap 32: J. Ickx (Ferrari), electrical trouble; lap 36: J. Stewart (Tyrrell), accident following driveshaft failure; lap 43: F. Cevert (Tyrrell), engine and gearbox trouble.

ROUND NINE

ITALIAN GRAND PRIX

Monza (Circuit length: 3.57 miles) 5th September, 1971
Race length: 196.35 miles (55 laps) Weather: hot and dry

Held at Monza in pre-war days and every year since 1949, the Italian race is – since the abandonment of Spa as a Grand Prix circuit – the fastest race in the Championship series and it almost always devolves into a flat-out 'blind', headed by a bunch of closely grouped cars that are constantly slip-streaming each other and swapping the lead. Consequently, it is never clear who will be the winner until the cars emerge from the last corner of the last lap. The 1970 race had proved a powerful mixture of tragedy and triumph; Jochen Rindt had lost his life in practice at the wheel of his Lotus 72 and the race winner was Clay Regazzoni, scoring a magnificent first World Championship race victory in his first season of Grand Prix racing. As far as the quality of the entry was concerned, the 1971 race was something of a disappointment and several well known faces were missing. Because of possible repercussions from Rindt's accident which could have resulted in the cars being impounded, Gold Leaf Team Lotus decided to give the race a miss and sent only the Lotus 56B gas-turbine car which was entered in the name of World Wide Racing, the Lotus subsidiary company that had fielded Soler-Roig's 'hire cars' in 1970. McLaren sent the two M19As straight on to the Canadian race and entered only an M14A and Beltoise was unable to appear for Matra because his licence was still suspended. And Ferrari almost failed to appear! The Commendatore had decreed that the cars should not run unless they were going to be fully competitive. However, in practice sessions at Monza and Vallelunga, the cars had turned in good times and Ferrari allowed them to run. Two other non-starters were Herbert Müller who should have appeared at the wheel of the ex-Walker Lotus 72, now owned by Jo Siffert, and Carlos Pace who was to have driven Frank Williams' old March 701.

THE ENTRY

Elf Team Tyrrell:

30. J. Stewart (Tyrrell-Cosworth, chassis no. 003)
2. F. Cevert (Tyrrell-Cosworth, chassis no. 002)

It seemed in very bad taste that at the circuit where Jochen Rindt had died, the number 1 should not have been left blank in the entry list as a tribute to the World Champion. It was allotted to Stewart who declined to use the number and took number 30 instead. At this race Stewart's car was fitted with the alloy spacer that increased the wheelbase by 4.3 in. In private practice before the official sessions Stewart tried his car with the radiator mounted at the extreme rear. For use in conjunction with this layout (and retained for the race) was a new inclined rear body cover running from behind the cockpit and surrounding the engine inlet trumpets and air-box. Both cars were raced with the now usual streamlined noses, but in practice Cevert also tried the old, narrow nose minus the integral front wings.

S.p.a. Ferrari SEFAC:

3. J. Ickx (Ferrari 312B/2, chassis no. 006).
4. C. Regazzoni (Ferrari 312B/2, chassis no. 005)

Almost inevitably Andretti was unable to race because of a USAC commitment. His car was present as a spare, as was the 1970 car, chassis no. 004, and this was in fact driven in the race by Ickx. For this race the Ferraris were fitted with new rear aerofoils that neatly blended in with the engine cover and oil cooler ducts. Of the rumoured 500 bhp development of the flat-12 engine, there was no sign.

World Wide Racing:

5. E. Fittipaldi (Lotus 56B-Pratt & Whitney, chassis no. 1)

The gas-turbine car was unchanged from its previous outings apart from a rather eye-catching gold and black paint finish.

Team Surtees:

7. J. Surtees (Surtees TS9-Cosworth, chassis no. 005 sponsored by Brooke Bond-Oxo Racing with Rob Walker)
8. R. Stommelen (Surtees TS9-Cosworth, chassis no. 001 sponsored by *Auto Motor und Sport* – Eifelland)
9. M. Hailwood (Surtees TS9-Cosworth, chassis no. 004)

Hailwood was brought into the Surtees Formula 1 team for the first time and Surtees drove the team's latest car with a streamlined nose. The car appeared in practice with side radiators, but Surtees stopped to have these removed after only six laps!

Motor Racing Developments:

10. G. Hill (Brabham BT34-Cosworth, chassis no. BT34/1)
11. T. Schenken (Brabham BT33-Cosworth, chassis no. BT33/3)

Both cars featured air deflectors in front of the exhaust pipes and Schenken's car was fitted with the full-width nose.

Équipe Matra:

12. C. Amon (Matra-Simca MS120B, chassis no. 04)

The team had brought along chassis no. 06 as a spare. Since the Matra's last appearance at the Nürburgring, the porting of the cylinder heads of the V-12 engine had been revised and it was claimed that power output had risen by some 20 bhp. The monocoque had also been strengthened.

Bruce McLaren Motor Racing:

14. J. Oliver (McLaren M14A-Cosworth, chassis no. M14A/2)

Frank Williams Racing Cars:

16. H. Pescarolo (March 711-Cosworth, chassis no. 03)

Yardley-BRM:

18. P. Gethin (BRM P160, chassis no. 01)
19. H. Ganley (BRM P160, chassis no. 04)
20. J. Siffert (BRM P160, chassis no. 02)
21. H. Marko (BRM P153, chassis no. 07)

Siffert had P160, chassis no. 03, as a spare and this was fitted with the short-stroke engine that had still not been raced.

STP-March:

22. N. Galli (March 711-Cosworth, chassis no. 04)
23. A. de Adamich (March 711-Alfa Romeo, chassis no. 01)
25. R. Peterson (March 711-Cosworth, chassis no. 06)

At this race the Alfa Romeo-powered car was looked after by Autodelta themselves. The Alfa engine used at this race was a more robust development with three, instead of five, main bearings. At this circuit the 711s ran without their prominent nose-mounted aerofoils.

Clarke Mordaunt Racing with Alistair Guthrie:

24. M. Beuttler (March 711-Cosworth, chassis no. 02)

Shell-Arnold Team:

26. J-P. Jarier (March 701-Cosworth, chassis no. 09)

This was the little-raced, silver-painted ex-Hubert Hahne car.

Jolly Club Switzerland:

27. S. Moser (Bellasi-Cosworth, chassis no. 01)

Two of the less competitive marques seen competing in the French Grand Prix held at the Paul Ricard circuit. Above is former World Champion Denis Hulme at the wheel of his McLaren M19A. Below is John Surtees with his own TS9 car. (Nigel Snowdon)

This photograph of the Tyrrells of Stewart and Cevert in the British Grand Prix has a remarkable mirage-like quality. Note the streamlined noses and high rear intakes adopted in mid-season. (Nigel Snowdon)

Ecurie Bonnier:

28. J. Bonnier (McLaren M7C-Cosworth, chassis no. M7C/1)

PRACTICE

BRM, Matra, Surtees and Tyrrell all turned out for unofficial practice on the Thursday, but the first official session was on the Friday afternoon and was held in extremely hot weather conditions. The Formula 1 lap record had stood since 1969 to the credit of Beltoise with a Matra MS80 in 1 min 25.2 sec (150.96 mph) and had been equalled during the 1970 race by Regazzoni. However, faster times had been recorded by Porsche 917s in both the 1970 and 1971 1000 Kilometre races at the circuit, the current outright record stood to the credit of the late Pedro Rodriguez in 1 min 24.0 sec and this record was certain to tumble. In the first session the Tyrrells were very much on top, Cevert was fastest in 1 min 23.41 sec and Stewart recorded second fastest time of 1 min 23.61 sec. The Ferrari team was in a tremendous state of confusion, despite the successful tests the cars seemed down on power and the fastest Maranello driver was Regazzoni in 1 min 24.45 sec. During the second of the afternoon sessions Siffert set the pace for BRM and turned in a fine lap in 1 min 23.27 sec. It was in the early part of this second session that Stommelen had a nasty accident. At the Curva del Vialone a rear tyre came off the rim, the TS9 went in a series of violent spins during which it ricochetted off the Armco and came to rest with a battered front sub-frame and wrecked suspension. Oliver was close behind with the McLaren and spun off while taking avoiding action. The M14A was only slightly damaged, but the fact that Team Surtees decided that the TS9 could not be repaired and that Stommelen would not start added to the already strained relations between Surtees and Stommelen.

On the Saturday there was one three-and-a-half-hour practice session and during this Ickx drove the 1970 car running on Goodyear instead of the usual Firestone tyres. With this car, which the Belgian infinitely preferred to the latest model, he turned in a lap in 1 min 22.82 sec which was initially credited as fastest lap in practice. Apart from the fact that several other teams had grave doubts as to whether the car had lapped that fast, the timekeepers had completely ignored a really superb lap by Amon with the now much improved Matra in 1 min 22.40 sec, and it was only under pressure that Amon's time was recognised. Marko was allowed to drive the spare BRM P160, but he preferred the older P153 car and decided to retain this for the race. Moser and the Bellasi did not practise until the Saturday because of fuel pump trouble and even then did not succeed in getting in many laps.

THE GRID

C. Amon (Matra) 1 min 22.40 sec		J. Ickx (Ferrari) 1 min 22.82 sec	
	J. Siffert (BRM) 1 min 23.03 sec		H. Ganley (BRM) 1 min 23.15 sec
F. Cevert (Tyrrell) 1 min 23.41 sec		R. Peterson (March) 1 min 23.46 sec	
	J. Stewart (Tyrrell) 1 min 23.49 sec		C. Regazzoni (Ferrari) 1 min 23.69 sec
T. Schenken (Brabham) 1 min 23.73 sec		H. Pescarolo (March) 1 min 23.77 sec	
	P. Gethin (BRM) 1 min 23.88 sec		H. Marko (BRM) 1 min 23.96 sec
J. Oliver (McLaren) 1 min 24.09 sec		G. Hill (Brabham) 1 min 24.27 sec	
	J. Surtees (Surtees) 1 min 24.45 sec		M. Beuttler (March) 1 min 25.01 sec
M. Hailwood (Surtees) 1 min 25.17 sec		E. Fittipaldi (Lotus) 1 min 25.18 sec	
	N. Galli (March) 1 min 25.19 sec		A. de Adamich (March) 1 min 25.73 sec
J. Bonnier (McLaren) 1 min 26.14 sec		S. Moser (Bellasi) 1 min 26.54 sec	
			J-P. Jarier (March) 1 min 28.19 sec

THE RACE

It was remarkable that all except four of the starters had bettered the existing Formula 1 lap record and thirteen drivers were faster than the pole position man (Rindt) in the 1969 race. As team manager Peter Warr commented, if the Lotus 56B gas-turbine had run in the 1969 race, which had been the original intention, it would have taken pole position, but now it was almost completely out-classed and back on the ninth row of the grid.

One race morning there was an additional hour of practice during which Siffert ran in a new engine in his P160, Stewart tried an extra-high fifth gear, Hill's Brabham broke its gearbox and Hailwood's Surtees blew up its engine (and was fitted with that removed from Surtees' own car during a routine change).

Both Amon and Ickx were engulfed at the start by the cars behind them and Regazzoni made a magnificent start from the fourth row of the grid to lead at the end of lap one from Siffert, Stewart, Ganley, Peterson, Ickx, Pescarolo, Amon, Gethin and Cevert. Regazzoni still led at the end of lap two, but Siffert was alongside the Ferrari and Peterson had slipped into third place ahead of Stewart. The first fifteen cars were all tightly bunched and at this stage of the race Regazzoni's lead meant very little apart from giving great pleasure to the very patriotic crowd. At the end of this lap, Marko brought his BRM into the pits with a rough-running engine, the mechanics richened up the mixture, but the car expired out on the circuit without completing another lap. On the following lap another retirement came when Surtees went out with a blown-up engine.

Peterson led on lap four from Stewart, Siffert, Regazzoni and Ickx and the Swedish driver stayed in front for four laps when Stewart with the Tyrrell went in front. On lap six there were two more retirements; poor Tim Schenken dropped out with a broken rear suspension sub-frame and Moser retired with a broken rear damper mounting. Pescarolo had his March well wound up and on lap nine he set a new circuit record of 1 min 23.8 sec. Regazzoni now moved in front again, but next time round the red March of Ronnie Peterson headed the pack. After going so well in practice, poor Chris Amon was having a miserable race, for chunking tyres were causing excessive understeer and because of overheating he was having to avoid slip-streaming other cars. Galli retired his March on lap twelve with electrical trouble. It was not until lap fifteen that Regazzoni took the lead again and then Cevert came through to hold first place. On lap sixteen the young Frenchman came round in front ahead of Peterson and Regazzoni and both Stewart and Ickx were missing. Ickx coasted his Ferrari into the pits with a broken engine and eventually Stewart arrived with a con-rod through the side of his Cosworth engine.

Peterson went into the lead again, heading Cevert, Regazzoni and Hailwood who had whistled through the field from fourteenth place. This state of affairs lasted only another lap and then Regazzoni pulled into the pits to retire with engine trouble – as on Ickx' car, the rubber engine damper between the crankshaft and the clutch had failed. Now the field was beginning to break up a little, with Peterson, Cevert and Hailwood in one tight bunch, followed after a short interval by a similar bunch consisting of Ganley, Siffert and Amon. Oliver and Gethin were in seventh and eighth places and then came Pescarolo, Hill and Beuttler. As the race progressed, so the second trio of runners closed up again and by half-distance they were running together. Hailwood took the lead on lap twenty-five and held it until Siffert came through to the front on lap twenty-eight.

Unfortunately the Swiss BRM driver found himself slowed by gearbox trouble (he eventually finished the race with the use of fourth gear only) and Peterson went ahead again. Pescarolo was in trouble with his March because of handling troubles and only after three pit stops was the trouble traced to a broken gearbox casing and the car retired. Now Amon, having accustomed himself to the Matra's rather odd handling, decided to have a go and on lap thirty-seven he came through to take the lead. For four laps the blue V-12 stayed in front and then Hailwood shot by on lap forty-two but Chris was revelling in the Matra's new-found power and he was back in the lead again next time round. By lap forty-eight Amon was still in front and it seemed that at long last he might have broken the jinx and was going to win his first ever World Championship race. The New Zealander decided to remove his oil-smeared top visor so that he could use the clean one underneath during the final laps of the race. Unfortunately both visors came off together and he found himself without any eye protection at all. In a matter of a few seconds the Matra had dropped to fifth place and Peterson again led from Cevert and Hailwood.

On lap fifty-one Hailwood was in front again, Gethin pushed his V-12 BRM through to second place and on the following lap took the lead. More trouble had followed for Amon and the Matra had now developed a vapour-lock in the fuel injection system and was running very roughly. Unnoticed in the excitement of the battle for the lead, Hill had retired his Brabham with gearbox trouble and Siffert had been lapped by almost the entire field. On lap fifty-three, with two laps to go, it was still Gethin in front, on lap fifty-four Peterson led and Gethin was back in fourth place. On the last lap Cevert was in the lead at Lesmo, Gethin took to the grass and with tyres smoking squeezed into second place ahead of Peterson at Parabolica and Gethin led out of the last corner to win the forty-second Italian Grand Prix by a hundreth of a second from Peterson, Cevert and Hailwood. For Gethin this was a magnificent first-ever World Championship race victory, it augured well for his future with the BRM and it seemed that with victory in two races in succession the Bourne team had at long last sorted out their many problems and could look forward to a period of consistent success.

Results:

1st, P. Gethin (BRM P160), 1 hour 18 min 12.60 sec (150.75 mph)
2nd, R. Peterson (March-711-Cosworth), 1 hour 18 min 12.61 sec
3rd, F. Cevert (Tyrrell-Cosworth), 1 hour 18 min 12.69 sec
4th, M. Hailwood (Surtees TS9-Cosworth), 1 hour 18 min 12.78 sec
5th, H. Ganley (BRM P160) 1 hour 18 min 13.21 sec
6th, C. Amon (Matra-Simca MS120B), 1 hour 18 min 44.96 sec
7th, J. Oliver (McLaren M14A-Cosworth), 1 hour 19 min 37.43 sec
8th, E. Fittipaldi (Lotus Turbine T56B), 1 lap in arrears
9th, J. Siffert (BRM P160), 2 laps in arrears
10th, J. Bonnier (McLaren M7C-Cosworth), 4 laps in arrears
11th, G. Hill (Brabham BT34-Cosworth), 8 laps in arrears – not running at finish
12th, J-P. Jarier (March 701-Cosworth), 8 laps in arrears

Fastest lap: H. Pescarolo (March 711-Cosworth), 1 min 23.8 sec (153.49 mph – record).
Previous lap record: J-P. Beltoise (Matra MS80-Cosworth), 1 min 25.2 sec (150.96 mph – set in 1969 race), equalled by C. Regazzoni (Ferrari 312B) in 1970 race.
1970 winner: C. Regazzoni (Ferrari 312B), 147.07 mph.

Retirements: Lap 3: H. Marko (BRM), engine trouble; lap 4: J. Surtees (Surtees), engine trouble; lap 6: T. Schenken (Brabham), rear sub-frame failure; S. Moser (Bellasi), broken shock absorber mounting; lap 12: N. Galli (March), electrical failure; lap 16: J. Ickx (Ferrari), engine trouble; J. Stewart (Tyrrell), engine trouble; lap 18: C. Regazzoni (Ferrari), engine trouble; lap 34: A. de Adamich (March), engine trouble; lap 41: H. Pescarolo (March), cracked gearbox casing; lap 42: M. Beuttler (March), engine trouble; lap 48: G. Hill (Brabham), gearbox seized.

ROUND TEN

CANADIAN GRAND PRIX

Mosport Park (Circuit length: 2.459 miles) 19th September, 1971
Race length: 157.38 miles (64 laps – Note: race stopped 16 laps earlier than scheduled 80 laps because of weather conditions)

Weather: cold and wet, gradually drying out with heavy mist in the closing stages

Originally first held as a Formula 1 race at Mosport Park in 1967 as part of the celebrations to mark Canada's centennial year, the Canadian Grand Prix had become a regular event in the racing calendar and formed the first of three trans-Atlantic rounds. The race alternated between the Mosport Park circuit, with a succession of fast curves, a sharp U-bend and two short straights, and the Mont Tremblant circuit near St. Jovite (about forty miles north of Montreal). It was the turn of Mosport Park, near Toronto, for the third time to form the setting for Canada's premier race and, like the first event, it was destined to be a thoroughly wet and miserable race.

THE ENTRY

Gold Leaf Team Lotus:

2. E. Fittipaldi (Lotus 72D-Cosworth, chassis no. R5)
3. R. Wisell (Lotus 72D-Cosworth, chassis no. R6)

S.p.a. Ferrari SEFAC:

4. J. Ickx (Ferrari 312B/2, chassis no. 006)
5. C. Regazzoni (Ferrari 312B/2, chassis no. 005)
6. M. Andretti (Ferrari 312B/2, chassis no. 007)

The 1970 car, 004, had as usual been brought along as a spare, together with 002. There was an unconfirmed rumour that on race day Ickx' car was fitted with new cylinder heads.

Motor Racing Developments:

8. T. Schenken (Brabham BT33-Cosworth, chassis no. BT33/3)
37. G. Hill (Brabham BT34-Cosworth, chassis no. BT34/1)

Once again Schenken's car was running with the streamlined nose.

Bruce McLaren Motor Racing:

9. D. Hulme (McLaren M19A-Cosworth, chassis no. M19A/2)

Penske-White Racing:

10. M. Donohue (McLaren M19A-Cosworth, chassis no. M19A/1)

The first of the M19As had now been sold to Roger Penske and had been repainted in his usual blue colours. Both cars now had conventional wishbone and link rear suspension and the rising-rate rear suspension had been abandoned.

Elf Team Tyrrell:

11. J. Stewart (Tyrrell-Cosworth, chassis no. 003)
12. F. Cevert (Tyrrell-Cosworth, chassis no. 002)

The original car, 001, had been brought along as a spare and all three cars were in short-chassis form.

Yardley-BRM:

14. J. Siffert (BRM P160, chassis no. 02)
15. P. Gethin (BRM P160, chassis no. 01)
16. H. Ganley (BRM P160, chassis no. 04)
28. G. Eaton (BRM P160, chassis no. 03)
31. H. Marko (BRM P153, chassis no. 07)

To field five cars was a mammoth task and team manager Tim Parnell had his hands full the whole time. This was the first race at which Marko had been included in the team as a works driver proper and not as a hirer. On the first practice day Gethin's car was fitted with a short-stroke engine.

STP-March:

17. R. Peterson (March 711-Cosworth, chassis no. 06)
18. N. Galli (March 711-Cosworth, chassis no. 04)
19. M. Beuttler (March 711-Cosworth, chassis no. 01)

Autodelta had not supported the team at this race and Beuttler had taken over the car usually driven by de Adamich, but fitted with a Clarke-Mordaunt engine. Peterson's car was tried in practice with a new 'shovel' nose.

Équipe Matra:

20. C. Amon (Matra MS120B, chassis no. 06)
21. J-P. Beltoise (Matra MS120B, chassis no. 05)

As at most of the 1971 races, only Amon's car was fitted with the more powerful engine having bifurcated exhaust ports.

Team Surtees:

22. J. Surtees (Surtees TS9-Cosworth, chassis no. 004 sponsored by Brooke Bond-Oxo Racing with Rob Walker)
24. R. Stommelen (Surtees TS9-Cosworth, chassis no. 002 sponsored by *Auto Motor und Sport* – Eifelland)

Ecurie Evergreen:

26. C. Craft (Brabham BT33-Cosworth, chassis no. BT33/2)

This was the car raced by Jack Brabham in 1970 and now bought from the works by Alain de Cadenet.

Frank Williams Racing Cars:

27. H. Pescarolo (March 711-Cosworth, chassis no. 03)

Gene Mason Racing:

33. S. Barber (March 711-Cosworth, chassis no. 05)

Pete Lovely Volkswagen Inc:

35. P. Lovely (Lotus 69 Special-Cosworth, chassis no. 69/5)

The American privateer who had raced his ex-works Lotus 49 in a number of Grands Prix in 1970 had now devised this interesting concoction consisting of a Lotus 69 Formula 2 car (that formerly driven by Hill) with the rear section of his old 49. A new nose had been fitted, together with a larger radiator, but unfortunately the car had insufficient fuel tankage to run through a Grand Prix without stopping.

PRACTICE

The race was held on the Sunday with official practice on the preceding Friday and Saturday amounting in all to a very generous seven hours. The first session on the Friday morning started in the wet, but the track gradually dried out to permit some fast times to be recorded. Although the Formula 1 lap record had stood to the credit of Ickx and Brabham with their BT26 cars and had been set in the 1969 race, in qualifying for the Can-Am race on the circuit in 1970 Dan Gurney had turned in a lap in 1 min 16.8 sec. Fastest in the first practice session were Stewart and Andretti both of whom recorded 1 min 18.5 sec and Fittipaldi with his Lotus was only a tenth of a second slower.

In dry, but still very cold and unpleasant conditions during the afternoon session Stewart worked his Tyrrell down to a fine 1 min 15.7 sec and Siffert was a tenth of a second slower for BRM. On the Saturday the weather had improved considerably and practice took place in bright, pleasantly warm weather. Now Siffert set the pace for BRM and turned in the fastest lap of the session in 1 min 15.5 sec, both Stewart (with the training car) and Cevert recorded times of 1 min 15.7 sec and no other driver was under the 1 min 16 sec mark. For the afternoon session Stewart reverted to his race car and, determined to beat Siffert for pole position, got the Tyrrell really in the groove to record 1 min 15.3 sec. Pescarolo with the Williams March had suffered two blown-up engines in practice and *le patron* was forced to resort to borrowing an engine for the race. Because of these troubles Pescarolo's best lap was an uncompetitive 1 min 21.9 sec and although Barber,

Lovely and Craft had all bettered this time, they were not allowed to start, whereas the Williams car had a guaranteed place on the grid. Pescarolo, however, crashed during an untimed practice session on race morning and although the car could have been straightened out in time for the start, the French driver had suffered abrasions and a strained neck. Howard Ganley crashed his BRM during the warming up laps and as a result of these incidents both Barber and Lovely joined the grid.

THE GRID

F. Cevert (Tyrrell) 1 min 15.7 sec	J. Siffert (BRM) 1 min 15.5 sec	J. Stewart (Tyrrell) 1 min 15.3 sec
C. Amon (Matra) 1 min 16.1 sec	E. Fittipaldi (Lotus) 1 min 16.1 sec	
M. Donohue (McLaren) 1 min 16.3 sec	R. Wisell (Lotus) 1 min 16.3 sec	R. Peterson (March) 1 min 16.2 sec
D. Hulme (McLaren) 1 min 16.4 sec	H. Ganley* (BRM) 1 min 16.3 sec	
M. Andretti (Ferrari) 1 min 16.9 sec	J. Ickx (Ferrari) 1 min 16.5 sec	J-P. Beltoise (Matra) 1 min 16.4 sec
G. Hill (Brabham) 1 min 17.2 sec	J. Surtees (Surtees) 1 min 17.1 sec	
C. Regazzoni (Ferrari) 1 min 17.5 sec	T. Schenken (Brabham) 1 min 17.4 sec	P. Gethin (BRM) 1 min 17.2 sec
N. Galli (March) 1 min 18.2 sec	H. Marko (BRM) 1 min 17.8 sec	
R. Stommelen (Surtees) 1 min 18.8 sec	M. Beuttler (March) 1 min 18.5 sec	G. Eaton (BRM) 1 min 18.4 sec
P. Lovely (Lotus) 1 min 21.1 sec	S. Barber (March) 1 min 19.8 sec	

* Failed to start because of accident on warming up lap.

Non-starters:

H. Pescarolo (March)	1 min 21.9 sec
C. Craft (Brabham)	1 min 20.3 sec

The start of the race was delayed as an result of an accident in an earlier Formula Ford event in which a driver ran into the back of an ambulance attending another accident and was killed. Rain had begun to fall and so the drivers were allowed a ten-minute session in which to acclimatise themselves to the conditions. The track was in such a slippery state that many of the cars spun off, Andretti went out of control and pushed Ganley's BRM into the guard-rail, rendering it *hors de combat*, and Hill retired to the pits for the suspension of his Brabham to be repaired.

Eventually, two hours after the scheduled time, the race was started and Stewart led away from the enormous cloud of spray that obscured the other runners. At Turn three Siffert was blinded by mud flung on to his visor by the wheels of other cars, had an excursion into the in-field and rejoined the circuit without damage. As the cars streamed past the pits at the end of the first lap, it was still Stewart in front and then came Peterson, Beltoise, Donohue, Fittipaldi, Cevert, Ickx and Wisell. Schenken's Brabham expired out on the circuit with failure of the spark box, the mechanics went out to the car, but by the time the trouble had been sorted out, the car was too far behind for it be worth continuing and he cruised round to the pits to retire. It was to be a thoroughly dismal day for the Brabham team and on only the second lap Graham Hill spun off, damaged the BT34's oil tank and crawled back to the pits to retire.

During the opening laps the positions among the leaders remained unchanged, but on lap four Peterson ran wide at a corner and scraped a guard-rail and this allowed Stewart to extend his lead to six seconds, and Beltoise pulled past the March to take second place. Peterson soon had the March back in second place, however, and began to close the gap on the leader. Regazzoni, never in the picture at this race, retired on lap seven after clouting a guard-rail. Following his first lap excursion Siffert had stopped at the pits to have the mud cleared away from the nose of the BRM and when he rejoined the race, he was in last place. By lap twelve Peterson was right on Stewart's exhausts, but he again nearly lost control, dropped back and then closed up again. All the way Ronnie was trying his hardest, pressing Stewart and just waiting for him to make a mistake. The opportunity Peterson had been waiting for come on lap seventeen, the red March thrust into the lead, but Stewart was back in front again almost immediately; next time round Peterson had another go at passing the World Champion, pushed through into the lead and stayed there. Now it was Stewart who was worrying the leader every inch of the way and then came Donohue, Ickx, Fittipaldi, Wisell, Cevert and Hulme.

The Scot's chance came on lap thirty-one and the March was pushed back to second place; next time round the two leaders lapped Eaton's slow BRM, the Canadian saw Stewart and let him through, but he had not seen Peterson and the March and the Bourne car collided. Peterson carried on with the front aerofoil askew, but dropped back to fourteen seconds behind the Tyrrell. The order at half-distance, forty laps, was Stewart – Peterson – Donohue – Hulme – Ickx – Wisell – Fittipaldi – Cevert – Amon – Surtees and everyone except Donohue had been lapped. The rain had now stopped and although the track was beginning to dry out, it was still very slippery and conditions were becoming misty. By lap fifty Ickx, failing to show the form that he had displayed in the wet at Zandvoort, had fallen right back to eighth place and Siffert had made up a lot of ground since his pit stop and was tenth ahead of Surtees.

As the race progressed, the mist became thicker and thicker; by lap sixty Stewart had extended his lead to thirty-six seconds and Peterson was nearly a minute ahead of Donohue. Because of the deteriorating conditions the officials had a conference, concluded that because more than 60 per cent of the race distance had been completed there would be no loss of Championship status and at the end of lap sixty-four – with sixteen laps to go to the full race distance – Stewart was shown the chequered flag. For the new World Champion's fans, Stewart had merely scored another victory, but it was certainly not one of his easiest. For the fourth time in 1971 Peterson had taken second place in a Championship race and here surely is a Champion in the making. Although a very experienced and accomplished driver in USAC and Sports Car races, Mark Donohue was new to Grand Prix racing and his fine third place – the best McLaren performance of the season – augured well for the Penske team in the future. Yet again Ferrari had disappointed and but for Siffert's off-course excursion the BRM team might well have featured high up in the results.

Results:

1st, J. Stewart (Tyrrell-Cosworth), 1 hour 55 min 12.9 sec, (81.96 mph)
2nd, R. Peterson (March 711-Cosworth), 1 hour 55 min 51.2 sec
3rd, M. Donohue (McLaren M19A-Cosworth), 1 hour 56 min 48.7 sec
4th, D. Hulme (McLaren M19A-Cosworth), 1 lap in arrears
5th, R. Wisell (Lotus 72D-Cosworth), 1 lap in arrears

6th, F. Cevert (Tyrrell-Cosworth), 2 laps in arrears
7th, E. Fittipaldi (Lotus 72D-Cosworth), 2 laps in arrears
8th, J. Ickx (Ferrari 312B/2), 2 laps in arrears
9th, J. Siffert (BRM P160), 3 laps in arrears
10th, C. Amon (Matra-Simca MS120B), 3 laps in arrears
11th, J. Surtees (Surtees TS9-Cosworth), 4 laps in arrears
12th, H. Marko (BRM P153), 4 laps in arrears
13th, M. Andretti (Ferrari 312B/2), 4 laps in arrears
14th, P. Gethin (BRM P160), 5 laps in arrears
15th, G. Eaton (BRM P160), 5 laps in arrears
16th, N. Galli (March 711-Cosworth), 7 laps in arrears
—, M. Beuttler (March 711-Cosworth), 8 laps in arrears – still running but not classified as a finisher
—, P. Lovely (Lotus 69 Special-Cosworth), 9 laps in arrears – still running but not classified as a finisher

Fastest lap: D. Hulme (McLaren M19A-Cosworth), 1 min 43.5 sec (85.53 mph)
Existing Formula 1 lap record: J. Ickx/J. Brabham (Brabham BT26-Cosworth), 1 min 18.1 sec (114.78 mph – set in 1969 race). Note: Dan Gurney (McLaren) set an outright circuit record of 1 min 18.0 sec in the 1970 Can-Am race.
1970 winner (race held at Mont Tremblant circuit): J. Ickx (Ferrari 312B), 101.27 mph.

Retirements: Lap 1: T. Schenken (Brabham), transistor box failure; lap 2: G. Hill (Brabham), accident; lap 7: C. Regazzoni (Ferrari), accident; lap 13: S. Barber (March), loss of oil pressure; lap 16: J-P. Beltoise (Matra), accident; lap 26: R. Stommelen (Surtees), loss of oil pressure.

ROUND ELEVEN

UNITED STATES GRAND PRIX

Watkins Glen (Circuit length: 3.377 miles) 3rd October, 1971
Race length: 199.243 miles (59 laps) Weather: warm and dry

Since the last Grand Prix at the circuit, Watkins Glen circuit had been extensively rebuilt. By the Six Hours' Sports Car race in July the original 2.3-mile circuit had been widened to a uniform width of thirty-six feet throughout, it had been completely resurfaced and certain of the corners had been remodelled. Now the second stage of the work had been completed; additional track extending to .94-mile had been joined on at the south-west part of the circuit and this section included four new, fairly slow corners. The start/finish line had been repositioned, new and elaborate pits, a four hundred foot long garage, new press facilities and new stands had been erected. To pay off existing debts and finance these major alterations to the circuit the Watkins Glen Grand Prix Corporation had raised a loan of 3.4 million dollars and had succeeded in creating what was now the finest road circuit in North America. The circuit was now very safe, the hypercritical Jackie Stewart had expressed complete satisfaction with it and the spectator facilities were excellent. There was, of course, no comparison between old and new lap times and the circuit in its new form was some 15 mph slower. Because of the cancellation of the Mexican Grand Prix, the United States race was the last in the 1971 series and attracted a very strong entry.

THE ENTRY

Gold Leaf Team Lotus:

2. E. Fittipaldi (Lotus 72D-Cosworth, chassis no. R5)
3. R. Wisell (Lotus 72D-Cosworth, chassis no. R6)

S.p.a. Ferrari SEFAC:

4. J. Ickx (Ferrari 312B/2, chassis no. 006)
5. C. Regazzoni (Ferrari 312B, chassis no. 005)
6. M. Andretti (Ferrari 312B, chassis no. 007)

The team had again brought the 1970 car, chassis no. 004, as a spare and Ickx in fact drove this in the race. Andretti was in difficulties because the USAC race scheduled to be held at Trenton (New Jersey) the previous weekend had been postponed because of rain and was now scheduled to be held the same day as the Grand Prix. Andretti's only hope of running at Watkins Glen depended on the postponement yet again of the Trenton race.

Bruce McLaren Motor Racing:

7. D. Hulme (McLaren M19A-Cosworth, chassis no. M19A/2)

Elf Team Tyrrell:

8. J. Stewart (Tyrrell-Cosworth, chassis no. 003)
9. F. Cevert (Tyrrell-Cosworth, chassis no. 002)
10. P. Revson (Tyrrell-Cosworth, chassis no. 001)

For this one race the spare Tyrrell had been entered for Revlon Cosmetics' heir and Can-Am Champion Peter Revson whose last Formula 1 drive had been with a 1.5-litre Lotus 24-BRM in 1964.

Équipe Matra:

11. C. Amon (Matra-Simca MS120B, chassis no. 06)
12. J-P. Beltoise (Matra-Simca MS120B, chassis no. 05)

Yardley-BRM:

14. J. Siffert (BRM P160, chassis no. 02)
15. P. Gethin (BRM P160, chassis no. 01)
16. H. Ganley (BRM P160, chassis no. 04)
17. H. Marko (BRM P160, chassis no. 03)
28. J. Cannon (BRM P153, chassis no. 07)

With an entry of five cars, BRM once again had their hands very full. Canadian John Cannon had hired a drive in the P153 when he heard shortly before the race that there would not be a March available. All the P160s except Ganley's car had the Mk II cylinder heads.

Team Surtees:

18. J. Surtees (Surtees TS9-Cosworth, chassis no. 005 sponsored by Brooke Bond-Oxo Racing with Rob Walker)
19. S. Posey (Surtees TS9-Cosworth, chassis no. 002)
20. M. Hailwood (Surtees-Cosworth, chassis no. 004)

Stommelen's unsuccessful year with Surtees came to an abrupt end when the young German contracted a jaw infection and was unable to drive. Surtees decided to find a replacement driver and asked both Gijs van Lennep and NART Ferrari driver Sam Posey to practise; only after the final practice session did he decide that the car would be driven by Posey. Surtees' Monza car re-appeared with side radiators, but these were now from a different manufacturer and featured louvres in the tops of the ducts.

Frank Williams Racing Cars:

21. H. Pescarolo (March 711-Cosworth, chassis no. 03)

Motor Racing Developments:

22. G. Hill (Brabham BT34-Cosworth, chassis no. BT34/1)
23. T. Schenken (Brabham BT33-Cosworth, chassis no. BT33/3)
24. C. Craft (Brabham BT33-Cosworth, chassis no. BT33/2)

For this one race the Ecurie Evergreen car was entered in the name of the works team.

STP-March:

25. R. Peterson (March 711-Cosworth, chassis no. 06)
26. N. Galli (March 711-Cosworth, chassis no. 04)

27. A. de Adamich (March 711-Alfa Romeo, chassis no. 01)

After missing the Canadian race, Autodelta were back again to support one of the March entries.

Ecurie Bonnier:

29. J. Bonnier (McLaren M7C-Cosworth, chassis no. M7C/1)

Pete Lovely Volkswagen Inc:

30. P. Lovely (Lotus 69 Special-Cosworth, chassis no. 69/5)

Penske-White Racing:

31. M. Donohue/D. Hobbs (McLaren M19A-Cosworth, chassis no. M19A/1)

Donohue was in exactly the same situation as Andretti and so Hobbs was nominated as alternative driver and in fact drove in the race.

Gene Mason Racing:

33. S. Barber (March 711-Cosworth, chassis no. 05)

Barber was purely a reserve and would only run if Andretti raced at Trenton, while all the other drivers had guaranteed starts accompanied by $6,000 guaranteed minimum (the amount awarded to the first driver to retire).

PRACTICE

At Watkins Glen there were two practice sessions, each of four hours, held on the Friday and the Saturday. When practice started, the circuit still had a liberal coating of dust and dried mud, a legacy of the rebuilding works, and it was only towards the end of the session that really fast times were recorded. Fastest of the session was Jackie Stewart in 1 min 42.84 sec, with Regazzoni second fastest in 1 min 43.23 sec and Fittipaldi third in 1 min 43.87 sec. Peterson tried out the new 'shovel' nose first seen at Mosport Park, but his practice was cut short when his 11-series Cosworth engine blew up. All the BRMs were plagued by locking brakes which resulted in flat spots on the Firestone tyres – a practice not to be encouraged at £25 a kick!

It was Stewart all the way again on the Saturday and the Scot clinched pole position with a fine, fast lap in 1 min 42.64 sec and Fittipaldi was there once again with a very creditable 1 min 42.66 sec which put him on the centre of the grid alongside the World Champion. Both Cannon and Ganley blew up their engines of their BRMs (a rare occurrence with these so very reliable V-12 power units) and Ickx' Ferrari suffered the same fate. The Belgian went out in the spare 1970 car and confirmed rumours in the Italian press that it was a better bet than the later version by deciding to retain it for the race.

THE GRID

D. Hulme (McLaren) 1 min 42.93 sec	E. Fittipaldi (Lotus) 1 min 42.66 sec	J. Stewart (Tyrrell) 1 min 42.64 sec
	F. Cevert (Tyrrell) 1 min 43.15 sec	C. Regazzoni (Ferrari) 1 min 43.00 sec
C. Amon (Matra) 1 min 43.97 sec	J. Ickx (Ferrari) 1 min 43.84 sec	J. Siffert (BRM) 1 min 43.47 sec
	J-P. Beltoise (Matra) 1 min 44.07 sec	R. Wisell (Lotus) 1 min 44.02 sec
J. Surtees (Surtees) 1 min 44.91 sec	H. Ganley (BRM) 1 min 44.43 sec	R. Peterson (March) 1 min 44.19 sec
	T. Schenken (Brabham) 1 min 45.11 sec	M. Hailwood (Surtees) 1 min 45.09 sec
G. Hill (Brabham) 1 min 45.45 sec	S. Posey (Surtees) 1 min 45.27 sec	H. Marko (BRM) 1 min 45.20 sec
	H. Pescarolo (March) 1 min 45.57 sec	P. Revson (Tyrrell) 1 min 45.52 sec
N. Galli (March) 1 min 46.61 sec	D. Hobbs (McLaren) 1 min 46.27 sec	P. Gethin (BRM) 1 min 45.73 sec
	S. Barber (March) 1 min 47.67 sec	J. Cannon (BRM) 1 min 47.47 sec
J. Bonnier (McLaren) 1 min 49.39 sec	C. Craft (Brabham) 1 min 48.70 sec	A. de Adamich (March) 1 min 47.95 sec
		P. Lovely (Lotus) 1 min 52.14 sec

Failed to start:

M. Andretti (Ferrari) 1 min 43.20 sec

On the morning of the race Roger Penske's Lear Jet waited at Trenton to fly Donohue and Andretti back to Watkins Glen, should the USAC race be postponed. Unfortunately for Formula 1 supporters, the weather was fine, the race went ahead as planned, Donohue's place in the McLaren was taken by Hobbs and there was a space on the grid for Barber who had gone quite well in practice.

The starter, in his lavender suit, dropped the flag, Hulme made the best start, but by the end of the first lap Stewart was out in front, heading Hulme, Cevert, Regazzoni, Siffert, Ickx, Amon, Fittipaldi and Wisell. Already four of the runners were in trouble. Barber had joined the race late, Craft spun at the corner before the pits, pushed the Brabham back to the pits and later rejoined the race, while Cannon spun off the track with his BRM and rejoined the race when the rest of the field was on its second lap; and a long time after the rest of the runners had gone by, poor Revson had brought the spare Tyrrell into the pits with the clutch slipping badly – the car was immediately pushed away into retirement.

Cevert passed Hulme and so the Tyrrells were once again in the first two places at the head of the field and Hulme was being pressed every inch of the way by Regazzoni and Ickx. Surtees brought his TS9 into the pits with ignition trouble and rejoined the race at the tail of the field while Wisell with the Lotus 72 lost his brakes, collided with the Armco barrier and abandoned the car, Fittipaldi, who had been holding sixth place ahead of Siffert, pulled into the pits with a sticking throttle and the tachometer 'tell-tale' at 11,000 rpm at the end of lap eleven and although he rejoined the race, he stopped again four laps later with a punctured rear tyre and had to make yet another stop because of wheel bearing trouble. Another retirement came on lap eleven when de Adamich's Alfa threw up a large stone which damaged the steering of Galli's March and four laps later Posey retired his Surtees with engine trouble.

As the race progressed Cevert, with the rest of the field close behind him, drew nearer and nearer to Stewart's Tyrrell which seemed to be handling badly. On lap fourteen the young Frenchman passed his team-mate to take the lead, on the same lap Ickx passed Hulme, almost lost control and went sideways and in the confusion Regazzoni, too, passed the New Zealander. Despite a sticking fuel relief valve which occasionally caused the BRM's engine to die at awkward moments, Siffert was beginning to speed up, and passed both Regazzoni and Stewart to hold third place behind Cevert and Ickx. By lap thirty the order was: 1st, Cevert; 2nd,

Ickx; 3rd, Siffert; 4th, Regazzoni; 5th, Stewart; 6th, Hulme; 7th, Peterson; 8th, Hailwood; 9th, Ganley; 10th, Schenken. Behind the Australian trailed Amon, whose Matra had a cracked brake disc and had lost the use of second gear, Gethin with a badly misfiring BRM and Graham Hill whose Brabham was understeering atrociously.

The vibration from Hulme's tyres was so bad that his vision was blurred and he was forced to stop at the pits on lap thirty-two. The tyres had slipped on the rims and although Hulme was able to rejoin the race, he was now way down the field. Three laps later Regazzoni went into a wild spin and before he rejoined the race he had lost four places, falling behind Stewart, Peterson, Hailwood and Ganley. Schenken stopped at the pits for a plug change, but on lap forty-one his Cosworth engine expired altogether. Peterson and Hailwood were now chasing Stewart hard, the Swedish driver slipped into fourth place on lap forty-five and just when it looked as though Hailwood was going to get to grips with the 1971 World Champion, the Surtees punctured a tyre and began to fall back. Instead of calling at the pits for a wheel change, Mike decided to press on.

On lap forty-nine second-place man, Ickx, coasted into the pits to retire his Ferrari with a bad oil leak and it was on the trail of oil left by the ailing Ferrari that Hulme, two laps in arrears, spun off into the Armco. Cevert, too, found himself in difficulties when he struck the oil and although the leading Tyrrell bounced off the Armco, the young Frenchman was able to carry on. The foolishness of Hailwood's decision to carry on with a deflating tyre resulted in spinning into the Armco in lap fifty-four and the Surtees was out of the race. Siffert, despite his engine misfiring at high revs, was clinging on to second place and then came Peterson, Ganley and Stewart. The 'slim-line' BRMs driven by Ganley and Marko have a fuel capacity of seven gallons less than the earlier cars and both ran very low on fuel. Marko made a quick stop to take on a few extra gallons, but when Ganley drove into the pits, he was waved on back into the race, thereby retaining his fourth place ahead of Stewart.

Cevert's victory (which won him $50,000) thoroughly vindicated the Tyrrell and made it clear that its successes were not simply due to Stewart's driving prowess. It was a particularly gratifying win for Cevert and a fine conclusion to what had been a very successful season. Second-place man Siffert (repeating Rodriguez' placing in the 1970 race) was bitterly disappointed that his car had been slowed by mechanical trouble and was convinced that he could have won the race if his car had been running properly.

Results:

1st, F. Cevert (Tyrrell-Cosworth), 1 hour 43 min 51.99 sec (115.09 mph)
2nd, J. Siffert (BRM P160), 1 hour 44 min 32.05 sec
3rd, R. Peterson (March 711-Cosworth), 1 hour 44 min 36.06 sec
4th, H. Ganley (BRM P160), 1 hour 44 min 48.74 sec
5th, J. Stewart (Tyrrell-Cosworth), 1 hour 44 min 51.99 sec
6th, C. Regazzoni (Ferrari 312B), 1 hour 45 min 8.42 sec
7th, G. Hill (Brabham BT34-Cosworth), 1 lap in arrears
8th, J-P. Beltoise (Matra-Simca MS120B), 1 lap in arrears
9th, P. Gethin (BRM P160), 1 lap in arrears
10th, D. Hobbs, (McLaren M19A-Cosworth), 1 lap in arrears
11th, A. de Adamich (March 711-Alfa Romeo), 2 laps in arrears
12th, C. Amon (Matra-Simca MS120B), 2 laps in arrears
13th, H. Marko (BRM P160), 2 laps in arrears
14th, J. Cannon (BRM P153), 3 laps in arrears
15th, M. Hailwood (Surtees TS9-Cosworth), 5 laps in arrears – classified but not running at finish
16th, J. Bonnier (McLaren M7C-Cosworth), 5 laps in arrears – classified but not running at finish
17th, J. Surtees (Surtees TS9-Cosworth), 5 laps in arrears
18th, S. Barber (March 711-Cosworth), 7 laps in arrears
19th, E. Fittipaldi (Lotus 72D-Cosworth), 10 laps in arrears
20th, P. Lovely (Lotus 69 Special-Cosworth), 10 laps in arrears

Fastest lap: J. Ickx (Ferrari 312B), 1 min 43.47 sec (117.50 mph – new lap record).
Existing lap record (old 2.3-mile circuit): J. Ickx (Ferrari 312B), 1 min 2.74 sec (131.97 mph).
1970 winner: E. Fittipaldi (Lotus 72C-Cosworth), 126.79 mph.

Retirements: Lap 1: P. Revson (Tyrrell), clutch trouble; lap 5: R. Wisell (Lotus), accident after loss of brakes; lap 11: N. Galli (March), broken front wheel and suspension damage; lap 15: S. Posey (Surtees), engine trouble; lap 23: H. Pescarolo (March), engine trouble; lap 30: C. Craft (Brabham), chassis damage; lap 41: T. Schenken (Brabham), engine trouble; lap 47: D. Hulme (McLaren), accident; lap 49: J. Ickx (Ferrari), alternator failure and oil leak; lap 54: J. Bonnier (McLaren), ran out of fuel; M. Hailwood (Surtees), accident.

4 World Championship Results

The Racing Formula

The present Grand Prix Formula (which remains in existence until at least the end of the 1975 season) is for single-seater cars of up to 3 litres unsupercharged and 1.5 litres supercharged. Commercial fuel is compulsory and minimum weight, without ballast, must be 500 kilogrammes. Cars must be fitted with self-starters, no oil may be added during a race and the width of the bodywork must not exceed that of the track. Except by special waiver of the Commission Sportive Internationale, race distances (prior to 1971) must not be less than 300 kilometres and not more than 400 kilometres.

Drivers' World Championship

Championship points are awarded on the basis of first, 9 points; 2nd, 6; third, 4; fourth, 3; fifth, 2; and sixth, 1 point. The season is divided into two equal sections. If there is an uneven number of qualifying events, the first section will contain one more event than the second section. Drivers may count the points obtained from all but one of the races in each section towards their total.

		Points
1st,	J. Stewart (Tyrrell)	62
2nd,	R. Peterson (March)	33
3rd,	F. Cevert (Tyrrell)	26
4th,	J. Ickx (Ferrari) J. Siffert (BRM)*	19
6th,	E. Fittipaldi (Lotus)	16
7th,	C. Regazzoni (Ferrari)	13
8th,	M. Andretti (Ferrari)	12
9th,	C. Amon (Matra) P. Gethin (McLaren and BRM) D. Hulme (McLaren) P. Rodriguez (BRM)* R. Wisell (Lotus)	9

14th,	H. Ganley (BRM) T. Schenken (Brabham)	5
16th,	M. Donohue (McLaren) H. Pescarolo (March)	4
18th,	M. Hailwood (Surtees) R. Stommelen (Surtees) J. Surtees (Surtees)	3
21st,	G. Hill (Brabham)	2
22nd,	J-P. Beltoise (Matra)	1

* Deceased

Manufacturers' World Championship

Points are awarded on the same basis as for the Drivers' Championship, the highest placed car only of each make being eligible for points.

		Points
1st,	Tyrrell	73
2nd,	BRM	36
3rd,	March	34
4th,	Ferrari	33
5th,	Lotus	21
6th,	McLaren	10
7th,	Matra	9
8th,	Surtees	8
9th,	Brabham	5

5 The Non-Championship Races

ARGENTINE GRAND PRIX

Buenos Aires Autodrome (Circuit length: 2.12 miles)
24th January, 1971
Race length: Aggregate of two 106-mile (50-lap) heats

It had always been the practice from 1947 onwards for the leading European drivers to travel to South America during the winter months for the 'Temporada' series of Formula Libre races. In 1953 the Argentine Grand Prix was given status as a World Championship Formula 1 race and until 1958 (and also in 1960), it was the first round of the Championship. Now, after an interval of eleven years, a Formula 1 Argentine Grand Prix had re-appeared in the calendar and the hope was, just as it had been with the 1000 Km Sports Car race held in 1970, that if all went well the race would be restored to the Championship series the following year. Because of the fatal accident to Ignazio Giunti in the Sports Car race held a fortnight previously, Ferrari scratched his entry of three of the 312B flat-12 cars and so the race lost much of its interest. Likewise Beltoise had left the country on £3,000 bail and was certainly most reluctant to appear again before an Argentinian crowd.

THE ENTRY

Formula 1

2. E. Fittipaldi (Lotus 72C-Cosworth, chassis no. R5 entered by Gold Leaf Team Lotus)
4. R. Wisell (Lotus 72C-Cosworth, chassis no. R3 entered by Gold Leaf Team Lotus)
6. W. Fittipaldi (Lotus 49C-Cosworth, chassis no. R10 entered by Gold Leaf Team Lotus)
8. C. Amon (Matra MS120, chassis no. 02 entered by Equipe Matra-Elf)

10. D. Bell (March 701-Cosworth, chassis no. 01 entered by Wheatcroft Racing)
12. J. Siffert (March 701-Cosworth, chassis no. 05 entered by Jo Siffert Racing)
14. H. Pescarolo (March 701-Cosworth, chassis no. 06 entered by Frank Williams Racing Cars)
16. C. Reutemann (McLaren M7C-Cosworth, chassis M7C/1 entered by Ecurie Bonnier)
18. R. Stommelen (Surtees TS7-Cosworth, chassis no. 002 entered by Team Surtees)
18. S. Moser (Bellasi-Cosworth, chassis no. 01 entered by Jolly Club)

Formula A/5000
22. D. Prophet (McLaren M10B-Chevrolet)
24. G. Spice (McLaren M10B-Chevrolet)
26. J. Bonnier (Lola T190-Chevrolet)
28. C. Marincovich/G. Young (McLaren M10B-Chevrolet entered by Luigi Chinetti)*
30. N. G. Veiga (Surtees TS5A-Chevrolet entered by Luigi Chinetti)*

* These two cars were to American Formula A, using fuel injection, and the remaining cars in the class were on carburettors.

Heat 1

After a paced lap behind a Mercedes 280SL the field of fifteen starters was released in almost perfect, fine, cool weather conditions. Stommelen with the blue and white Surtees went straight into the lead and at the end of the first lap he headed Siffert, Pescarolo, Wisell, Emerson Fittipaldi and Amon. While the German pulled out a good lead, Siffert strove to hold off the rest of the runners and Fittipaldi's Lotus 72, its handling affected by the loss of a nose fin, gradually fell back. Amon succeeded in taking third place from Wisell and began to battle with Pescarolo and on a few occasions succeeded in getting in front for a short while. Fittipaldi dropped behind all the other Formula 1 cars except Moser's Bellasi and he then came into the pits where three laps were lost while a new nose fin was fitted. Once the car rejoined the race, it ran well, although completely out of contention, and Fittipaldi tucked in behind Stommelen for the remaining laps.

Results:

1st, R. Stommelen (Surtees), 1 hr 3 min 57.97 sec (99.48 mph) 2nd, J. Siffert (March), 1 hr 4 min 4.25 sec; 3rd, H. Pescarolo

(March), 1 hr 4 min 4.59 sec; 4th, C. Amon (Matra), 1 hr 4 min 4.91 sec; 5th, R. Wisell (Lotus), 1 hr 4 min 5.83 sec; 6th, C. Reutemann (McLaren), 1 hr 4 min 26.63 sec; 7th, D. Bell (March); 8th, W. Fittipaldi (Lotus); 9th, D. Prophet (McLaren); 10th, E. Fittipaldi (Lotus) 11th, S. Moser (Bellasi); 12th, G. Spice (McLaren).

Retirements: Lap 11: N. G. Veiga (Surtees), engine oil seal failure; lap 12: C. Marincovich (McLaren), broken fuel injection pump; lap 22: J. Bonnier (Lola), flat battery.

Heat 2

After an interval of forty-five minutes the second heat was under way, but without Emerson Fittipaldi whose Lotus 72 had lost its oil pressure and with the mechanics still working in the pits on Moser's Bellasi. This time Siffert roared away from Stommelen, pursued by Pescarolo, Reutemann and Amon. The New Zealander soon began to turn the pressure on, passing Reutemann on lap two and Pescarolo on lap three; just as he was about to have a go at passing Stommelen, the young German was trying to overtake Siffert, the Matra and the Surtees collided and Stommelen shot off the road. Stommelen rejoined the race, but the impact had broken several of the gearbox studs and he retired the car on lap ten. Amon carried on undismayed by this incident, chased Siffert hard and on lap ten out-braked him to take the lead. A lap later 'Seppi' was passed by both Pescarolo and Reutemann and on lap twelve both Bell and Wilson Fittipaldi went ahead of the March. Wisell stopped at the pits to complain about the handling of his Lotus, Moser joined the race many laps in arrears, and Wilson Fittipaldi retired with engine failure on lap twenty-one. Lap twenty-five saw Bell move up to third place ahead of Reutemann, but then came two March retirements in quick succession. Siffert went out on lap thirty-six with a broken rear suspension upright and two laps later Bell was out with engine failure. At the chequered flag Amon was twenty-two seconds ahead of Pescarolo and this gave him a comfortable win on aggregate. This was Amon's first Formula 1 victory since the 1970 *Daily Express* Trophy race and the only one he scored during the 1971 season.

Results:

1st, C. Amon (Matra), 1 hr 4 min 14.38 sec (99.18 mph); 2nd, H. Pescarolo (March), 1 hr 4 min 36.56 sec; 3rd, C. Reutemann (McLaren), 1 hr 4 min 45.97 sec; 4th, D. Prophet (McLaren), 48 laps; 5th, G. Spice (McLaren), 47 laps; 6th, G. Young, (McLaren), 47 laps; 7th, J. Bonnier (Lola), 46 laps.

Retirements: Lap 10: R. Stommelen (Surtees), gearbox damage following accident; lap 21: W. Fittipaldi (Lotus), engine failure; lap 24: S. Moser (Bellasi), engine failure; lap 34: R. Wisell (Lotus), accident; lap 36: J. Siffert (March), broken rear suspension upright; lap 38: D. Bell (March), engine failure.

Results on Aggregate

1st, C. Amon (Matra-Simca MS120), 2 hr 8 min 19.29 sec (99.18 mph)
2nd, H. Pescarolo (March 701-Cosworth), 2 hr 8 min 41.15 sec
3rd, C. Reutemann (McLaren M7C-Cosworth), 2 hr 9 min 12.60 sec
4th, D. Prophet (McLaren M10B-Chevrolet), 96 laps
5th, D. Bell (March 701-Cosworth), 88 laps
6th, J. Siffert (March 701-Cosworth), 86 laps
7th, R. Wisell (Lotus 72C-Cosworth), 84 laps
8th, G. Spice (McLaren M10B-Chevrolet), 84 laps
9th, W. Fittipaldi (Lotus 49C-Cosworth), 71 laps
10th, J. Bonnier (Lola T190-Chevrolet), 68 laps

Fastest lap: C. Amon, 1 min 15.05 sec (101.25 mph – set in Heat 2, new circuit record).

RACE OF CHAMPIONS

Brands Hatch (Circuit length: 2.65 miles) 21st March, 1971
Race length: 132 miles (50 laps)

First held in 1965 when the winner was the late Mike Spence with a Lotus 33, the Race of Champions has proved over the years an interesting and worthwhile 'try-out' before the European season proper gets under way. In 1967 Dan Gurney scored the first ever victory with the V-12 Eagle, Bruce McLaren won the 1968 race with the McLaren M7A on its race debut, Stewart's victory with the Matra MS80 in 1969 was also on the model's race debut and in 1970 Stewart again won, giving the new March 701 its first victory. Once again in 1971 a strong entry was received and, unlike some Formula 1 races held during the year, there was no need to bolster up the entry with Formula 5000 cars. The only new models to appear at the race were the 'lobster-claw' Brabham BT34 and the gas-turbine Lotus 56B which had originally been expected to appear at the end of the 1970 season. Three drivers, Ray Allen, Mike

Buettler and Tony Trimmer, were making their Formula 1 debuts and John Miles was having his first of two drives during the season for BRM.

THE ENTRY

1. G. Hill (Brabham BT34-Cosworth, chassis no. BT34/1 entered by Motor Racing Developments)
2. T. Schenken (Brabham BT33-Cosworth, chassis no. BT33/1 entered by Motor Racing Developments)
3. J. Miles (BRM P153, chassis no. 07 entered by Yardley-BRM)
4. H. Ganley (BRM P153, chassis no. 03 entered by Yardley-BRM)
5. C. Regazzoni (Ferrari 312B/2, chassis no. 005 entered by S.p.a. Ferrari SEFAC)
6. E. Fittipaldi (Lotus 56B-Pratt & Whitney, chassis no. 1 entered by Gold Leaf Team Lotus)
7. R. Wisell (Lotus 72C-Cosworth, chassis no. R3 entered by Gold Leaf Team Lotus)
8. T. Trimmer (Lotus 72C-Cosworth, chassis no. R5 entered by Gold Leaf Team Lotus)
9. D. Hulme (McLaren M19A-Cosworth, chassis no. M19A/1 entered by Bruce McLaren Motor Racing)
10. P. Gethin (McLaren M14A-Cosworth, chassis no. M14A/1 entered by Bruce McLaren Motor Racing)
12. R. Peterson (March 711-Cosworth, chassis no. 03 entered by Frank Williams Racing Cars)
14. R. Allen (March 701-Cosworth, chassis no. 06 entered by Frank Williams Racing Cars)
15. M. Beuttler (March 701-Cosworth, chassis no. 11 entered by Clarke Mordaunt Racing with Alistair Guthrie)
16. J. Surtees (Surtees TS9-Cosworth, chassis no. 001 entered by Team Surtees sponsored by Brooke Bond-Oxo Racing with Rob Walker)
17. J. Stewart (Tyrrell-Cosworth, chassis no. 001 entered by Elf Team Tyrrell)

THE RACE

In practice Stewart lapped in 1 min 24.6 sec – all of 1.2 seconds faster than the existing lap record – and alongside him on the front row of the grid were Hulme (1 min 25.5 sec) and Regazzoni (1 min 26.0 sec). Peterson was at the wheel of the new March built for Frank Williams, but the car was not completed until the Saturday, missed practice and in addition to starting from the back of the grid, Ronnie was given a ten-second handicap. At the time of the start the track was still wet in places after rain in the morning and there were prospects of further rain. Team managers were in a dilemma as to which were the best tyres to fit and while both Stewart and Hulme ran on intermediate tyres, Ferrari and Brabham gambled on the rain holding off and both Regazzoni and Hill ran with dry-weather tyres.

Initially Stewart and Hulme pulled away into the distance from Regazzoni, Hill and Surtees and Peterson soon began to pick up places from the slower runners. After only a single lap Trimmer stopped at the pits with fuel pressure trouble and although he rejoined the race, he retired on lap four. Another retirement followed on lap eight when the fuel injection system on Beuttler's March failed. Peterson's race through the field was short-lived and he retired on lap thirteen when one of the shafts for the inboard front brakes broke. As the track dried out, so Regazzoni closed up on Hulme, moved into second place on lap twenty and then started to chase Stewart. The rain was holding off and it now seemed that those teams that had opted for dry-weather tyres had gambled the right way. Five laps later Graham Hill with the new Brabham BT34 was through into third place and on the next lap Regazzoni took the lead from Stewart. Although Stewart was driving right on the limit, he had no hopes of staying with the Ferrari and as Hulme's engine developed a mis-fire he dropped further and further behind Hill. On lap thirty Hulme pulled into the pits to have the ignition box changed, but the car sounded just as rough when it rejoined the race and four laps later the New Zealander retired his McLaren.

Now Hill had closed right up on Stewart who succeeded in holding the Brabham off through the corners by dint of adopting lines other than the conventional and was able to accelerate away from the turquoise-green car along the straights – Stewart's car had the latest 11-series Cosworth engine, but Hill's car had a 1970 unit fitted. On lap thirty-five, after one of his best races for a long time, Hill brought the new Brabham into the pits to retire with suspected valve-spring failure. Although the 312B/2 was now laying a trail of blue smoke, the Ferrari pit did not seem at all anxious and the new car swept on to score its first race victory and Regazzoni's second Formula 1 win, 23.6 seconds ahead of Stewart's ill-handling Tyrrell. Although Surtees brought his TS9 home in third place, it was ailing by the chequered flag with low oil pressure, it had lost its water from a pipe holed by contact with the track and was a lap behind the winner.

Results

1st, C. Regazzoni (Ferrari 312B/2), 1 hr 13 min 35.0 sec (108.04 mph)
2nd, J. Stewart (Tyrrell-Cosworth), 1 hr 13 min 58.6 sec
3rd, J. Surtees (Surtees TS9-Cosworth), 1 lap in arrears
4th, T. Schenken (Brabham BT33-Cosworth), 2 laps in arrears
5th, H. Ganley (BRM P153), 2 laps in arrears
6th, R. Allen (March 701-Cosworth), 2 laps in arrears
7th, J. Miles (BRM P153), 2 laps in arrears

Fastest lap: G. Hill (Brabham), 1 min 26.7 sec (110.03 mph).

Retirements: Lap 5: T. Trimmer (Lotus), fuel pump failure; lap 8: M. Beuttler (March), fuel metering unit drive failure; lap 14: R. Peterson (March), inboard brake drive-shaft failure; lap 34: E. Fittipaldi (Lotus gas-turbine), suspension failure; lap 34: D. Hulme (McLaren), ignition trouble; lap 35: G. Hill (Brabham), engine failure); lap 38: P. Gethin (McLaren), water leak; lap 44: R. Wisell (Lotus), engine failure.

QUESTOR GRAND PRIX

Ontario Motor Speedway, California (Circuit length: 3.10 miles)
28th March, 1971
Race length: Aggregate of two 102.2 miles (32 laps) heats

Held at Ontario in California (and not to be confused with the Canadian Ontario) on a circuit laid out in the infield of an Indianapolis-type speedway track and incorporating most of the main straight of that track, the Questor Grand Prix was a new and lucrative addition to the calendar sponsored by the Questor Corporation whose diverse range of products includes automobile components, sporting goods and even baby chairs. Held in two heats, the race was run to a complicated points system with the first finisher in each heat scoring 40 points, second finisher, 35, third, 32, fourth, 30, fifth, 28, sixth, 26, seventh, 24, and then one point less for each following position down to one point for thirtieth place. The race was open to both Formula 1 and Formula A cars.

THE ENTRY

Formula 1 Cars

2. E. Fittipaldi (Lotus 7C-Cosworth, chassis no. R5 entered by Gold Leaf Team Lotus)

3. R. Wisell (Lotus 72C-Cosworth, chassis no. R3 entered by Gold Leaf Team Lotus)
4. J. Ickx (Ferrari 312B, chassis no. 001 entered S.p.a. Ferrari SEFAC)
5. M. Andretti (Ferrari 312B, chassis no. 002 entered by S.p.a. Ferrari SEFAC)
6. D. Hulme (McLaren M19A-Cosworth, chassis no. M19A/1 entered by Bruce McLaren Motor Racing)
7. P. Gethin (McLaren M14A-Cosworth, chassis no. M14A/1 entered by Bruce McLaren Motor Racing)
8. J. Stewart (Tyrrell-Cosworth, chassis no. 001 entered by Elf Team Tyrrell)
10. C. Amon (Matra MS120B, chassis no. 04 entered by Equipe Matra)
12. P. Rodriguez (BRM P160, chassis no. 01 entered by Yardley Team BRM)
14. J. Siffert (BRM P160, chassis no. 02 entered by Yardley Team BRM)
15. H. Ganley (BRM P153, chassis no. 03 entered by Yardley Team BRM)
17. D. Bell (March 701-Cosworth, chassis no. 06 entered by Frank Williams Racing Cars)
18. H. Pescarolo (March 711-Cosworth, chassis no. 03 entered by Frank Williams Racing Cars)
19. G. Hill (Brabham BT34-Cosworth, chassis no. BT34/1 entered by Motor Racing Developments)
20. T. Schenken (Brabham BT33-Cosworth, chassis no. BT33/1 entered by Motor Racing Developments)
21. R. Peterson (March 711-Cosworth, chassis no. 02 entered by STP-March)
25. J. Cannon (March 701-Cosworth, chassis no. 03 entered by STP)

Formula A Cars

Lola T192 Chevrolet 5-litre cars: driven by Mark Donohue, Bob Bondurant, Al Unser, Lou Sell and Tony Adamowicz

Lola T190 Chevrolet 5-litre cars: driven by Bobby Unser and Ron Grable

McLaren M10B-Chevrolet 5-litre car: driven by A. J. Foyt

Surtees TS8-Chevrolet 5-litre cars: driven by Peter Revson and Sam Posey

Lotus 70-Ford 5-litre car: driven by George Follmer

Eagle-Plymouth 5-litre car: driven by Swede Savage

ASD American-Chevrolet 5-litre car: driven by Gus Hutchison

Reserve Entries

Lotus 49B-Cosworth, chassis no. R11 driven by Pete Lovely
Lola T190-Chevrolet 5-litre driven by Jack Byers
McLaren M10B-Chevrolet 5-litre driven by David Hobbs
Note: none of the reserve entries started the race

Heat One

There were a grand total of thirty cars formed up for the rolling start and heading the long line-out in pole position was the Tyrrell of Jackie Stewart which had lapped in 1 min 41.257 sec, while, alongside him, Amon with the Matra had turned in a lap in 1 min 41.275 sec.

Jackie Ickx with the Ferrari went straight into the lead at the start, heading Stewart and these two drivers still led at the end of the first lap from Amon, Hulme, Hill and Siffert. Siffert spun halfway round the circuit on lap two. Hulme spun on the next lap and at the end of lap three Follmer retired his Lotus with a broken rocker. Donohue, heading the Formula A category, was pressing Graham Hill hard for fourth place and on lap five Stewart snatched the lead from Ickx. Now Hill slowed off with loss of oil pressure, on lap nine Donohue went through into fourth place closely followed by Andretti's Ferrari and the Brabham pulled off the track enveloped in a cloud of oil smoke. The ASD was overheating and constantly stopping at the pits and Rodriguez was stationary in the pits while a rear wishbone was changed on his BRM.

After ten laps the order was Stewart – Ickx – Amon – Donohue – Andretti – Siffert. On lap twelve Savage crashed the Eagle and received head injuries, Revson retired his Surtees with gearbox trouble and Posey's Surtees was eliminated by overheating. Andretti overtook Donohue's Lola, Amon was falling behind the second-place Ferrari of Ickx. Then the Ferrari suffered a puncture, stopped for a wheelchange and rejoined the race in sixteenth place. Both Al Unser and Bondurant retired with engine blow-ups and Wisell retired his Lotus with a seized engine, as did Pescarolo his March with a collapsed sub-frame, the result of an earlier collision with Schenken's Brabham. Now Amon began to close up on Stewart, but all his efforts came to nothing when the Matra punctured a tyre and after a quick pit stop he rejoined the race in tenth place. Andretti had speeded up with the Ferrari, by lap twenty-nine he was right on Stewart's exhausts and the following lap the flat-12 car swept by into the lead. Donohue had stopped at the pits on lap thirty with fuel-feed problems and although the mechanics were unable to sort out the trouble, he rejoined the race to creep round to the finish. At the chequered flag Andretti was three seconds ahead of Stewart, and Siffert crossed the line in third place.

Results:

1st, M. Andretti (Ferrari), 56 min 3.05 sec (109.40 mph); 2nd, J. Stewart (Tyrrell), 56 min 6.05 sec; 3rd, J. Siffert (BRM), 56 min 48.38 sec; 4th, D. Hulme (McLaren); 5th, J. Ickx (Ferrari); 6th, C. Amon (Matra); 7th, T. Schenken (Brabham); 8th, H. Ganley (BRM); 9th, M. Donohue (Lola); 10th, R. Grable (Lola); 11th, P. Gethin (McLaren); 12th, B. Unser (Lola); 13th, D. Bell (March); 14th, L. Sell (Lola).

Heat Two

A total of twenty-two cars formed up on the grid for Heat Two These included A. J. Foyt, who had retired his McLaren in the first heat complaining about the handling and was still not any happier about it, and Jo Siffert whose BRM had been patched up after it had crossed the line in the first heat with fractured rear suspension mounting plates. Peterson had retired his March in the first heat with a damper pulled away from the mounting and he joined the second heat when it was half-over.

As the grid moved off, Andretti nosed ahead initially, but then Stewart came through to lead and the end of the first lap the order was Stewart, Andretti, Siffert, Ickx, Hulme, Amon and Donohue. On lap two Ickx tried to out-brake Siffert into one of the turns, the Ferrari went out of control and pushed the BRM off the course. Both cars rejoined the race, the BRM's monocoque was dented and the Ferrari had collected a slow puncture which resulted in Ickx spinning off again soon afterwards. A wheel was damaged and Ickx was out of the race. By the end of lap five Stewart had pulled out a three second lead over Andretti and Donohue, after moving up to third place, dropped back behind Amon and Schenken because of a recurrence of the fuel-feed trouble. Siffert was rapidly making up ground after the earlier incident, passed Schenken and began to hare after Hulme. On lap ten Andretti took the lead from Stewart and at the end of that lap the order was Andretti – Stewart – Amon – Hulme – Siffert – Rodriguez – Schenken – Grable – Ganley – Pescarolo – Gethin. Fittipaldi retired his Lotus with the gearbox seized in fourth gear and Bobby Unser pulled off with his Lola.

Now Andretti was gradually drawing away from Stewart who was being worried by Amon, and Siffert moved ahead of Hulme. Rodriguez then passed Hulme and moved up into fourth place when

Siffert suddenly slowed off because a bolt had fallen out of a lower rear wishbone on the BRM. With a rear wheel awry, Siffert decided to carry on to the finish. Pescarolo retired when the sub-frame on the March started to collapse again and Bell was eliminated by a cracked rear upright extension. Rodriguez closed right up on Amon who was still trying to find a way past Stewart, but then Rodriguez had a nasty moment when he lost control, the BRM shot off the road and then carried on – and on the following lap Rodriguez set the fastest lap of the race in 1 min 42.78 sec (111.50 mph). At the chequered flag Andretti was twelve seconds ahead of Stewart and was clear winner of the race on aggregate. This was Ferrari's third Formula 1 victory of the season, Andretti's second, and just as in Race of Champions at Brands Hatch, tyres had played a crucial part in the victory, for it was clear that the Ferraris were handling much better at Ontario on their Firestones than was the Goodyear-shod Tyrrell. In the second heat the first Formula A car home was Grable's Lola and this driver/car combination also won the category on aggregate.

Results:

1st, M. Andretti (Ferrari), 55 min 45.36 sec (109.98 mph); 2nd, J. Stewart (Tyrrell), 55 min 57.66 sec; 3rd, C. Amon (Matra), 55 min 57.94 sec; 4th, P. Rodriguez (BRM); 5th, D. Hulme (McLaren); 6th, T. Schenken (Brabham); 7th, R. Grable (Lola); 8th, P. Gethin (McLaren); 9th, J. Cannon (March); 10th, T. Adamowicz (Lola); 11th, H. Ganley (BRM); 12th, L. Sell (Lola); 13th, J. Siffert (BRM); 14th, G. Hutchison (ASD American).

Results on Aggregate

1st, M. Andretti (Ferrari 312B), 1 hr 51 min 48.41 sec (no aggregate speed issued), 80 points ($39,400)
2nd, J. Stewart (Tyrrell-Cosworth), 1 hr 52 min 4.32 sec, 70 points ($25,250)
3rd, D. Hulme (McLaren M19A-Cosworth), 1 hr 53 min 16.98 sec, 58 points ($17,400)
4th, C. Amon (Matra MS120B), 1 hr 53 min 29.68 sec, 58 points ($14,350)
5th, T. Schenken (Brabham BT33-Cosworth), 63 laps, 50 points ($13,550)
6th, J. Siffert (BRM P160), 60 laps, 50 points ($12,950)
7th, R. Grable (Lola T190-Chevrolet), 63 laps, 45 points ($8,000)
8th, P. Gethin (McLaren M14A-Cosworth), 63 laps, 43 points ($11,850)

This fine view of the 312B/2 flat-12 Ferrari at the Nürburgring highlights its clean-cut, powerful lines. At the wheel is Jackie Ickx who retired on the second lap when he spun off into the Armco. (Nigel Snowdon)

One of the fastest drivers at the present time and a potential World Champion, Jackie Ickx was out of luck in 1971 and took fourth place in the Championship. (Nigel Snowdon)

After a brilliant first Formula 1 season in 1970, Clay Regazzoni was another victim of Ferrari unreliability in 1971 and time and time again mechanical trouble terminated his fast drives. (Nigel Snowdon)

9th, H. Ganley (BRM P153), 61 laps 43 points ($11,350)
10th, P. Rodriguez (BRM P160), 53 laps, 41 points ($12,150)
11th, J. Ickx (Ferrari 312B), 34 laps, 39 points ($11,250)
12th, J. Cannon (March 701-Cosworth), 60 laps, 38 points ($6,250)
13th, L. Sell (Lola T192-Chevrolet), 59 laps, 36 points ($6,000)
14th, M. Donohue (Lola T192-Chevrolet),* 36 laps, 34 points ($5,750)
15th, D. Bell (March 701-Cosworth),* 46 laps, 32 points ($9,850)
16th, R. Unser (Lola T190-Chevrolet),* 40 laps, 32 points ($5,250)
17th, T. Adamowicz (Lola T190-Chevrolet), 43 laps, 30 points ($5,000)
18th, R. Peterson (March 711-Cosworth), 43 laps, 30 points ($9,100)
19th, G. Hutchison (ASD American-Chevrolet), 52 laps, 29 points ($4,500)

* Not running at the finish.

Fastest lap: P. Rodriguez, 1 min 42.7 sec (111.80 mph – new lap record).
No Previous Lap Record for this circuit.

ROTHMANS INTERNATIONAL TROPHY RACE

Oulton Park (Circuit length: 2.761 miles) 9th April, 1971
Race length: 110.4 miles (40 laps)

This race was a new addition to the motor racing calendar and the combination of three factors, the large number of other early season Formula 1 races, a shortage of Cosworth engines following the ravages of the Questor race a fortnight before, and preparations for the Spanish Grand Prix reduced the number of entrants to twelve and four of these were not truly competitive.

THE ENTRY

2. H. Ganley (BRM P153, chassis no. 03 entered by Yardley-BRM)
3. P. Rodriguez (BRM P160, chassis no. 01 entered by Yardley-BRM)
4. J. Siffert (BRM P153, chassis no. 05 entered by Yardley-BRM)
5. J. Surtees (Surtees TS9-Cosworth, chassis no. 002 entered by Team Surtees sponsored by Brooke Bond-Oxo Racing with Rob Walker)

6. P. Gethin (McLaren M14A-Cosworth, chassis no. M14A/2 entered by Bruce McLaren Motor Racing)
8. M. Beuttler (March 701-Cosworth, chassis no. 11 entered by Clarke Mordaunt Racing with Alistair Guthrie)
10. E. Fittipaldi (Lotus 72C-Cosworth, chassis no. R5 entered by Gold Leaf Team Lotus)
11. R. Wisell (Lotus 56B-Pratt & Whitney, chassis no. 1 entered by Gold Leaf Team Lotus)
14. C. Williams (March 701-Cosworth, chassis no. 06 entered by Frank Williams Racing Cars)
15. A. Rollinson (March 701-Cosworth, chassis no. 07 entered by Jo Siffert Automobiles)
16. J. Stewart (Tyrrell-Cosworth, chassis no. 001 entered by Elf Team Tyrrell)
17. T. Trimmer (Lotus 49C-Cosworth, chassis no. R6 entered by Gold Leaf Team Lotus)

An additional entry was Henri Pescarolo with Frank Williams' March 711, but the car failed to arrive. The only new developments were to be seen on two of the Lotus entries. Fittipaldi's 72C had a new single-plane rear aerofoil and a new and more rounded oil tank mounted on the back of the gearbox. The gas-turbine car was now fitted with ducts for the front and rear brakes, bump stops on the dampers and new low-profile Firestone tyres.

PRACTICE

During the first session all three Lotus entries were in trouble, but the unluckiest was Trimmer with the old 49C who landed badly after taking off over a bump, smacked the barrier at Clay Hill and damaged the monocoque and rear sub-frame. The sub-frame was replaced with that from R10 which was on display at a Lotus dealer in Bradford! Stewart and Gethin were joint fastest in 1 min 25.8 sec. During a final untimed session late in the afternoon Cyd Williams went out of control after cresting a bump and collided with the Bailey bridge over the circuit. The driver was taken to hospital unconscious (fortunately it proved to be only concussion) and with a broken knee and the car was a write-off.

THE RACE

Rain was threatening just before the start of the race, but all the teams gambled on the weather staying fine – which in fact it did. On the warming-up lap Siffert's BRM collected a nail in a tyre, the mechanics started to change the wheel on the grid, but the officials insisted on the car being moved to the pits so that the race could start and 'Seppi' eventually joined in three-quarters of a lap in arrears.

Rodriguez was away first at the fall of the flag, heading Surtees, Gethin and Fittipaldi. By the end of the first lap the Mexican was clear of Surtees and after a poor start Stewart was still in fifth place. Stewart had moved up a place next time round, Trimmer stopped at the pits to sort out a sticking throttle and rejoined the race in last place behind Siffert, and Surtees was beginning to drop back. At the end of lap five Surtees came into the pits to retire with piston failure and Fittipaldi stopped out on the circuit on the next lap with transistor box failure. A mechanic went out to the car to replace this component and Fittipaldi rejoined the race many laps in arrears. With ten laps over, the order was Rodriguez, Gethin, Stewart, Ganley and then came Wisell with the gas-turbine Lotus. Beuttler stopped at the pits for attention to the loose nose of his March, rejoining the race behind Siffert, and 'Seppi' retired at the end of lap thirteen because of a broken rotor arm. Beuttler was now sixth, but he retired at the end of lap sixteen, and Wisell came into the pits to retire at the end of lap seventeen – a tyre had burst and damaged the suspension.

At half-distance, with twenty laps completed, the order was Rodriguez, Gethin (having fallen back a little after accidentally switching the ignition off), Stewart, Ganley, Rollinson and Trimmer and these six, together with Fittipaldi's Lotus, comprised the surviving runners. Rodriguez was hurling the BRM through the bends, revelling in the twists and turns of Oulton, on lap twenty-six he set a new circuit record of 1 min 25.0 sec and although Gethin later matched this lap time he was unable to catch the BRM. As for Stewart, plagued by a car that was not handling too well and tending to mis-fire, the best he could do was to hold on to third place. Ganley was lapped, Fittipaldi was many laps behind and Rollinson and Trimmer were hardly in the race. As he took the flag at the end of lap forty, Rodriguez was 4.6 seconds ahead of Gethin's McLaren. Rodriguez' performance in this short race had been superb, especially so because he had not raced at Oulton Park before.

Results:

1st, P. Rodriguez (BRM P160), 57 min 33.4 sec (115.13 mph)
2nd, P. Gethin (McLaren M14A-Cosworth), 57 min 38.0 sec
3rd, J. Stewart (Tyrrell-Cosworth), 57 min 45.6 sec
4th, H. Ganley (BRM P153), 1 lap in arrears
5th, A. Rollinson (March 701-Cosworth), 4 laps in arrears

6th, A Trimmer (Lotus 49 C-Cosworth), 4 laps it arrears
7th, E. Fittipaldi (Lotus 72C-Cosworth), 13 laps in arrears

Fastest lap: P. Rodriguez and P. Gethin, 1 min 25.0 sec (116.93 mph – new lap record).
Previous lap record: J. Stewart (Tyrrell-Cosworth), 1 min 26.6 sec (114.78 mph – set in Gold Cup race, 1970)

Retirements: Lap 6: J. Surtees (Surtees), engine trouble; lap 14: J. Siffert (BRM), broken rotor arm; lap 17: M. Beuttler (March), broken radiator mounting; lap 18: R. Wisell (Lotus), suspension failure.

GKN/DAILY EXPRESS INTERNATIONAL TROPHY RACE

Silverstone (Circuit length: 2.927 miles) 8th May, 1971
Race length: Aggregate of 75.4 miles (26 laps) heats

Apart from the British Grand Prix itself, the *Daily Express* Trophy race at Silverstone is the oldest of the British Formula One races, dating back to 1949 when it was won by Alberto Ascari at the wheel of a 1500 cc supercharged Ferrari and dominated the following year by the all-conquering Alfa Romeo 158s. In 1955 it was the scene of a memorable clash between the new British Connaught and Vanwall Grand Prix cars and the Italian Maseratis (with victory going to one of the Italian cars driven by Peter Collins) and a Vanwall driven by Stirling Moss scored the marque's first major victory in the 1956 race. The race has remained the most important of the year's non-Championship races, but since 1969 it has been somewhat debased by the inclusion of Formula 5000 cars, sixteen of which ran in the 1971 event.

THE ENTRY

Formula 1 Cars:

1. J. Stewart (Tyrrell-Cosworth chassis no. 003 entered by Elf Team Tyrrell)
2. E. Fittipaldi (Lotus 56B-Pratt & Whitney, chassis no. 1 entered by Gold Leaf Team Lotus)
3. R. Wisell (Lotus 72C-Cosworth, chassis no. R3 entered by Gold Leaf Team Lotus)
4. G. Hill (Brabham BT34-Cosworth, chassis no. BT34/1 entered by Motor Racing Developments)
5. A. Rollinson (Surtees TS7-Cosworth, chassis no. 001 entered by Team Surtees)

6. P. Gethin (McLaren M14A-Cosworth, chassis no. M14A/2 entered by Bruce McLaren Motor Racing)
7. P. Rodriguez (BRM P160, chassis no. 01 entered by Yardley-BRM)
8. J. Siffert (BRM P160, chassis no. 02 entered by Yardley-BRM)
11. R. Peterson (March 711-Alfa Romeo, chassis no. 01 entered by STP-March)
12. H. Pescarolo (March 711-Cosworth, chassis no. 03 entered by Frank Williams Racing Cars)
14. C. Amon (Matra MS120B, chassis no. 06 entered by Équipe Matra)
15. J-P. Beltoise (Matra MS120B, chassis no. 05 entered by Équipe Matra)
16. J. Surtees (Surtees TS9-Cosworth, chassis no. 001 entered by Team Surtees sponsored by Brooke Bond-Oxo Racing with Rob Walker)
17. H. Ganley (BRM P153, chassis no. 07 entered by Yardley-BRM)
18. M. Beuttler (March 701-Cosworth, chassis no. 11 entered by Clarke Mordaunt Racing with Alistair Guthrie)
21. T. Schenken (Brabham BT33-Cosworth, chassis no. BT33/1 entered by Motor Racing Developments)

In addition to Stewart's race car, the Tyrrell team had brought along car 001 as a spare; this was fitted with the experimental Girling 'twin-disc' brakes. Since its last outing at Oulton Park the Lotus turbine had been fitted with larger brakes and the 72C driven by Wisell had a one-piece rear aerofoil. Peterson's March was the same car (and engine) as used by de Adamich at Barcelona. Galli should have driven this, but was prevented from doing so by the hand injury he suffered at Monza and there should have been a Cosworth-powered car for Peterson, but a shortage of engines prevented this. Amon's Matra was a new car with the side fuel tanks blended into the monocoque, as first seen at Barcelona. Unlike the BRM drivers, Stommelen was reluctant to run at both Spa and Silverstone the same weekend, so Team Surtees fielded the original TS7 car for Rollinson. Ferrari had entered two cars, but these were scratched from the race.

Formula 5000 Cars:

Originally twenty-two Formula 5000 cars were accepted as entries, but only sixteen turned up. McLaren M18-Chevrolets were driven by Brian Redman (Sid Taylor Team Castrol car), Jean-Pierre Jaussaud (Barry Newman car), and Ulf Norinder, while Ray Allen (entered by Epstein Team Trojan), David Prophet, Gordon Spice and John Myerscough drove McLaren M10-Chevrolet cars. Tony Dean had his ex-works McLaren M7A fitted with a Chevrolet engine. There were three Lolas; the works development T192 driven by Frank Gardner, Mike Walker with Doug Hardwick's T192 and Kaye Griffiths with a T190. Mike Hailwood drove the works Surtees TS8-Chevrolet and the field was completed by Jock Russell with his Lotus 70-Ford, Trevor Taylor with the Leda, Robs Lamplough with his Lamplola-Ford, Fred Saunders with his Crossle-Rover and Bob Miller's Dulon-Chevrolet.

In practice Chris Amon was fastest in 1 min 20.0 sec, Jackie Stewart was alongside on the grid with a lap in 1 min 20.2 sec and Emerson Fittipaldi, the Lotus turbine at long last running on a circuit to which it was really suited, was third fastest in 1 min 21.0 sec. Fastest of the Formula 5000 boys was Mike Hailwood who turned in 1 min 23.6 sec, faster than several of the Formula 1 cars.

HEAT ONE

Race day was dry and sunny with quite a strong wind. At the start of the first heat Pescarolo's March was in trouble because of low fuel pressure, he went straight into the pits when the flag fell, the engine revived itself and he shot back into the race. Stewart streamed into the lead at the start, followed by Surtees, Beltoise, Amon and Fittipaldi. Initially Peterson was sixth, but he fell back after a plug lead came off. Stewart began to pull out a lead, Surtees fell back and was sandwiched between the two Matras and Fittipaldi retired at the end of lap two because a wishbone had torn away from its mounting point. Peterson shot into the pits at the end of that lap two and shot out again in a matter of seconds with the plug lead back in place.

On lap three Stewart set a new lap record of 1 min 20.7 sec and on the next lap Amon pushed Surtees back to fourth place. Rodriguez and Siffert were now sixth and seventh. On lap five Graham Hill, going well with the 'lobster-claw' Brabham took fourth place from Surtees, but on that same lap Amon's engine cut out and on the next lap he stopped at the pits; the mechanics worked on the fuel system and the New Zealander rejoined the race two laps in arrears. Now Rodriguez pushed the P160 BRM past Surtees and closed up on Hill's third-place Brabham. Siffert's BRM began to drop back and on lap seven he pulled into the pits to retire. Hill and Rodriguez surged past Beltoise's Matra and on lap fourteen

Surtees went ahead of the French V-12 car to take fourth place. Amon stopped again at the pits to have a punctured tyre changed.

Rodriguez was chasing Hill hard for second place and eventually took on the inside at Woodcote on lap twenty. Peterson had been making up ground rapidly after his pit stop, but on lap twenty-five, just after he had overtaken Gardner's Lola for fourteenth place, the March's throttle jammed open on the approach to Becketts. The March plunged into the bank on the outside of the circuit, two wheels were torn off – one of them splitting Peterson's crash helmet. Although the driver was taken unconscious to hospital, his injuries proved to be only minor. At the chequered flag Stewart was over ten seconds ahead of Rodriguez, Hill finished third and Redman, in tenth place, led the Formula 5000 category.

Results:
1st, J. Stewart (Tyrrell), 128.68 mph; 2nd, P. Rodriguez (BRM P160); 3rd, G. Hill (Brabham BT34); 4th, J. Surtees (Surtees TS9); 5th, J-P. Beltoise (Matra-Simca MS120B); 6th, P. Gethin (McLaren M14A); 7th, R. Wisell (Lotus 72); 8th, H. Ganley (BRM P153); 9th, T. Schenken (Brabham BT33); 10th, B. Redman (McLaren M18); 11th, A. Dean (McLaren M7A); 12th, M. Hailwood (Surtees TS8); 13th, A. Rollinson (Surtees TS7); 14th, F. Gardner (Lola T192); 15th, H. Pescarolo (March 711); 16th, J-P. Jaussaud (McLaren M18); 17th, M. Beuttler (March 701); 18th, R. Peterson (March 711), did not finish; 19th, G. Spice (McLaren M10B), did not finish; 20th, U. Norinder (McLaren M18); 21st, C. Amon (Matra-Simca MS120B); 22nd, J. Russell (Lotus 70); 23rd, F. Saunders (Crossle 15F); 24th, R. Miller (Dulon LD8).

Retirements: Lap 3: E. Fittipaldi (Lotus 56B), suspension failure; lap 4: R. Lamplough (Lamplola), oil leak; T. Taylor (Leda), handling problems; lap 6: R. Allen (McLaren M10B), accident; lap 8: J. Siffert (BRM P160), engine trouble; lap 18: J. Myerscough (McLaren M10B), oil leak; lap 21: D. Prophet (McLaren M10B), overheating; lap 25: G. Spice (McLaren M10B), gearbox trouble; R. Peterson (March 711), accident.

HEAT TWO

In the interval between the heats the Lotus team had repaired the gas-turbine car, which started from the back of the grid, Ganley, having driven for most of the first heat without a clutch, now had this fully operative and Schenken's Brabham had the 13-in. rear wheels used in the first heat replaced by 15-in. wheels. The grid was formed up in Heat One finishing order.

When the flag fell, Rodriguez made an electric start and led away from Stewart, the Scot was alongside the BRM as the two cars approached Copse, then the Tyrrell's throttle jammed open and the dark blue car skidded straight into the bank. The car was very badly damaged, but Stewart escaped with a strained arm. Ganley's BRM and Rollinson's Surtees collided at Becketts and although the BRM was out of the race with wrecked rear suspension, Rollinson was able to carry on. At the end of the first lap Rodriguez led from Surtees, Hill, Gethin, Redman (going magnificently with his Formula 5000 McLaren), Amon, Beltoise and Pescarolo. Hill moved into second place ahead of Surtees on lap four and Beltoise and Amon were now fourth and fifth with the Matras. Graham, turning in his best drive of the season, now closed right up on Rodriguez and was chasing him hard.

On lap seven Beltoise retired with a con-rod through the side of the engine; Redman punctured a tyre on debris from Beltoise's blown-up engine, after the wheel-change the McLaren was reluctant to start, it eventually fired and then succumbed at Becketts to electrical trouble. Hill went past Rodriguez into the lead on lap twelve, and at the end of the next lap the Mexican pulled into the pits with a punctured tyre. He lost almost a lap while the wheel was changed and rejoined the race immediately in front of Hill. Surtees was trying hard to hold off Amon and on lap fourteen turned in fastest time of the heat in 1 min 20.6 sec. Wisell was now fourth ahead of Gethin, Fittipaldi, Pescarolo, Hailwood and Schenken. Hailwood's TS8 Surtees had jammed in top gear which made his performance all the more remarkable. Despite his pit stop Rodriguez was in twelfth place and going very strongly.

On lap twenty-three two of the leading contenders dropped out of the race. Surtees retired with a broken front rocking arm and Wisell was eliminated by sudden and inexplicable engine failure. As a result of these two retirements Fittipaldi's drive through the field had brought him third place in the heat, Hailwood finished sixth and won the Formula 5000 category and Rodriguez had climbed back to eighth place, having been lapped by Hill in the closing stages of the race. Graham Hill was the clear winner on aggregate and there could hardly have been a winner more popular with the crowd.

Results:

1st, G. Hill (Brabham BT34), 129.14 mph; 2nd, C. Amon (Matra-Simca MS120B); 3rd, E. Fittipaldi (Lotus 56B); 4th, P. Gethin (McLaren M14A); 5th, H. Pescarolo (March 711); 6th, M.

Hailwood (Surtees TS8); 7th, T. Schenken (Brabham BT33); 8th, P. Rodriguez (BRM P160); 9th, A. Dean (McLaren M7A); 10th, J-P. Jaussaud (McLaren M18); 11th, F. Gardner (Lola T192); 12th, M. Beuttler (March 701); 13th, A. Rollinson (Surtees TS7); 14th, U. Norinder (McLaren M18); 15th, J. Surtees (Surtees TS9 did not finish); 16th, F. Saunders (Crossle 15F did not finish; 17th, G. Spice (McLaren M10B); 18th, R. Wisell (Lotus 72 did not finish); 19th, R. Miller (Dulon LD8).

Retirements: Lap 1: J. Stewart (Tyrrell), accident; H. Ganley (BRM), accident; lap 8: R. Lamplough (Lamplola), water pump failure; J.-P. Beltoise (Matra-Simca MS120B), engine failure; lap 10: B. Redman (McLaren M18); lap 16: J. Russell (Lotus 70), low oil pressure; lap 23: R. Wisell (Lotus 72), engine failure; lap 24: F. Saunders (Crossle 15F), ran out of fuel; J. Surtees (Surtees TS9), suspension failure.

Results on Aggregate:

1st, G. Hill (Brabham BT34-Cosworth), 1 hour 11 min 3.2 sec (128.53 mph)
2nd, P. Gethin (McLaren M14A-Cosworth), 1 hour 12 min 37.0 sec
3rd, T. Schenken (Brabham BT33-Cosworth), 1 hour 13 min 7.9 sec
4th, P. Rodriguez (BRM P160), 51 laps
5th, M. Hailwood (Surtees TS8-Chevrolet), 51 laps
6th, H. Pescarolo (March 711-Cosworth), 51 laps
7th, A. Dean (McLaren M7A-Chevrolet), 50 laps
8th, J-P. Jaussaud (McLaren M18-Chevrolet), 50 laps
9th, F. Gardner (Lola T192-Chevrolet), 50 laps
10th, M. Beuttler (March 701-Cosworth), 50 laps
11th, J. Surtees (Surtees TS9-Cosworth), 49 laps
12th, C. Amon (Matra-Simca MS120B), 49 laps
13th, R. Wisell (Lotus 72C-Cosworth), 48 laps
14th, A. Rollinson (Surtees TS7-Cosworth), 48 laps
15th, U. Norinder (McLaren M18-Chevrolet), 47 laps
16th, G. Spice (McLaren M10B-Chevrolet), 47 laps
17th, F. Saunders (Crossle 15F-Rover), 46 laps
18th, R. Miller (Dulon LD8-Chevrolet), 44 laps

Fastest lap: J. Stewart (Tyrrell-Cosworth), 1 min 20.5 sec (130.90 mph – new lap record).
Previous lap record: J. Stewart (Matra MS80-Cosworth), 1 min 21.3 sec (129.61 mph – set in 1969 British Grand Prix)
1970 winner: C. Amon (March 701-Cosworth), 124.19 mph.

JOCHEN RINDT GEDÄCHTNIS-RENNEN

Hockenheim Motordrom (Circuit length: 4.218 miles)

13th June, 1971

Race length: 146.64 miles (35 laps)

Because of the cancellation of the Belgian Grand Prix, there was an interval of four weeks between Monaco and Zandvoort and with the return of the German Grand Prix to the Nürburgring there were prospects of no Formula 1 racing at all at Hockenheim in 1971. Accordingly the Badischer Motor Sport Club decided to fill this gap in the calendar and the fact that the Le Mans race was the same weekend had only a negligible effect, for the only team racing in both Formula 1 and at Le Mans was Matra and the only drivers at the Sarthe circuit were Amon, Beltoise, Pescarolo, Rodriguez and Siffert. Hulme and Stewart, however, were both competing in the Can-Am race at Mosport. Fittipaldi missed the race because of injuries suffered in a road accident in France. Matra, Tyrrell and Brabham all gave the race a miss, but the latter only because Hill's Brabham BT34 could not be repaired in time following its Monaco prang.

THE ENTRY

2. J. Surtees (Surtees TS9-Cosworth, chassis no. 001 entered by Team Surtees sponsored by Brooke Bond-Oxo Racing with Rob Walker)
3. R. Stommelen (Surtees TS9-Cosworth, chassis no. 002 entered by Team Surtees sponsored by *Auto Motor und Sport* – Eifelland)
4. J. Ickx (Ferrari 312B, chassis no. 003 entered by S.p.a. Ferrari SEFAC)
5. C. Regazzoni (Ferrari 312B, chassis no. 004 entered by S.p.a. Ferrari SEFAC)
7. D. Walker (Lotus 72D-Cosworth, chassis no. R5 entered by Gold Leaf Team Lotus)
8. R. Wisell (Lotus 72D-Cosworth, chassis no. R3 entered by Gold Leaf Team Lotus)
10. R. Peterson (March 711-Alfa Romeo, chassis no. 06 entered by STP-March)
11. A. Soler-Roig (March 711-Cosworth, chassis no. 04 entered by STP-March)
12. N. Galli (March 711-Alfa Romeo, chassis no. 01 entered by STP-March)
15. R. Allen (March 701-Cosworth, chassis no. 06 entered by Frank Williams Racing Cars)

16. H. Ganley (BRM P153, chassis no. 06 entered by Yardley-BRM)
17. J. Miles (BRM P153, chassis no. 07 entered by Yardley-BRM)
19. S. Barber (March 711-Cosworth, chassis no. 05 entered by Gene Mason Racing)
21. P. Gethin (McLaren M14A-Cosworth, chassis no. M14A/2 entered by Bruce McLaren Motor Racing)
22. M. Beuttler (March 701-Cosworth, chassis no. 11 entered Clarke Mordaunt Racing with Alistair Guthrie)
23. X. Perrot (March 701-Cosworth, chassis no. 05 entered by Jo Siffert Automobiles)
24. R. Lamplough (BRM P133, chassis no. 05 entered by R. Lamplough Racing)
25. B. Terbeck (BRM P126, believed to be chassis no. 02 entered by R. Lamplough Racing)

Originally Ferrari had also entered a car for Andretti, but this was scratched when Andretti decided to rest after suffering slight burns in the USAC race at Milwaukee. Lotus had also entered three cars, with Walker at the wheel of the 56B gas-turbine car and Tony Trimmer with Fittipaldi's Lotus 72D. However, after the gas-turbine suffered an internal fire in practice, it was scratched from the race and Walker took over Trimmer's car. Since its last outing the 56B had been fitted with larger fuel tanks. Peterson's car was fitted with the March team's own Alfa engine and the Swedish driver also had a Cosworth-powered car, chassis no. 02 as a spare. BRM had brought as a spare P160 car, chassis no. 03, the latest to be built. The two old BRMs driven by Lamplough and Terbeck had been bought at low price from the works and Terbeck's car failed to start after engine failure in practice.

Practice was dominated by the Ferraris and Ickx was fastest of all in 1 min 56.8 sec, 3.7 sec faster than his own lap record set in the 1970 German Grand Prix and 2.9 sec faster than his practice time then. Regazzoni was .9 of a second slower. As a tribute to Jochen Rindt, pole position on the grid was left vacant and so Ickx alone on the front row headed the two by two grid formation.

THE RACE

Ickx made a superb start at the fall of the flag and accelerated away from the rest of the field with Regazzoni second and at the end of the first lap the two Ferraris were fifty yards clear of Peterson and then came Ganley, Wisell, Gethin, Surtees and Galli. On this circuit and with this opposition the Ferraris were in complete control of the race, but although Ickx stayed in front for the remaining thirty-four laps, a silly mechanical fault put Regazzoni completely out of contention. As the Ferraris started lap three, the Swiss driver's car suddenly cut out completely. A mechanic came out to the car, but by the time the trouble had been traced to the electrically operated rev limiter which had earthed itself and Clay was back in the race, he was ten laps in arrears.

Wisell came through to challenge and pass Peterson and they drew nearer and nearer the leading Ferrari until lap thirteen when the Lotus suddenly eased off. The Swedish Lotus driver brought the 72D into the pits next time round with brake trouble and he rejoined the race after the brakes had been bled. On Peterson's March the clutch had failed completely and hampered by having to make clutchless gear changes he began to fall back again. Early retirements had been Gethin who stopped with the McLaren on lap four with broken throttle linkage, Miles who retired his BRM on lap seven because of a cracked cylinder liner and Allen retired his March with a leaking fuel tank on lap fifteen.

Surtees passed Ganley for third place on lap thirteen, Galli was fifth with his rather badly smoking March and then came Stommelen who had taken nine laps to pass Walker and Barber. In fact he had by-passed the chicane while doing so and this was to result in a one-minute penalty. The remainder of the entry were never in the picture, trailing round rather hopelessly and with Lamplough bringing up the tail of the field. Throughout the race Ickx kept up the pressure, lapping faster than his previous lap record and reducing it to 1 min 58.5 sec. Peterson was almost a minute behind at the chequered flag, but this was the best performance to date by a Tipo 33/3 Alfa-engined car.

Results:

1st, J. Ickx (Ferrari 312B), 1 hr 10 min 11.7 sec (126.20 mph)
2nd, R. Peterson (March 711-Alfa Romeo), 1 hr 11 min 5.5 sec
3rd, J. Surtees (Surtees TS9-Cosworth), 1 hr 11 min 28.7 sec
4th, H. Ganley (BRM P153), 1 hr 11 min 43.8 sec
5th, N. Galli (March 711-Alfa Romeo), 1 hr 11 min 56.9 sec
6th, S. Barber (March 711-Cosworth), 1 lap in arrears
7th, R. Stommelen (Surtees TS9-Cosworth), 1 lap in arrears*
8th, A. Soler-Roig (March 711-Cosworth), 1 lap in arrears
9th, D. Walker (Lotus 72D-Cosworth), 1 lap in arrears

* On time Stommelen finished sixth, but he was penalised one minute for missing the chicane when his brakes locked up.

10th, R. Wisell (Lotus 72D-Cosworth), 2 laps in arrears
11th, X. Perrot (March 701-Cosworth), 4 laps in arrears
12th, R. Lamplough (BRM P133), 4 laps in arrears
13th, M. Beuttler (March 701-Cosworth), 7 laps in arrears
14th, C. Regazzoni (Ferrari 312B), 10 laps in arrears

Fastest lap: J. Ickx, 1 min 58.8 sec (127.82 mph – new circuit record).

Previous lap record: J. Ickx, 2 min 00.5 sec (126.02 mph – set in the 1970 German Grand Prix)

Retirements: Lap 4: P. Gethin (McLaren), broken throttle control rod; lap 6: J. Miles (BRM), broken cylinder liner; lap 15: R. Allen (March), fuel metering unit trouble.

INTERNATIONAL GOLD CUP RACE

Oulton Park (Circuit length: 2.761 miles) 21st August, 1971
Race length: Aggregate of two 55.22 miles (20 laps) heats

One of the oldest established of non-Championship Formula 1 races, the Gold Cup was first held in 1954 when the winner was Stirling Moss with a works Maserati and he repeated this victory in 1955 with a works car. In 1956–7 and 1964–5 the race was held for Formula 2 cars and in 1958 it was a Sports Car event. Twice in succession Jack Brabham has won the race with his own cars (1966–7) and in 1968 the victor was Stewart with the Matra who defeated the works Ferraris. The following year a Brabham had again won the race, but this time the driver was Jackie Ickx. In 1970 John Surtees scored the first victory to be achieved by his own Formula 1 car and he again entered the race in 1971. As in 1969 and 1970 the field was made up by a number of Formula 5000 cars.

THE ENTRY

Formula 1 Cars:

32. J. Surtees (Surtees TS9-Cosworth, chassis no. 004 entered by Team Surtees sponsored by Brooke Bond-Oxo Racing with Rob Walker)
33. H. Ganley (BRM P153, chassis no. 07 entered by Yardley-BRM)
34. P. Gethin (BRM P160, chassis no. 01 entered by Yardley-BRM)

35. M. Beuttler (March 711-Cosworth, chassis no. 02 entered by Clarke Mordaunt Racing with Alistair Guthrie)
36. J.-P. Jarier (March 711-Cosworth, chassis no. 09 entered by Goodwin Racing Services)
37. H. Pescarolo (March 711-Cosworth, chassis no. 03 entered by Frank Williams Racing Cars)
38. T. Trimmer (March 701-Cosworth, chassis no. 06 entered by Frank Williams Racing Cars)
39. C. Craft (Brabham BT33-Cosworth, chassis no. BT33/2 entered by Ecurie Evergreen)

Formula 5000 Cars:

1. B. Redman (McLaren M18-Chevrolet entered by Sid Taylor Team Castrol)
3. F. Gardner (Lola T300-Chevrolet entered by Lola Cars Ltd)
8. R. Allen (McLaren M10B-Chevrolet entered by Team Trojan)
11. T. Taylor (Leda LT25-Chevrolet entered by Malaya Garage Racing Division)
15. M. Hailwood (Surtees TS8-Chevrolet entered by Team Surtees)
21. D. Prophet (McLaren M10B-Chevrolet entered by Bugle Prophet)
22. G. McRae (McLaren M10B-Chevrolet entered by Crown Lynn Potteries)
26. A. Rollinson (Surtees TS8-Chevrolet entered by Alan McKechnie)
41. R. Miller (Dulon LD8-Chevrolet)
44. G. Spice (McLaren M10B-Chevrolet entered by Gordon Spice Cash & Carry Ltd)
66. F. Saunders (Crossle 15F-Rover entered by Mermaid Racing)
77. M. Walker (Lola T192-Chevrolet entered by Doug Hardwick)

HEAT I

In pole position on the grid was Gethin's BRM which had turned in a fastest lap of 1 min 24.6 sec and alongside him were Pescarolo and Ganley both of whom had recorded 1 min 25.0 sec. Because of fuel injection trouble Beuttler's March made the grid at only the very last moment. When the flag fell, the March lunged forward, stalled and refused to fire again. McRae missed the start because of a last-minute plug change and joined the race two laps in arrears. Pescarolo went straight into the lead, heading the BRMs of Gethin, Ganley and Surtees. Spice collided with Craft at the Esso hairpin and the McLaren disappeared over the banking and out of the race, Trimmer came into the pits at the end of the first lap for the gear linkage to be adjusted and Miller and Jarier (whose March was running very roughly) brought up the tail of the field. Allen retired on lap two when an oil pump belt fell off, Taylor squashed the monocoque of the Leda against the bank at Knickerbrook when a tyre punctured on lap four and Gethin stopped at the pits at the end of lap five because locking brakes had worn a flat spot on one of the tyres. At the chequered flag Pescarolo led comfortably with the red March and Ganley took second place, hard pressed in the closing stages by Surtees who had equalled the circuit record on lap twelve.

Results:
1st, H. Pescarolo (March), 28 min 48.2 sec (115.30 mph); 2nd, H. Ganley (BRM), 28 min 52.6 sec; 3rd, J. Surtees (Surtees), 28 min 54.0 sec; 4th, F. Gardner (Lola), 29 min 19.6 sec; 5th, P. Gethin (BRM), 29 min 19.8 sec; 6th, M. Hailwood (Surtees), 29 min 27.8 sec; 7th, A. Rollinson (Surtees); 8th, C. Craft (Brabham); 9th, M. Walker (Lola); 10th, D. Prophet (McLaren); 11th, F. Saunders (Crossle); 12th, R. Miller (Dulon); 13th, J-P. Jarier (March).

Retirements: Lap 1: M. Beuttler (March), fuel injection system; G. Spice (McLaren), accident; lap 4: T. Taylor (Leda), accident; lap 15: B. Redman (McLaren), overheating; lap 16: G. McRae (McLaren), electrical fire; lap 18: T. Trimmer (March), accident.

HEAT 2

A total of fifteen cars formed up on the grid for the second heat and this time Surtees led away from Pescarolo, Gethin and Ganley. These four Formula 1 cars stayed at the head of the field until lap three when Gethin collided with Pescarolo, damaging the BRM's steering, and pulled into the pits to retire. Although Pescarolo had only to keep Surtees in his sights to win overall, his brakes were playing up and he was having difficulty in keeping Ganley at bay. On lap seven the March spun off at Knickerbrook and tore a rear wheel off against the bank. Third place was now inherited by Frank Gardner with the Formula 5000 Lola and in the closing stages of the race neither of the leading 3-litre cars was running well; the BRM's handling was badly affected by one of the front suspension lugs working loose and Surtees slowed off because the TS9 was running on only seven cylinders. However, while his engine was still *au point*, Surtees set a new lap record of 1 min 24.8 sec and at the chequered flag he was still almost thirteen seconds ahead of the BRM. This was Surtees' third Gold Cup victory (he won the race with a Formula 2 Lola in 1965) and the second ever at the wheel of one of his own cars. However the 1971 Gold Cup race was probably the least interesting of all Formula 1 events held during the year.

Results:

1st, J. Surtees (Surtees), 28 min 44.6 sec (115.27 mph); 2nd, H. Ganley (BRM), 28 min 57.4 sec; 3rd, F. Gardner (Lola), 29 min 27.0 sec; 4th, A. Rollinson (Surtees), 29 min 33.0 sec; 5th, C. Craft (Brabham), 29 min 33.8 sec; 6th, G. McRae (McLaren), 29 min 41.0 sec; 7th, M. Walker (Lola); 8th, G. Spice (McLaren); 9th, D. Prophet (McLaren); 10th, J-P. Jarier (March); 11th, F. Saunders (Crossle).

Retirements: Lap 4: P. Gethin (BRM), accident damage; lap 7: H. Pescarolo (March), accident; lap 14: M. Hailwood (Surtees), accident damage.

Results on Aggregate:

1st, J. Surtees (Surtees TS9-Cosworth), 57 min 38.6 sec (114.96 mph)
2nd, H. Ganley (BRM P153), 57 min 50.0 sec
3rd, F. Gardner (Lola T300-Chevrolet), 58 min 46.6 sec
4th, A. Rollinson (Surtees TS8-Chevrolet), 59 min 15.2 sec
5th, C. Craft (Brabham BT33-Cosworth), 59 min 30.8 sec
6th, M. Walker (Lola T192-Chevrolet), 60 min 18.2 sec
7th, D. Prophet McLaren (M10B-Chevrolet) 38 laps.
8th, F. Saunders (Crossle 15F-Rover), 36 laps
9th, G. McRae (McLaren M10B-Chevrolet), 35 laps.
10th, J.-P. Jarier (March 701-Cosworth), 34 laps
11th, M. Hailwood (Surtees TS8-Chevrolet) ,33 laps – not running at the finish
12th, R. Miller (Dulon LD8-Chevrolet), 32 laps

Fastest lap: J. Surtees, 1 min 24.8 sec (117.21 mph – new circuit record).

ROTHMANS WORLD CHAMPIONSHIPS VICTORY RACE

Brands Hatch (Circuit length: 2.65 miles) 24th October, 1971

Race length: Scheduled length of 106 miles (40 laps), but race halted on lap fifteen following Siffert's crash with positions classified as at the end of lap fourteen (31.1 miles)

Supposedly held as a sort of tribute race to the victories of Jackie

Stewart and Tyrrell in the World Championships, this reason was simply a pretext for adding a Formula 1 race to the Motor Show 200 meeting programme and none the worse for that. A good entry of fourteen Formula 1 cars was received and it seemed in the circumstances rather unnecessary to include Formula 5000 cars in the entry. What should have been a closely fought and exciting climax to an excellent Formula 1 year ended in tragedy when, for no apparent reason, Jo Siffert's BRM went out of control and crashed and the very popular Swiss driver lost his life.

THE ENTRY

1. J. Stewart (Tyrrell-Cosworth, chassis no. 003 entered by Elf Team Tyrrell)
2. F. Cevert (Tyrrell-Cosworth, chassis no. 002 entered by Elf Team Tyrrell)
4. R. Peterson (March 711-Cosworth, chassis no. 06 entered by STP-March)
5. J. Siffert (BRM P160, chassis no. 02 entered by Yardley-BRM)
6. P. Gethin (BRM P160, chassis no. 01 entered by Yardley-BRM)
7. H. Ganley (BRM P160, chassis no. 04 entered by Yardley-BRM)
8. E. Fittipaldi (Lotus 72D-Cosworth, chassis no. R5 entered by Gold Leaf Team Lotus)
10. J. Oliver (McLaren M19A-Cosworth, chassis no. M19A/2 entered by Bruce McLaren Motor Racing)
11. G. Hill (Brabham BT34-Cosworth, chassis no. BT34/1 entered by Motor Racing Developments)
12. T. Schenken (Brabham BT33-Cosworth, chassis no. BT33/3 entered by Motor Racing Developments)
14. C. Reutemann (Brabham BT33-Cosworth, chassis no. BT33/1 entered by Motor Racing Developments)
15. H. Pescarolo (March 711-Cosworth, chassis no. 03 entered by Frank Williams Racing Cars)
16. J. Surtees (Surtees TS9-Cosworth, chassis no. 004 entered by Team Surtees sponsored by Brooke Bond-Oxo Racing with Rob Walker)
17. M. Hailwood (Surtees TS9-Cosworth, chassis no. 002 entered by Team Surtees sponsored by Brooke Bond-Oxo Racing with Rob Walker)

The only team to produce anything new at Brands Hatch was the Motor Racing Developments organisation, for Schenken's car had a new one-piece full-width nose and cockpit with high sides and the team also fielded a new driver – Carlos Reutemann, to be a regular team member in 1972, who was being given a 'shake-down' with the team. His first Formula 1 drive had been with Bonnier's McLaren at the Argentine race early in the year. The BRMs driven by both Siffert and Gethin had the Mk II cylinder heads. Neither Ferrari nor Matra entered the race and the entry from Tecno was cancelled, allegedly because of faulty bag fuel tanks.

Formula 5000 Cars

McLaren M18-Chevrolet: Reine Wisell (deputising for Brian Redman at the wheel of the Sid Taylor car now running in works colours).
McLaren M10B-Chevrolet: Guy Edwards, Keith Holland, David Prophet, Ray Allen, Teddy Pilette (entered by Racing Team VDS) and Gordon Spice.
Lola T300-Chevrolet: Frank Gardner (works car)
Lola T192-Chevrolet: Mike Walker
Lola T190-Chevrolet: Ian Ashley
Leda LT25-Chevrolet: Trevor Taylor
Surtees TS8-Chevrolet: Alan Rollinson
Crossle 15F-Rover: Fred Saunders

Practice was dominated by the BRMs of Siffert and Gethin which were fastest in an identical time of 1 min 22.8 sec – thereby bettering the lap record set by Jack Brabham in the 1970 Race of Champions by three seconds.

THE RACE

When the flag fell for the start of the race, Gethin shot into the lead and he was still leading at the end of the first lap from Fittipaldi, Hailwood, Peterson, Siffert and Stewart. As they went through Druids on lap two Pescarolo and Wisell collided and both the March and the F5000 McLaren were out of the race. Then at Bottom Bend Peterson and Hailwood bounced off each other and spun. Fortunately all the following cars managed to avoid them and both drivers set off for their pits for wheel-changes. Peterson was soon back in the race, almost a lap in arrears, but Hailwood was eliminated by damaged suspension as he made his way back to the pits. By the end of lap five Stewart was in third place ahead of Schenken, Siffert, Surtees, Cevert and Ganley and Rollinson, in twelfth place, led the Formula 5000 class. Fittipaldi was right on Gethin's exhausts and trying hard to get past.

Siffert was now beginning to pick up places and on lap eleven he took fourth place from Schenken and started to chase after Stewart. On lap fifteen a great pall of smoke hung over Hawthorn, and Surtees, looking very pale, the bodywork of his car damaged and with a flat tyre pulled into the pits. No other cars came by. Siffert's BRM had gone out of control just before Hawthorn, crashed into the bank and exploded in a cloud of flames and smoke. The driver, unconscious, had perished almost immediately. The other cars had come to rest on the circuit, the track blocked, but Surtees, whose car had been showered with debris, had carried on to the pits. The cause of the accident is not known and the refusal of Louis Stanley, managing director of BRM, to release the remains of the car to the Royal Automobile Club for examination has not helped the organising body of motor sport in the United Kingdom in carrying out its investigations. The race was stopped at this point and the results decided on the positions at the end of lap fourteen.

Results:

1st, P. Gethin (BRM P160), 19 min 54.4 sec (111.82 mph)
2nd, E. Fittipaldi (Lotus 72D-Cosworth), 19 min 54.6 sec
3rd, J. Stewart (Tyrrell-Cosworth), 19 min 59.8 sec
4th, J. Siffert (BRM P160) 20 min 7.2 sec
5th, T. Schenken (Brabham BT33-Cosworth), 20 min 10.0 sec
6th, J. Surtees (Surtees TS9-Cosworth), 20 min 10.4 sec
7th, F. Cevert (Tyrrell-Cosworth), 20 min 19.2 sec
8th, G. Hill (Brabham BT34-Cosworth), 20 min 26.0 sec
9th, C. Reutemann (Brabham BT33-Cosworth), 20 min 27.8 sec
10th, A. Rollinson (Surtees TS8-Chevrolet), 20 min 50.8 sec*
11th, F. Gardner (Lola T300-Chevrolet), 20 min 51.0 sec
12th, M. Walker (Lola T192-Chevrolet), 20 min 52.4 sec
13th, G. Spice (McLaren M10B-Chevrolet), 21 min 4.6 sec
14th, T. Pilette (McLaren M10B-Chevrolet), 21 min 5.8 sec
15th, K. Holland (McLaren M10B-Chevrolet), 21 min 6.6 sec
16th, R. Peterson (March 711-Cosworth), 21 min 10.2 sec
* Winner, Formula 5000 Category.

Fastest lap: E. Fittipaldi, 1 min 24.0 sec (113.57 mph – circuit record).

Retirements: Lap 2: R. Wisell (McLaren), accident; H. Pescarolo (March), accident; lap 3: F. Saunders (Crossle), fire; M. Hailwood (Surtees), accident; lap 6: H. Ganley (BRM), engine failure; lap 10: T. Taylor (Leda), overheating; lap 14: J. Oliver (McLaren), brake trouble.

Part Two
The Sports Car Year

6 The Cars and Teams

The 1971 season was not exceptional by any standard, as one vital ingredient for exciting motor racing was lacking, the absence at most races of any serious opposition to the overwhelming Porsche onslaught. It was, however, a memorable season for the efficiency of the John Wyer team (as in 1970), the sheer speed of the 917s (now able to lap Spa-Francorchamps at 160 mph), the consistent reliability of the Alfa Romeo Tipo 33/3 cars which won three races after the Porsche power had disintegrated, and the pace and superb handling characteristics of the new Ferrari 312P which must be the hot favourite to dominate Prototype racing in 1972.

PORSCHE

1971 was the second year of the collaboration between the Porsche factory and the Gulf Oil Corporation-sponsored JW Automotive Engineering Ltd headed by John Wyer. In all the Gulf-Porsche 917s won five of the season's eleven Championship races. The Porsche Konstruktionen AG team of Salzburg had now withdrawn from racing, but their two cars were taken over by the Martini Racing Team, managed by Hans-Dieter Dechent and sponsored by the aperitif company. Despite the handicap of having only three cars (as they fielded two at each race except Sebring and the Osterreichring where they were loaned a works car this meant that one car always had to run in successive races), the team won at Sebring and at Le Mans (at the Sarthe Circuit they were also loaned cars by the Stuttgart works). In addition a Martini-entered, but works-prepared 908/3 won the Nürburgring 1,000 Km race.

Although Ferrari ceased racing the 5-litre 512 cars and concentrated on development of the 312P flat-12 Prototype with a view to racing the model seriously when a 3-litre capacity limit was to be imposed, development still continued on the 917s and was concentrated in three directions, engine improvements, new body styles and braking improvements.

Engine Modifications

At the beginning of the season both the Gulf and Martini teams used the familiar 4907 cc (86 × 70.4 mm) engine developing 575/590 bhp at 8,500 rpm that had first appeared at Monza in 1970. This was essentially a very reliable engine that gave little trouble during the year except that it still had a tendency to develop crankcase oil leaks. At the Daytona race only the Martini team used the original 4,494 cc (85 × 66 mm) engines and although this was said to be in the interests of reliability, there may well have been other reasons such as a shortage of 5-litre units at that point in the season.

Porsche engineers had, however, been endeavouring to improve both the power and reliability of the 917 engine and from Brands Hatch onwards the Gulf team used a new version of the 5-litre flat-12. This was a 4,999 cc unit with nickel-silicon alloy cylinder liners (as developed for use with the NSU Wankel engine) to reduce oil consumption and engine wear and this new engine was said to develop around 620 bhp. At Le Mans, however, the Gulf and Martini teams used the older 4907 cc engines because it had been decided to use 5-speed gearboxes (4-speed 'boxes were used in 1970 and in 1971 first gear was in fact needed only for starting from the pits) as it was thought that this would prove a more reliable combination. Throughout the year the Martini drivers complained that their cars were down on power compared with their Gulf rivals and it seems probable that the only occasion on which the private team used the 4999 cc engine was at the Osterreichring. The 1971 917s also had crankshafts machined from a single billet (instead of welded in the middle) and with some of the valve gear parts made in titanium.

During the year it became known that Porsche had been working on a 16-cylinder engine for the 917 and it seems likely that this would have been used if the opposition from Ferrari had proved really intense. The 917 flat-12 in turbocharged form is to be used in Can-Am racing in 1972 and the 16-cylinder unit may possibly appear in due course in these races.

New Body Styles

At the Daytona race the JW team brought along a spare car with a new and slightly longer tail surmounted by tail-fins. This tail was intended to break up air turbulence and improve stability and it was worth some 300 rpm on the straight. The only races in which the Wyer team used this tail were Monza and Le Mans (where it was fitted to the Attwood/Müller 'third-string' car), but it was used by the Martini team at Spa and the Osterreichring in addition to these two races.

The most advanced body developments were first seen at the Le Mans Test Weekend where three new styles were revealed. These had been produced under the direction of Charles Deutch, designer of the very aerodynamic Peugeot-powered CD cars that had run at Le Mans in the early 'Sixties, who had been engaged by Porsche as an aerodynamic consultant.

The first and most important of these body styles was what might be described as the standard 1971 *Lang* body. This was slightly longer and around thirty-five kg heavier than the Kurz body. It had titanium suspension components and Bilstein de Carbon shock absorbers. There was a very long, smooth tail, tail-fins, the rear wheels partially covered in, a rear spoiler and cut-off end to the tail. With Jack Oliver at the wheel this car lapped the Sarthe circuit in 3 min 13.6 sec (something over eight seconds better than the lap record). As a result of these satisfactory tests, two of these cars ran under the Wyer banner in the 24 Hours race and one was entered by the Martini team.

The second car was a short car with bulbous nose, a short tail with tail fins and similar suspension to the *Lang* model. This car, which was nick-named the 'pig', was driven in the Three Hours race held at the Test Weekend by Kauhsen/van Lennep and in the 24 Hours race by Kauhsen/Jöst. In both races it ran under the Martini banner. The third new car to appear in April was based on the 917 *Lang* driven into second place in the 1970 race, but now fitted with a very short, stubby nose and a long tail with open end. This car was not raced in June. These three cars were all painted plain white and the only Gulf car at the circuit in April was a standard 917 to which a number of modifications were made during testing.

Brake Improvements

At the Buenos Aires race at the beginning of the season the Gulf cars were fitted with a new pattern of brake disc made from beryllium and ventilated both laterally and radially. Apart from Sebring (an exceptionally hard circuit on brakes) where the front discs were changed to those of the original pattern after the beryllium discs revealed in practice a tendency to crack round the ventilation holes and for dust to build up, these were used by the JW team throughout the season.

Two further braking developments were seen at the Austrian race at the end of June. On the spare Gulf car the Wyer team tried out front Girling twin-discs, similar to, but rather larger than those fitted to the Tyrrell Formula 1 cars. The brake development tried on the Martini car was rather more revolutionary and was also used in the race. Neither the Porsche technicians, nor the Martini drivers, were prepared to talk about the new brakes, but it is known that they had a transistorised anti-locking device which allowed drivers to brake much deeper into corners. Although they were said to function satisfactorily, except on the rare occasions when the electrics played up, neither of the drivers, Larrousse or Marko, seemed very happy with these brakes.

Other Developments

At the BOAC race at Brands Hatch the Gulf cars were fitted with alloy hubs similar to those used on the 908 Prototypes, but after one of the hubs expanded during the race and caused difficulty in removing a wheel, these were abandoned. From Daytona onwards the 917s used a new and sturdier gearbox casing which weighed rather more than the original. The 1971 cars were, however, fitted with lighter body panels and weight was much the same as for the 1970 cars.

Specification of the 917

Engine: air-cooled flat-12 with a capacity of 4,907 cc (86 × 70.4 mm) or 4,999 cc (86.8 × 70.4 mm developing 590/620 bhp at 8,500 rpm, with twin overhead camshafts per bank of cylinders and Bosch fuel injection and ignition. *Transmission;* 4 or 5-speed gearbox with baulk-ring synchromesh and in unit with the final drive. *Chassis:* multi-tubular space-frame with glue-attached glass-fibre panels. *Front suspension:* double wishbones and combined coil spring/damper units. *Rear suspension:* links, radius arms and combined coil spring/damper units. *Wheelbase:* 7 ft 6.6 in. *Front track:* 4 ft 10.6 in. *Rear track:* 4 ft 9.4 in. *Overall length* (*Kurz*)*:* 15 ft 8.9 in. *Weight* (*Kurz* with fuel): 1976 lb.

The 908/3

In the Targa Florio and the Nürburgring 1,000 Km race Porsche once again fielded the lightweight 908/3 models. These cars, light, with superb handling and derived from the 909 'Bergspyder' hill climb car, were largely unchanged from 1970, but were fitted with tail fins, were slightly lighter and at the Nürburgring were fitted with larger oil tanks. Their handling was reckoned to be better than that of the Alfa Romeo Tipo 33/3s, mainly because they broke away more progressively, but they could no longer match the top-end performance of their Italian V-8 rivals. In the Targa

Florio the Porsche entry completely disintegrated, while the cars that appeared at the Nürburgring were not up to the team's usual high standards of preparation and both cars supplied to the Gulf team were handling atrociously. If the works Ferrari 312P had not retired with serious overheating, the Porsche entries would have been soundly trounced in this race.

Porsche Drivers

For 1971 the John Wyer team signed up Derek Bell to partner Jo Siffert and Jack Oliver to partner Pedro Rodriguez. For the Targa Florio Wyer dropped Bell and Oliver from the team and replaced them with two drivers who knew the Little Madonie Circuit well, Brian Redman and Herbert Müller. Unfortunately Redman crashed and suffered bad burns which prevented him from fulfilling his second engagement with the team at Le Mans and here the third car was driven by Müller and Dickie Attwood. When Jack Oliver found that the Austrian 1,000 Km race clashed with a commitment in the Can-Am series, he opted to cross the Atlantic and was summarily dropped from the Wyer team. His place was taken at the Osterreichring and Watkins Glen by Dickie Attwood. Following Pedro Rodriguez' fatal accident in the Nuremberg 200 race, Gijs van Lennep joined the team and he partnered Siffert at Watkins Glen and Derek Bell in the non-Championship races at Barcelona and Montlhéry.

The Martini team was led by Vic Elford, a Salzburg driver in 1970, and he was partnered by Frenchman Gerard Larrousse who had finished second at Le Mans in 1970. The second Martini car was driven by Austrian Helmut Marko (third at Le Mans in 1970) and Gijs van Lennep (who drove the AAW Team 917 in 1970). Brian Redman drove for the Martini team at Brands Hatch only.

Private 917s

With several teams and drivers competing in the Interserie races with the new 917 Can-Am 5,000 Spyder conversion, few privately entered 917s took part in Championship races. At Buenos Aires and in the European rounds Team Auto Usdau, financed by a Mannheim Mercedes-Benz dealer, fielded a 4.5-litre car used in the making of the Le Mans film for Willibert Kauhsen and Reinhold Jöst and at Le Mans these drivers appeared at the wheel of one of the Martini entries. Zitro Racing Cars of Geneva raced a very pristine, but also very slow 4.5-litre 917 for Dominique Martin and Gerard Pillon and David Piper entered his car in a couple of races.

The 312P

For 1971 Ferrari completely abandoned the 5-litre Sports Cars and concentrated his efforts on the brand-new 312P Prototype with a 3-litre flat-12 engine and transmission, monocoque chassis and neat, compact body lines having excellent aerodynamics. Without doubt the 312P was the fastest of the 3-litre Prototypes, simply running away from the opposition at the Nürburgring, but not able to match the speed of the 917s on fast courses such as Monza and Spa. But throughout the season the 312P was plagued by the most atrocious fortunes. On its debut at Buenos Aires the car collided with the Matra MS660 which Jean-Pierre Beltoise was pushing back to the pits and driver Ignazio Giunti suffered a horrible death. A new car with heavier 16-gauge monocoque to comply with the 1972 Regulations was built in time to run at Sebring, but here the car retired, it was delayed a collision with the British Dulon-Porsche at Brands Hatch, it was eliminated by crashes at the Monza, Spa and Osterreichring races and it retired when leading at both the Nürburgring and Watkins Glen. At the end of the season two cars were fielded in the non-Championship Kyalami Nine Hours race and they dominated this event to take the first two places. With a very strong team of drivers consisting of Ickx, Regazzoni, Andretti, Ronnie Peterson, Brian Redman and Tim Schenken, Ferrari's chances of success in the 1972 Championship could hardly be better.

The 512M

Although Ferrari did not race the 5-litre cars in 1971 (except at the first round of the Interserie in May), work had steadily been progressing on an improved version of the 1970 512S car which was known as the 512M. This had first appeared in October, 1970 in the Austrian 1,000 Km race and the following month it won the Kyalami Nine Hours race. In its finalised form the car was much more potent than its predecessor and most of the cars belonging to private owners were converted to this specification.

The 512M featured a new nose and a cutaway tail similar to that of the Porsche 917. The chassis was much lighter, with less tubes, others of lighter gauge and the almost complete elimination of the front sub-frame. The engine featured chromed alloy cylinder liners, improved inlet and exhaust manifolding, fuel injection changes and now had a power output of around 600 bhp. In addition the rear brakes were larger. If a works-backed team had been running these cars, they might well have achieved a great deal of success, but, as it was, with the exception of the Penske-prepared car (referred to below), the 512Ms lacked the team organisation and the drivers to achieve good results. 512M cars were raced by the North American Racing Team, Scuderia Filipinetti, Herbert Müller Racing, Ecurie Francorchamps, Escuderia Montjuich and David Weir.

Without doubt the most potent of all the private Ferraris was the beautifully rebuilt 512M car entered by Roger Penske Racing as the Sunoco-Ferrari on behalf of its owner, Kirk White of Philadelphia. Among a whole host of modifications this car featured a special pressurised refuelling system, the oil and water reservoirs filled by compressed air and a vacuum device on the brake master cylinders to draw the fluid back from the brakes and the pistons back into the calipers to facilitate pad changes. A much larger rear aerofoil was fitted. The V-12 engines were specially rebuilt and developed by Traco Engineering and the car was finished in blue with yellow wheels. The drivers were Mark Donohue and David Hobbs. The car had the speed to match the 917s at Daytona and Sebring and it led them at Watkins Glen, but it was plagued by ill luck and its chances of victory in both of the early-season American races were ruined by accidents.

Another interesting variant of the 512M was the special car also known as a 512F developed by Mike Parkes for Scuderia Filipinetti. The cockpit was lower and narrower than standard, the windscreen was much more steeply sloping and the radiators (mounted as usual ahead of the rear wheels) were much more exposed. Instead of the normal twin tanks, there was a single fuel tank on the right-hand side of the car, the oil radiators were at the back, the water radiators were replaced by aluminium ones and a larger aerofoil was fitted. This car ran only at Le Mans.

ALFA ROMEO

The Alfa Romeo Tipo 33/3s entered by Carlo Chiti's Autodelta team on behalf of the works were, on the surface, largely unchanged, but over the winter months a great deal of development work had been carried out, the engines were more powerful, all the old unreliability had disappeared and in 1971 the cars were the most reliable of all. Modifications for 1971 were limited to reducing weight, slightly improving the aerodynamics and there was a new and stronger gearbox. With a strong team of drivers consisting of Andrea de Adamich, Henri Pescarolo, Rolf Stommelen, 'Nanni' Galli, Nino Vaccarella and Toine Hezemans, plus Vic Elford and Ronnie Peterson who drove for the team at Watkins Glen only, the team enjoyed a tremendous run of success, winning the Prototype class of eight of the nine races entered and winning outright at Brands Hatch, in the Targa Florio and at Watkins Glen.

Specification of the Tipo 33/3

Engine: 90-degree V-8 with a capacity of 2993 cc (86 × 64.4 mm) with twin overhead camshafts per bank of cylinders, four valves per cylinder, Lucas fuel injection, Marelli 'Dinoplex' ignition and a power output of 430 bhp at 9,000 rpm. *Transmission:* 5-speed gearbox in unit with the final drive. *Chassis:* Sheet-alloy monocoque chassis with front suspension by double wishbones and coil springs and rear suspension by links, radius arms and coil spring/damper units. *Wheelbase:* 7 ft 7.3 in. *Front track:* 4 ft 7.5 in. *Rear track:* 4 ft 7 in. *Weight:* 1,532 lb.

In practice for the Targa Florio race there appeared a completely new version of the Alfa Romeo Tipo 33 known as the 33/TT/3. This was clearly derived from Porsche 908/3 practice and the car was shorter, lower, narrower and lighter than the ordinary 33, it had a central monocoque box-section and a light aluminium tubular framework, there was a redesigned and lighter gearbox mounted ahead of the rear axle and the car weighed only 580 kg. The 'TT' stood for 'telaio tubolare' (tubular chassis), although it was nick-named by the Italian press, 'Tipo Tedesco' (German type).

The 33/TT/3 again ran in practice only at the Nürburgring and hopes of fielding it either at the Osterreichring or Watkins Glen were dashed when Galli crashed it in practice at both circuits. It is interesting, however, that the model's lap times were generally slower than those of the ordinary cars. The car ran in practice only at the Imola 500 Km race and was scratched from the race proper and of two cars entered in the Paris 1,000 Km race, one was too badly damaged in testing at the Paul Ricard Circuit to run at Montlhéry and the other crashed on the warming-up lap. So the season ran out without the new model ever being raced, but it is the Tipo 33/TT/3, later with a new flat-12 engine that forms the backbone of Autodelta efforts in 1972.

MATRA

Once again Équipe Matra fielded the MS660 model powered by their own V-12 engine, but most of the team's racing budget was expended on Grand Prix racing and the Prototype ran only in the Buenos Aires, Le Mans and Paris 1,000 Km races. It was driven in the latter two events by Amon/Beltoise, but at Buenos Aires the Frenchman was partnered by Jabouille.

7 The Championship Races

ROUND ONE

BUENOS AIRES 1,000 KILOMETRES RACE

Buenos Aires Autodrome 10th January, 1971
(Circuit length: 3.79 miles). Weather: dry and very cold.

Between 1954 and 1958 the Buenos Aires 1,000 Kilometres race had been a round in the Sports Car Championship and after a year's interval it was again held in 1960. All these early races were dominated by Ferraris and Maseratis, the works Jaguars and Mercedes-Benz 300SLRs never appeared in the race and the Aston Martin team only once, in 1954. Private Jaguars entered by the Ecurie Ecosse ran in the Argentine in both 1954 and 1957, taking a fourth place on each occasion. After an interval of ten years the Buenos Aires race was revived, but although still run at the famous Autodrome, the circuit was different from those used for the early races. This non-Championship 1970 race was supported by the works Matra and Autodelta teams and was won by a Matra 630/650 Spyder driven by Beltoise and Pescarolo. Following this successful 'dummy run', the race was given World Championship status in 1971 and attracted a strong entry with representation from all the leading teams.

THE ENTRY (Principal Contenders)

Group 5 Sports Cars:

JW Automotive Engineering Ltd:
Porsche 917 5.0-litre cars driven by Jo Siffert/Derek Bell and Pedro Rodriguez/Jack Oliver. These were ordinary 1970 cars unchanged apart from the latest Porsche beryllium brake discs and running in 5-speed form.

Martini Racing Team:
Porsche 917 5.0-litre cars driven by Vic Elford/Gerard Larrousse

and Helmut Marko/Gijs van Lennep. The two silver and blue cars were running with 4-speed gearboxes.

Alex Soler-Roig:

Porsche 917 4.5-litre driven by Alex Soler-Roig, Carlos Reutemann and Emerson Fittipaldi. Fittipaldi was due to drive a works Alfa Romeo Tipo 33/3, but switched to this car after writing the Alfa off during unofficial practice.

Team Auto Usdau:

Porsche 917 4.5-litre driven by Willi Kauhsen and Reinhold Jöst. Kauhsen was taken ill with influenza on the Friday before the race and so he arranged for the car to be co-driven by local man Engel Monguzzi. The car was one that had been used during the making of the Le Mans film and was still finished in rather scruffy Gulf colours. On the driver's door there was a message from Steve McQueen, reading, 'Finished! Thanks for staying together!'

Zitro Racing Cars:

Porsche 917 4.5-litre driven by Dominique Martin and local man Pablo Brea.

Scuderia Filipinetti:

Ferrari 512M 5-litre driven by Mike Parkes and Joakim Bonnier. During unofficial practice on the Wednesday Ronnie Peterson, who had been entered at the wheel of the Filipinetti Lola, had a go with this car, but lost control at the Ascari curve, a fast bend on the back part of the circuit, hit the Armco almost head-on and spun down the course for some 300 yards. Peterson blamed his accident on a punctured tyre. Initially the car seemed wrecked beyond immediate repair, but with the mechanics working flat-out in shifts the car was got ready for the start.

North American Racing Team:

Ferrari 512S 5-litre driven by Sam Posey and Nestor Garcia Veiga. After the locally built Berta Prototype joined the list of non-starters because of a blown-up engine, Luiz di Palma was nominated as reserve driver.

Hughes De Fierlandt:

Ferrari 512S 5-litre driven by de Fierlandt and Taf Gosselin.

Ronnie Peterson justified his role as March team-leader by taking second places at Monaco, Silverstone, Monza and Mosport, (Nigel Snowdon)

Fellow Swedish driver Reine Wisell had a far less happy time with Team Lotus and few good places came his way. (Nigel Snowdon)

Clay Regazzoni with the Ferrari 312P in practice for the Spa 1000 Kilometres race. The car was eliminated in the race by a collision with the British Dulon Prototype. (Nigel Snowdon)

Escuderia Montjuich:

Ferrari 512S 5-litre driven by José Juncadella and Carlos Pairetti.

Group 6 Prototypes:

S.p.a. Ferrari SEFAC:

Ferrari 312P 3-litre driven by Ignazio Giunti and Arturo Merzario. This was Ferrari's brand new car with a Formula 1 flat-12 engine and running gear and was quite obviously a very serious contender for outright victory.

Autodelta:

Alfa Romeo Tipo 33/3 3-litre cars driven by Toine Hezemans/Emerson Fittipaldi, Rolf Stommelen/'Nanni' Galli and Henri Pescarolo/Andrea de Adamich. The first of these cars non-started following Fittipaldi's crash during unofficial practice.

Equipe Matra:

Matra MS660 3-litre driven by Jean-Pierre Beltoise/Jean-Pierre Jabouille. Francois Cevert should have co-driven with Beltoise, but he had injured a shoulder in a road accident in France.

Ecurie Evergreen:

McLaren M8C-Cosworth 3-litre driven by Chris Craft/Trevor Taylor and Lola T210-Cosworth 1.8-litre driven by Alain de Cadenet/Nasif Estefano.

Scuderia Filipinetti:

Lola T212-Cosworth 1.8-litre driven by Ronnie Peterson/Jorge Cupeiro.

As mentioned, the Cosworth-powered Berta non-started after blowing up its newly rebuilt engine and two other Berta cars, both powered by Renault Torino 2.6-litre engines, also failed to make the start.

PRACTICE

Following unofficial practice sessions on the Wednesday and the Thursday, the first timed session was due to take place on the Friday morning. However the ravages of the earlier sessions were such that this first Friday practice was cancelled to give the entrants a chance to sort out their crumpled machinery and the timed sessions were, therefore, between 3 and 7 pm on both the Friday and the Saturday.

In addition to Fittipaldi's crash with the Alfa and Peterson's

accident with the Ferrari, Oliver went off the road with his Gulf 917, wrecking the front end of the car and parts to repair this had to be flown from England. On the Friday Stommelen went off the road with his Alfa and the titanium front suspension was wrecked. There were no local facilities for welding titanium and so Autodelta had to make do with bolting everything up again as tightly as possible and hoping for the best.
Fastest in practice were:

1. Rodriguez/Oliver (Porsche 917 5-litre) . 1 min 52.70 sec
2. Giunti/Merzario (Ferrari 312P 3-litre) . 1 min 52.74 sec
3. Siffert/Bell (Porsche 917 5-litre) . . 1 min 53.40 sec
4. Elford/Larrousse (Porsche 917 5-litre) . 1 min 53.93 sec
5. de Adamich/Pescarolo (Alfa Romeo Tipo 33/3 3-litre) 1 min 54.43 sec
6. Beltoise/Jabouille (Matra MS660 3-litre) . 1 min 54.65 sec
7. Stommelen/Galli (Alfa Romeo Tipo 33/3 3-litre) 1 min 55.57 sec
8. Bonnier/Parkes (Ferrari 512M 5-litre) . 1 min 55.81 sec
9. Posey/Veiga/di Palma (Ferrari 512S 5-litre) 1 min 55.84 sec
10. Marko/van Lennep (Porsche 917 5-litre) . 1 min 56.29 sec

THE RACE

The start was scheduled to take place at 8.30 am on the Sunday, but, ten minutes late, the twenty-two starters completed a slow, paced lap behind Juan Fangio's Mercedes 280SL and when the flag was dropped, Giunti's Ferrari out-accelerated the 917s and led away into the first right-hand bend. The small red Ferrari continued to hold the lead through the twisting parts of the circuit and then Rodriguez forged his way by on the long straight. At the end of the first lap the order was Rodriguez, Giunti, Siffert, Elford, Parkes, Beltoise, de Adamich and Stommelen. Marko's 917, which had started the race with a suspected burnt piston (the team had no spare engine), called in at the pits at the end of lap one, it rejoined the race, but retired out on the circuit without completing another lap.

Although Rodriguez, the left-hand headlamps of his 917 ablaze (there had been no time to repair those on the right-hand side following the practice shunt), soon pulled clear of the 312P, it was not until lap six that Siffert went through into second place. Two laps later Elford moved into third place ahead of the Ferrari and on the following lap when Siffert used his wipers to clear his screen fogged by oil fumes from the Ferrari, he only made the mess worse and Elford slipped by into second place. On the next lap Siffert made a quick pit stop to have the screen cleaned and rejoined the race in thirteenth place.

By lap ten Rodriguez had a four-second lead over Elford, Giunti was still a comfortable third and then came Parkes, Beltoise, de Adamich and Stommelen. Elford, whose car seemed to be handling rather better than that of the race leader, closed right up on Rodriguez and on lap twenty-one when the Mexican was baulked by a back-marker that he was lapping, the British driver nipped through into the lead. Elford was now well in the groove, lapping faster and faster, on lap twenty-eight he set a new circuit record of 1 min 51.08 sec (disallowed after his disqualification) and by lap thirty he had extended his lead to fourteen seconds. Siffert was now back in fourth place behind Giunti's Ferrari.

Elford's lead was short-lived, however, and on lap thirty-one his 917 developed fuel starvation. The engine died altogether out on the circuit and it took Elford two minutes to re-start the car by which time he was just over a lap behind Rodriguez. When the Sports Cars stopped to refuel, Giunti's Ferrari took the lead and now headed Beltoise, Stommelen and de Adamich. On lap thirty-seven Beltoise's Matra ran out of fuel on the circuit about a quarter of a mile from the pits. The Frenchman, not realising that it would be a breach of the race regulations and result in disqualification, started to push the MS660 back to towards the pits. Despite the obvious dangers of pushing a car round the course, none of the marshalls stopped Beltoise who continued to shove the car uphill and crossed over on corners to take advantage of the camber. Most of the drivers lapped Beltoise several times and knew roughly whereabouts on the course he was likely to be. Disaster struck when Giunti was motoring in Parkes' slipstream and as they rounded a corner, the Italian pulled out to the right to overtake the 512M. Unfortunately Beltoise was pushing the Matra across the road, the French car was directly in the Ferrari's path and Giunti had no chance to avoid it.

The collision shot the 312P some two hundred yards down the track and the Ferrari burst into flames. Some two minutes had elapsed before Merzario, who had sprinted down from the pits, was able to pull his team-mate from the car. Giunti had suffered bad burns and serious head injuries and on arrival at hospital he was found to be dead. Although the cars had initially streamed past the blazing wreck, they were eventually stopped on the red flag. Then one of the local drivers went past the flag, others followed and the race started again. In the confusion the electronic time-keeping went completely awry, the official lap scorers were muddled, what the precise race positions were no one seemed to know and after this terrible accident few cared. It was clear that Rodriguez was still leading the race, but he stopped at the pits on lap forty-three because of a punctured rear tyre and minor body damage caused when he went off the course. By the time this had been sorted out and the Mexican was back in the race, he had dropped to ninth place. Now Siffert led from Parkes with the Filipinetti Ferrari with Stommelen third. Pescarolo lost two laps with his Alfa while damaged bodywork was taped up. Next in trouble was Elford with a recurrence of the fuel starvation trouble and he stopped out on the course. Two of the Martini mechanics went out to the car to repair the trouble, but this was contrary to the race regulations and resulted in the 917's disqualification.

By lap fifty Siffert still led from the Filipinetti Ferrari by a margin of two minutes, Stommelen was third and Peterson was fourth and driving a brilliant race with the Filipinetti Lola. The Fittipaldi/Reutemann Porsche 917 retired with oil leaking into the clutch and the Jöst/Monguzi car was disqualified after running out of fuel on the circuit. The Parkes/Bonnier Ferrari lost its second place and two laps while a vibration was traced to the loss of a balancing weight from a rear wheel and by half-distance the order was: 1st, Siffert/Bell; 2nd, Stommelen/Galli; 3rd, Rodriguez/Oliver; 4th, de Adamich/Pescarolo; 5th, Posey/Veiga; 6th, Peterson/Cupeiro.

During the latter part of the race neither of the Gulf cars was quite *au point*. The Siffert/Bell car was suffering from clutch trouble and was consuming fuel at a greater rate than anticipated and the Rodriguez/Oliver car was handling badly, probably as a result of the minor accident earlier in the race. On lap 140 the Filipinetti Lola, still going magnificently and in fifth place with Peterson at the wheel, crashed at the hairpin bend, probably because of a puncture. It was just a few minutes later that Bonnier collided with another car and as he approached the pits and the left-hand front of the body disintegrated. The car went into a slide which Bonnier just about held and then went into the pits for extensive body repairs.

At the chequered flag the two Gulf 917s were credited with first and second places with the Alfas third and fourth. That these placings were correct seems very unlikely—David Yorke's lap chart in the Gulf pit gave Stommelen/Galli second place with the 917 of Rodriguez/Oliver third and Yorke confirmed that he had deliberately slowed this car down in the later stages of the race. Autodelta entered a protest, but this was rejected and in any case the Italian team had reason to be content with their second successive victory in the Prototype category (the last was at the 1970

Austrian race in which Pescarolo/de Adamich had finished second). Because of Giunti's fatal accident and because of the shortcomings of the race organisation both before and after the accident, the Argentine race was the unhappiest and probably the least efficiently organised of all 1971 Championship races. Eventually several of the marshalls were hauled over the coals following the enquiry into the accident and poor Beltoise had his licence suspended. In the Argentine he was charged with manslaughter and left the country on bail. But to what extent was the French driver really to blame for this accident? In the heat of the moment he had made a wrong decision without any awareness of the possible consequences of his action. It was surely the marshalls' job to prevent such behaviour and the brunt of the responsibility for the disaster that occurred must lie with them.

Results:

1st, J. Siffert/D. Bell (Porsche 917 5-litre), 165 laps, 5 hours 25 min 25.92 sec (115.722 mph),*
2nd, P. Rodriguez/J. Oliver (Porsche 917 5-litre), 164 laps,
3rd, R. Stommelen/N. Galli (Alfa Romeo Tipo 33/3 3-litre), 163 laps,
4th, A. de Adamich/H. Pescarolo (Alfa Romeo Tipo 33/3 3-litre), 161 laps,
5th, J. Juncadella/C. Pairetti (Ferrari 512S 5-litre), 155 laps,
6th, T. Gosselin/H. de Fierlandt (Ferrari 512S 5-litre), 153 laps,
7th, M. Parkes/J. Bonnier (Ferrari 512M 5-litre), 150 laps,
8th, S. Posey/L. di Palma/N. Veiga (Ferrari 512S 5-litre), 148 laps,
9th, C. Craft/T. Taylor (McLaren M8C-Cosworth 3-litre), 147 laps,
10th, D. Martin/P. Brea (Porsche 917 4.5-litre), 145 laps,
11th, D. Weir/J. del Rio (Lola-Cosworth 1.8-litre), 143 laps,
12th, R. Peterson/J. Cupeiro (Lola-Cosworth 1.8-litre), 130 laps,
13th, D. Rouveyran/C. Ruesch (Lola-Cosworth 1.8-litre), 129 laps.
*Class winners.

Fastest lap: J. Siffert, 1 min 51.53 sec (122.78 mph—new lap record).

NOTE: V. Elford (Porsche 917 5-litre) recorded a lap in 1 min 51.08 sec (123.28 mph), but this was disallowed because he was disqualified later in the race.

Principal retirements: Marko/van Lennep (Porsche 917 5-litre), engine trouble; Beltoise/Jabouille (Matra 660 3-litre), ran out of fuel/accident; Giunti/Merzario (Ferrari 312P 3-litre), fatal accident; Elford/Larrousse (Porsche 917 5-litre), disqualified; Fittipaldi/Reutemann (Porsche 917 4.5-litre), oil leaking into clutch.

ROUND TWO

DAYTONA CONTINENTAL 24 HOURS RACE

Daytona Speedway (Circuit length: 3.81 miles) 30th/31st January
Weather: dry and warm

The first race at Daytona for Sports Cars was in 1962 when the victor was Dan Gurney at the wheel of his very special Lotus 19B (a development of the cars raced by Stirling Moss and others for the works and U.D.T.-Laystall in 1960–2), but powered by a Ford 4.7-litre engine. In that year and 1963 the race was held as a three-hour event, but it was extended to 2,000 kilometres in 1964. In both 1963 and 1964 Ferraris won the race and in the following year's event a Ford GT40, driven by Ken Miles and Lloyd Ruby, scored the model's first ever victory. The race was extended to twenty-four hours in 1966, a retrograde step that turned the race into perhaps the most tedious and least interesting in the Championship series. Such is the rate of mechanical attrition in this race that a car can spend a couple of hours in the pits undergoing major repair work and still win the race. In 1969 the winning Lola (the only car of this marque to win a Championship race) spent nearly two hours in the pits and the following year the second-place 917 Porsche of Siffert/Redman lost eighty minutes while the clutch was replaced. Fortunately, unlike the organisers of the Le Mans race, the Daytona organisers are falling in line with the new requirement of the FIA that races counting towards the Championship should not last longer than six hours and so future races are likely to be much more lively events. With lap speeds (in practice) of around 130 mph and parts of the course on which 200 mph is comfortably exceeded, Daytona is America's fastest road course and with its two banked curves it is now unique amongst road racing circuits.

THE ENTRY

Group 5 Sports Cars:

J W Automotive Engineering Ltd:

Porsche 917 5-litre cars driven by Jo Siffert/Derek Bell and Pedro Rodriguez/Jack Oliver. These were normal 1970 cars running with 4-speed gearboxes. As a spare the team had brought along a car fitted with a slightly longer tail of reduced drag profile and with two large stabilising fins. Although this tail increased the 917's speed along the straights, it affected stability on the banking and was not used in the race.

Martini Racing Team:

Porsche 917 4.5-litre cars driven by Helmut Marko/Rudi Lins and Vic Elford/Gijs van Lennep. Both of these cars were also fitted with 4-speed gearboxes and it was said that the smaller engines were used in the interests of reliability. This team had also brought along a spare training car. Because of shipping delays the new engines did not arrive in time for Thursday's practice which determined the first ten places on the grid.

Penske–White Racing:

Sunoco-Ferrari 512M 5-litre driven by Mark Donohue and David Hobbs. This was the completely rebuilt car described fully on page 157.

North American Racing Team:

Ferrari 512M 5-litre cars driven by Sam Posey/Peter Revson and Greg Young/Masten Gregory and a 512S 5-litre driven by Ron Bucknum/Tony Adamowicz.

Hughes De Fierlandt:

Ferrari 512S 5-litre driven by de Fierlandt and Taf Gosselin.

Escuderia Montjuich:

Ferrari 512S 5-litre driven by Arturo Merzario/José Juncadella.

Group 6 Prototypes:

North American Racing Team:

Ferrari 312P 3-litre driven by Luigi Chinetti, jnr and Garcia Veiga. This was one of the team's two 1969 coupés rebodied with a very simple, but rather ugly open body.

Although there were forty-eight starters (and sixty plus entries weeded down during qualifying by their inability to lap within 130% of the fastest time, really fast cars were conspicuous by their absence. The NART 312P was the only Prototype entered and the Ferrari, Autodelta and Matra teams had all given the race a miss.

PRACTICE

In practice for the 1970 race Andretti with the works Ferrari 512S had taken pole position on the grid with a lap in 1 min 51.6 sec

(122.90 mph), but since then the circuit had been resurfaced in many places and times were likely to be much faster. Although Rodriguez initially set the pace for Gulf on the Wednesday with a lap in 1 min 45.2 sec, Donohue with the silver-blue Ferrari replied with 1 min 44.4 sec and on the Thursday morning improved on this with a lap in 1 min 43.7 sec. That the race would be a fight between the Gulf cars and the Sunoco Ferrari seemed beyond doubt. During the last hour of Thursday's practice, when the weather was at its coolest, Rodriguez tried really hard to better the Ferrari's time and driving right on the limit snatched pole position by a narrow margin with a time of 1 min 43.68 sec. But it seemed that Donohue and the Penske car had the legs of its German rivals and the American went out to record laps of 1 min 42.57 sec and 1 min 42.42 sec (133.90 mph). Rodriguez went out again to see what he could produce in reply, but the 917 was only just getting nicely wound up when the chequered flag brought a halt to the session. On the Thursday the Martini drivers were out in the training car with a very tired engine and narrow wheels and recorded slow times.

Fastest during official qualifying for places on the grid were:

1.	Donohue/Hobbs (Ferrari 512M 5-litre) .	1 min 42.42 sec
2.	Rodriguez/Oliver (Porsche 917 4.5-litre) .	1 min 43.68 sec
3.	Posey/Revson (Ferrari 512M 5-litre) .	1 min 43.95 sec
4.	Siffert/Bell (Porsche 917 5-litre) . .	1 min 44.44 sec
5.	Young/Gregory (Ferrari 512M 5-litre) .	1 min 46.65 sec
6.	Bucknum/Adamowicz (Ferrari 512S 5-litre)	1 min 50.20 sec
7.	Merzario/Juncadella (Ferrari 512S 5-litre)	1 min 51.21 sec
8.	de Fierlandt/Gosselin (Farrari 512S 5-litre)	1 min 54.14 sec
9.	de Lorenzo/Yenko (Chevrolet Corvette 7-litre)	1 min 57.19 sec
10.	Greenwood/Barber/Lang (Chevrolet Corvette 7-litre)	1 min 59.00 sec

On the Friday the Martini cars recorded the following times:

Elford/van Lennep	1 min 45.39 sec
Lins/Marko	1 min 45.56 sec

THE RACE

The weather was dry and windy as the forty-eight cars moved off in a rolling start just before 3 pm. Donohue and the Penske Ferrari took an immediate and expected lead with Rodriguez and the Gulf-Porsche in hot pursuit, headlamps ablaze. Although the Ferrari pulled out a lead initially, when the two cars started to lap the slowest back-markers, Pedro revealed his superior high-speed traffic driving, closed right up on the Ferrari and moved into the lead on lap thirteen. But it was short-lived, the Ferrari went in front again on the next lap and soon opened the gap up to around one-and-a-half seconds. Siffert was in a comfortable third place and then came the Ferraris of Gregory and Revson. Already one of the Martini cars was in trouble; Marko's 917 was in collision with another, slower contender and he came into the pits with the left-hand rear badly battered. A lot of time was lost while the suspension was repaired and the bodywork patched and the car eventually rejoined the race. Revson's Ferrari stopped at the pits for attention to its brake lights, Merzario stopped to report that the oil pressure was low and after only sixteen laps Gregory retired his Ferrari with a broken con-rod.

Just before the two leading cars stopped to refuel at the end of lap thirty, Rodriguez went ahead again, but when they stopped, Penske pit-work was slicker, the Ferrari pulled out of the pits in fractionally over twelve seconds and Rodriguez' stop took eight seconds longer. Siffert took the lead while these two cars were refuelling, but when he stopped at the end of lap thirty-seven, Donohue and Rodriguez resumed in the first two places. At the end of the first hour, the leading positions remained unchanged, but when the Ferrari made its second routine pit stop, time was lost while both rear tyres were changed, the Porsche's second stop was slightly quicker and Rodriguez resumed the race with an advantage of three seconds. At this point in the race Siffert, yet to make his second stop, led the field, but Donohue soon closed the gap on Rodriguez and passed him and went back into the lead when Siffert stopped to refuel on lap seventy-five. Derek Bell relieved Siffert but the car's stop was a fairly long one while the rear tyres were changed and on lap eighty-seven Bell was lapped by the race leader.

With two hours and forty minutes of racing over, Donohue made his third pit stop with the Sunoco-Ferrari. Because of a faulty rectifier, the stop lasted all of four-and-a-half minutes while the trouble was traced and then only a few laps later the car was back in the pits again for a stop of eight minutes while the alternator terminals were sorted out. The net result of these two long stops by the Penske car was that, for the time being at least, the two Gulf cars were comfortably ensconced in the first two places and the Ferrari was four laps in arrears, and had lost third place to the Elford/van Lennep 917. When Bell accelerated down the pits road after his routine stop at the end of lap 113, the car left an ominous trail of oil along the road. Derek nursed the car round to bring it back to the pits at the end of the next lap, but it was pushed away into retirement because of a broken con-rod.

At the four-hour mark, with one sixth of the race over, the order was: 1st, Rodriguez/Oliver; 2nd, Elford/van Lennep (four laps behind); 3rd, Donohue/Hobbs; 4th, de Fierlandt/Gosselin; 5th, Posey/Revson; 6th, Chinetti/Veiga; 7th, Marko/Lins (having climbed back from 31st place at the end of the first hour). However, in a matter of minutes the de Fierlandt/Gosselin Ferrari had retired with fuel injection trouble. The Posey/Revson car was slowed by electrical trouble and the other surviving NART Ferrari 512S of Bucknum/Adamowicz had lost a lot of time with body repairs after it had been forced off the road by a slower car and it was also plagued by electrical problems.

As midnight approached the Chevrolet Corvette of Costanzo/Heina went out of control on the banking and crashed into the infield. Shortly afterwards Elford, travelling at around 200 mph, reached the scene of this incident, a tyre burst (almost certainly on debris left in its wake by the Corvette), the 917 crunched into the retaining wall and shot down the banking on to the grass. As the yellow warning lights flashed, the field eased its pace, but a Porsche 911 collided with the Penske Ferrari. Donohue drove back to the pits with the nose and left-hand side of the Ferrari badly shattered and the car eventually rejoined the race in fourth place and, at the half-way mark, all of fifty-three laps in arrears.

Shortly afterwards the surviving Martini car pulled into the pits with gearbox trouble and the mechanics started to repair the transmission with parts from Elford's crashed car (under the race regulations it was forbidden to change the actual gearbox casing). Another retirement during the night hours was Posey's NART Ferrari which blew up its engine when travelling at full cry on the banking. In the early hours of Sunday morning rain began to fall, by 6 am the circuit was thoroughly soaked, most of the entry spun at least once and Oliver brought the leading 917 in for Rodrigues, the maestro of wet weather racing, to take over the wheel. Fortunately the rain did not last long and by 8 am the track had completely dried out.

With eighteen hours' racing under their tyres, Rodriguez/Oliver still led at 9 am, but their 917 was not completely healthy, as it had developed an oil leak and had a split exhaust pipe. In second place was the Bucknum/Adamowicz Ferrari 512S. This car lost its tail section completely on the straight, went out of control and spun on the banking and a very pale Adamowicz brought it into the pits for the tail from the retired Posey/Revson car to be fitted. Marko's 917 burst a tyre on the banking and scraped to rest against the retaining wall where it remained a hazard until the Martini mechanics had scrambled up the banking (which is at an angle of 31°) and changed both right-hand wheels. The car was then driven back to the pits and retirement. At the time of the accident the surviving Martini car had climbed back to fifth place and had still been running very well.

At 11.30 am Rodriguez brought the leading Gulf 917 into the pits with the gearbox jammed in top. There was no alternative but for the mechanics to strip the 'box and replace the seized cogs. An hour and thirty-two minutes were lost while the mechanics worked on the red hot gearbox and replaced the damaged components. During the Porsche's pit stop the second-place NART Ferrari of Bucknum/Adamowicz, still slowed by its electrical troubles, had made up lost ground on the stationary leader and by the time the Gulf car rejoined the race at 1.05 pm, the Ferrari was three laps ahead. Rodriguez was at the wheel of the Porsche, he accelerated furiously down the pits road, turned in a lap with a stone cold car from a standing start in 1 min 49.5 sec and began a furious chase of the ailing race leader. After only forty-four minutes of furious driving the Mexican had brought the 917 through to first place. Now rain started to fall again, both Rodriguez and Donohue, still in third place with the Penske Ferrari, stopped to fit wet-weather tyres. The rain did not last long, both drivers stopped again to change back to dry-weather tyres and the NART Ferrari slipped into the lead once more. Rodriguez, however, was soon back in front and at the chequered flag, after twenty-four hours of rather dreary and uninspiring racing, was a lap ahead of the Bucknum/Adamowicz 512S. Despite a pit stop twenty-five minutes before the chequered flag for the fuel-pump drive to be replaced for the third time during this race, the Donohue/Hobbs Ferrari took a gallant third place, sixty-one laps ahead of the fourth-place Chevrolet Corvette. Motor racing is full of ifs and buts, yet it is clear that but for its unfortunate collision with the Porsche 911, the Penske-Ferrari would have scored Ferrari's first Sports Car World Championship victory since the 1970 Sebring race.

Results:

1st, P. Rodriguez/J. Oliver (Porsche 917 5-litre), 688 laps, 2,621.28 miles (109.203 mph),*
2nd, R. Bucknum/T. Adamowicz (Ferrari 512S 5-litre), 687 laps,
3rd, M. Donohue/D. Hobbs (Ferrari 512M 5-litre), 674 laps,
4th, A. de Lorenzo/D. Yenko (Chevrolet Corvette 7-litre), 613 laps,*
5th, L. Chinetti/G. Veiga (Ferrari 312P 3-litre), 584 laps,*
6th, D. Hines/O. Costanzo (Chevrolet Corvette 7-litre), 581 laps,
7th, J. Duval/G. Nicholas/R. Bailey (Porsche 914/6 2-litre), 579 laps,

8th, S. Vehr/J. Buffam/I. Kramer (Porsche 914/6 2-litre), 571 laps,
9th, J. Locke/J. Netterstrom/B. Everett (Porsche 911T 2-litre), 570 laps,
10th, J. Greenwood/A. Barber/R. Lang (Chevrolet Corvette 7-litre), 554 laps,
11th, V. Gimondo/C. Dietrich (Chevrolet Camaro 5-litre), 542 laps,*
12th, C. Baker/R. Grossman/S. Brown/C. Reynolds (Chevron B16-Cosworth 1.8-litre), 534 laps.

*Class winners.

1970 winners: P. Rodriguez/L. Kinnunen (Porsche 917 5-litre), 114.87 mph.

Principal Retirements: de Fierlandt/Gosselin (Ferrari 512S 5-litre), engine trouble; Posey/Revson (Ferrari 512M 5-litre), engine blow-up; Gregory/Young (Ferrari 512M 5-litre), broken con-rod; Siffert/Bell (Porsche 917 5-litre), broken con-rod; Elford/van Lennep (Porsche 917 5-litre), accident; Lins/Marko (Porsche 917 5-litre), accident.

ROUND THREE

SEBRING 12 HOURS RACE

Sebring (Circuit length: 5.2 miles) 20th March, 1971
Weather: dry and warm.

The 1971 Sebring race was the twentieth in the series which dated back to 1952. In that year the victor was a private Frazer Nash, the American marque Cunningham scored its only major International victory in the 1953 race, the following year a 1500 cc Osca entered by Briggs Cunningham scored the Bologna concern's sole major win and a Jaguar driven by Mike Hawthorn and Phil Walters was the winner in 1955. Other marques to score rare victories over the years at the Florida circuit have been Maserati who achieved one of only two race victories with their monstrous 4.5-litre V-8 car in 1957 and a win by Chaparral in 1965. Ferrari has won the race on eight occasions, and both Ford and Porsche have now won it three times. Sebring had started life as a purely military airfield, but it is now also the municipal airport for the town of Sebring and each year the race completely disrupts business flying. It seemed that the 1971 race would be the last to be held over the traditional course, for the organisers had been given notice that the race could not again be run. Plans were well under way, however, for the construction of a new course alongside the present circuit and incorporating the existing pits, paddock and pits straight.

THE ENTRY

Group 5 Sports Cars:

J W Automotive Engineering Ltd:

Porsche 917 5-litre cars driven by Jo Siffert/Derek Bell and Pedro Rodriguez/Jack Oliver. These cars were in identical trim to those raced at Daytona apart from 5-speed gearboxes. Initially the cars were fitted with the beryllium brake discs ventilated radially and laterally, but it was found in practice that because of high surface pressures cracks were developing near the lateral ventilation holes and there was a build-up of pad dust so the team reverted to the normal radially ventilated discs at the front.

Martini Racing Team:

Porsche 917 5-litre driven by Vic Elford/Gerard Larrousse. Because of the ravages suffered at Daytona, the German team could field only one car (the Daytona training car) and this was fitted with a 4-speed gearbox and the normal radially ventilated brakes.

Roger Penske Racing:

Sunoco-Ferrari 512M 5-litre driven by Mark Donohue/David Hobbs. Since Daytona this beautifully prepared car had been fitted with a new body made in California and with a new and larger rear aerofoil.

North American Racing Team:

Ferrari 512M 5-litre driven by Peter Revson/Swede Savage.
Ferrari 512S 5-litre cars driven by Ronnie Bucknum/Sam Posey and Chuck Parsons/David Weir.
Ferrari 365 GTB 4 Daytona driven by Harley Cluxton/Bob Grossmann.

Apart from the beautiful road-going 'Daytona' which was brand new (and being raced complete with air conditioning!), the NART Ferraris were a rather tatty, shabby collection, looking rather ill-prepared and with the major handicap that there were simply not enough mechanics to look after all the cars.

Young America:

Ferrari 512M 5-litre driven by Greg Young/Masten Gregory. This was the car that had run for the same drivers under the

NART banner at Daytona, but the team was now fully organised with their own mechanics.

Of the five 512 cars entered in this race, only the Sunoco-sponsored car was likely to be able to challenge the 917s. The Penske team however, was not without its problems, for their better engine had blown up while being tested and the car had to be raced with the less powerful spare unit, Donohue had sprained his ankle while helping to load the car at Philadelphia and there was some doubt as to whether he would be able to drive (Penske himself was all set to come out of retirement and co-drive the car) and the transporter broke down on its way to the circuit and had to be towed the last sixty-five miles.

Group 6 Prototypes:

S.p.a. Ferrari SEFAC:

Ferrari 312P 3-litre driven by Jackie Ickx and Mario Andretti. The Maranello team was back with a new version of the car that had crashed at Buenos Aires and this was some 100 lb heavier than the original, partly because of strengthening of the monocoque and partly because of the addition of lighting equipment for the 12 Hours race.

Autodelta:

Alfa Romeo Tipo 33/3 3-litre cars driven by Nino Vaccarella/Toine Hezemans, 'Nanni' Galli/Rolf Stommelen and Andrea de Adamich/Henri Pescarolo. These cars were in very much the same trim as they had appeared at Buenos Aires and they were expected to do well if the 917s ran into trouble.

North American Racing Team:

Ferrari 312P 3-litre driven by Luigi Chinetti, jnr/George Eaton.

As usual at the American rounds, the Group 4 Grand Touring class was dominated by the 7-litre Chevrolet Corvettes, three of which were entered.

PRACTICE

Practice was divided into two sessions, each of two hours, on both the Thursday and Friday, together with a night practice session on the Thursday. On the Thursday morning Derek Bell had only covered about ten laps with his Gulf 917 when the left-hand rear wheel collapsed round the rim and the car spun down the road for some four hundred yards, fortunately without striking anything solid. As a result of this incident all the other JW 917 wheels were crack-tested and two more had to be discarded. Although no one approached Kinnunen's circuit record of 2 min 32.77 sec during the Thursday morning, in the afternoon Andretti lapped the new Ferrari in 2 min 32.47 sec. On the Friday Donohue had the Penske Ferrari really wound up and snatched pole position with a lap in 2 min 31.65 sec (123.44 mph). Neither of the JW 917s was going as well as expected and Siffert and Bell were far from happy with the handling of their car.

Fastest in practice were:

1.	Donohue/Hobbs (Ferrari 512M 5-litre) .	2 min 31.65 sec
2.	Ickx/Andretti (Ferrari 312P 3-litre) . .	2 min 32.47 sec
3.	Rodriguez/Oliver (Porsche 917 5-litre) .	2 min 33.84 sec
4.	Elford/Larrousse (Porsche 917 5-litre) .	2 min 34.81 sec
5.	Galli/Stommelen (Alfa Romeo Tipo 33/3 3-litre)	2 min 34.99 sec
6.	Siffert/Bell (Porsche 917 5-litre) . .	2 min 35.18 sec
7.	Revson/Savage (Ferrari 512M 5-litre) .	2 min 35.50 sec
8.	Young/Gregory (Ferrari 512M 5-litre) .	2 min 37.40 sec
9.	Bucknum/Posey (Ferrari 512S 5-litre) .	2 min 29.37 sec
10.	Vaccarella/Hezemans (Alfa Romeo Tipo 33/3 3-litre)	2 min 39.85 sec

THE RACE

When the green flag fell for the start at 11 am, Donohue went straight into the lead followed by Rodriguez, Siffert, Elford and Andretti. In this race, however, the Sunoco-Ferrari was unable to break away from the Gulf 917 driven by the Mexican. Siffert came through to take second place from his team-mate and after ten laps Donohue was 4.9 seconds ahead of the Swiss driver. Rodriguez was still in third place, Elford was fourth and then came Andretti and Revson. By lap fourteen Elford had closed right up on Rodriguez and was all set to move up into third place when a Lola T212 crossed his line at one of the corners and the two cars collided. Elford lost a lap in the pits while a wheel was changed and the front of the body was taped up. Not long afterwards Parsons shunted his 512S into a sandbank when the throttles jammed open and although the car rejoined the track, it had to be retired because of damaged oil cooler mountings.

On lap twenty-two Siffert set a new lap record of 2 min 30.46 sec—following which he was shown an 'ease-off' signal by the Gulf pit—and the leading cars were now in the throes of their first pit stops. Donohue had stopped on lap twenty, Rodriguez six laps later and

Andretti with the 3-litre Ferrari stopped on lap thirty. A miscalculation had apparently been made in the Gulf pit and on lap twenty-five Siffert ran out of fuel on the far side of the circuit Contrary to the rule that a driver may only return to the pits for fuel on foot, 'Seppi' hitched a lift back to the pits on the pillion of a motor-cycle. For this breach of the rules Siffert/Bell were penalised four laps and on top of this nineteen laps were lost while Siffert collected the fuel and foot-slogged it back to the car again. When Rodriguez stopped to refuel, Andretti took the lead and Donohue went back in front again when it was the 312P's turn to stop. While Siffert was sorting out his fuel problems, another Ferrari was in trouble; Young lost control of his 512M at the hairpin bend and the car rolled over. After some twenty seconds five marshalls lifted the Ferrari on to its side and just as Young crawled out from under the wreckage, the car burst into flames.

As the race progressed and with the second round of pit stops completed, a definite pattern had emerged. Although the Penske Ferrari was travelling faster than the Rodriguez/Oliver 917 which in turn was faster than the Ickx/Andretti Ferrari Prototype, the Penske car was needing a pit stop every twenty laps, the Gulf car every twenty-six laps and the Ferrari every thirty laps. All three cars were taking approximately the same length of time for stops and the Ferrari, needing only seven stops in all (to the eleven of the Penske car) must inevitably win, always provided, of course, that mechanical derangements or accidents did not upset these calculations. By the end of the third hour the works Ferrari had pulled out a lead of over a minute from the Penske Ferrari which in turn led Rodriguez/Oliver 917 by the fairly narrow margin of 4.2 seconds.

By the fourth hour the works Ferrari had extended its lead to a full lap, aided by an unscheduled stop for new brake pads by the Porsche and time lost by difficulty in removing a wheel on the Sunoco car. It was during this hour that the whole face of the race changed. Rodriguez was in second place, hard-pressed by Donohue, when the two cars collided at the chicane leading on to the main back straight. According to Donohue, he was already past the 917 when Rodriguez hit him 'not once, but twice.' Pedro claimed that Donohue had pulled past him and then cut across the front of the 917. The right-hand front wing of the 917 was badly shattered and rejoined the race, having lost two laps while the mechanics cut away the ragged glass-fibre—the car raced during the night hours with a spot-lamp jury-rigged on the nose. The damage to the Sunoco-Ferrari was much more severe, the breather on Penske's special refuelling system was damaged and nineteen laps were lost before the car eventually rejoined the fray. Furthermore it now needed to stop to refuel every fifteen or sixteen laps and its chances of winning the race had completely disappeared. Eventually Penske lodged three protests against the Gulf team; that Siffert should have been disqualified and not penalised for breaking the regulations when he ran out of fuel; that Bell had not switched off his engine during a refuelling stop (in fact the stop in question had merely been to close the door which was not shut properly); and finally that the right-hand wing on Rodriguez' car did not cover the wheel. All these protests were rejected by the stewards, but the atmosphere at the prize-giving was far from cordial.

Shortly before the Penske Ferrari rejoined the race, the small, red Maranello works car had succumbed to transmission trouble and the Martini Porsche of Elford/Larrousse had been delayed in the pits at the five-hour mark because the brake pistons had jammed during a pad change. The result was that the Alfa Romeo Tipo 33/3s of Stommelen/'Nanni' Galli and de Adamich/Pescarolo now led the race. The second-place car was also shared by Vaccarella following the retirement of his own car with fuel injection metering unit failure. Not long afterwards the second-place Alfa dropped to fourth because of alternator trouble, but nearly eight hours' racing had elapsed before the Elford/Larrousse 917 came through to take the lead. A rear tyre burst on the Bucknum/Posey Ferrari and although Bucknum tried to nurse the car back to the pits, the wheel collapsed and dragging that corner of the car along the ground damaged the suspension and wore a hole in the bottom of the engine, causing the oil to escape and the engine to seize up.

During the last few hours of the race the two Gulf cars and the Penske Ferrari were roaring through the field to make up lost ground, but at the chequered flag the Elford/Larrousse Martini-entered 917 was three clear laps ahead of the Alfa of Galli/Stommelen, with team-mates de Adamich/Pescarolo/Vaccarella in third spot. Rodriguez/Oliver had climbed back to fourth place, Siffert/Bell were fifth and the Donohue/Hobbs Penske-entered Ferrari took a rather unhappy sixth place.

Results:

1st, V. Elford/G. Larrousse (Porsche 917 5-litre), 260 laps, 1352 miles (112.50 mph),*

2nd, R. Stommelen/N. Galli (Alfa Romeo Tipo 33/3 3-litre), 257 laps,

3rd, N. Vaccarella/A. de Adamich/H. Pescarolo (Alfa Romeo Tipo 33/3 3-litre), 248 laps,

4th, P. Rodriguez/J. Oliver (Porsche 917 5-litre), 248 laps,

5th, J. Siffert/D. Bell (Porsche 917 5-litre), 248 minus 4 penalty laps,
6th, M. Donohue/D. Hobbs (Ferrari 512M 5-litre), 243 laps,
7th, J. Greenwood/R. Smothers (Chevrolet Corvette 7-litre), 218 laps,*
8th, G. Eaton/L. Chinetti, Jnr. (Ferrari 312P 3-litre), 213 laps,
9th, J. Locke/B. Everett (Porsche 911T 2.2-litre), 203 laps,*
10th, D. Hines/R. Johnson (Chevrolet Corvette 7-litre), 199 laps,
11th, Tisdelle/Kirill (Porsche 911S 2.2-litre), 195 laps,
12th, H. Cluxton/R. Crossman (Ferrari 365GTB4 4.4-litre), 195 laps. *Class winners.

Fastest lap: J. Siffert, 2 min 30.46 sec (124.43 mph—new lap recrod)
Previous lap record: J. Siffert (Porsche 917), 2 min 33.11 sec (122.27 mph—set in 1970 race)

1970 winners: M. Andretti/I. Giunti/N. Vaccarella (Ferrari 512S 5-litre), 107.29 mph.

Principal retirements: Revson/Savage (Ferrari 512M), electrical failure; Parsons/Weir (Ferrari 512S), throttle jammed/accident; Vaccarella Hezemans (Alfa Romeo Tipo 33/3), fuel injection trouble; Gregory/Young (Ferrari 512M), accident; Ickx/Andretti (Ferrar, 312P), transmission failure; Bucknum/Posey (Ferrari 512S)i puncture/loss of oil.

ROUND FOUR

BOAC 1,000 KILOMETRES RACE

Brands Hatch (Circuit length: 2.65 miles) 4th April, 1971
Weather: damp and cold

In contrast with previous years when the Brands Hatch race attracted fields that were among the strongest seen in the Championship series, the 1971 BOAC race was weak in numbers as far as both Sports Cars and Prototypes were concerned. Matra had not competed since the terrible accident in the Buenos Aires race, there was not enough money in the kitty to attract either the Penske-White 512M or the North American Racing Team Ferraris and very few owners of private 917s and 512S cars seemed interested in competing. The result was a handful of the top class cars that competed regularly in the Championship series backed up by two Lola T70-Chevrolet coupés that were too tatty to pass the scrutineers and a whole brigade of Chevrons and Lolas in the under 2-litres classes.

Group 5 Sports Cars:

J W Automotive Engineering Ltd:

Porsche 917 5-litre cars driven by Jo Siffert/Derek Bell and Pedro Rodriguez/Jack Oliver. The cars entered were those that had appeared at Buenos Aires, fitted with 4-speed gearboxes and back on the beryllium brake discs that had been discarded at Sebring. The team had also brought along one of the cars raced at Daytona as a spare. For this race the JW team adopted a NASCAR-style quick-filling fuel nozzles with five churns feeding into one nozzle by gravity. Although it was anticipated that this system would provide lightning refuelling stops, it was very experimental and the normal fillers were left in position on the cars in case it should be decided to use these after all.

Martini Racing Team:

Porsche 917 5-litre cars to be driven by Vic Elford/Gerard Larrousse (one of the Daytona cars rebuilt) and Gijs van Lennep/Kurt Ahrens (the Sebring winner, looking very second-hand, which did not arrive until the Friday). Ahrens also failed to arrive and his place was taken by Brian Redman. Before the race the team switched the driver pairings so that Redman co-drove with Elford and van Lennep with Larrousse. None of the drivers was happy with the handling of the Daytona car, but there was not much that could be done about it. The van Lennep/Larrousse car ran with high ram intake snorkels which gave power output a slight boost at the expense of fuel consumption.

Team Auto Usdau:

Porsche 917 4.5-litre driven by Willi Kauhsen/Reinhold Jöst. Since the Buenos Aires race this car had been repainted yellow.

Herbert Müller Racing:

Ferrari 512M 5-litre driven by Herbert Müller and René Herzog. This was a car used in the filming of 'Le Mans' now brought up to full 512M specification.

Escuderia Montjuich:

Ferrari 512M 5-litre driven by José Juncadella and David Hobbs (the latter deputising for Arturo Merzario). Since the car's last appearance this too had been rebuilt to the latest specification.

In the 2-litre Sports Car class a total of five of the pretty and effective Chevron B16 coupés was entered, but one of these was subsequently transferred to the Prototype category because it ran with a 1.6-litre Cosworth FVA engine instead of the 1.8-litre FVC unit with which the model was homologated.

Group 6 Prototypes:

S.p.a. Ferrari SEFAC:

Ferrari 312P 3-litre driven by Jackie Ickx/Clay Regazzoni. Since Sebring the car had been converted to the lighter 'Sprint' trim (without headlamps, etc) in which form it weighed around 600 kg.

Autodelta:

Alfa Romeo Tipo 33/3 3-litre cars driven by Andrea de Adamich/ Henri Pescarolo and Rolf Stommelen/Toine Hezemans. Since their last appearance the Tipo 33/3s had been fitted with new gearboxes which had an oil radiator, yet were twenty-two pounds lighter than those previously fitted.

Team Auto Usdau:

Porsche 908/2 Spyder 3-litre driven by Dieter Spoerry/Hans Wiegel. This was another ex-Le Mans film car and had also been painted yellow.

In the 2-litre Prototype class a strong entry was received. The fastest cars in the class were the DART-entered Chevron B19-Cosworth FVC driven by John Miles/Graham Birrell and the Scuderia Filipinetti-entered Lola T212-Cosworth FVC driven by Jo Bonnier/Peter Westbury. Among other interesting cars was the sole Huron (out of three entered) driven by Roger Enever and Shaun Jackson and sponsored by Camel Filters, the Dulon LD 11P with Porsche 910 engine driven by Ridelagh/McGovern and the Martin-BMW of Brian Martin/Ed Swart. Three Lola T210s (the 1970 version of the T212) and two other Chevron B19s were also entered in the class.

PRACTICE

Practice on the Friday afternoon saw very few cars circulating and not much in the way of fast times. Ickx and Regazzoni with the works Ferrari were taking things gently with a new engine in the car, but both they and the Autodelta boys seemed perfectly happy with the way their mounts were performing. Not so the Porsche 917 drivers; the Gulf cars were constantly in and out of the pits for minor adjustments and changes and both they and the Martini cars were weaving about badly. Elford commented that when he braked his car, he needed a clear twenty feet of road's width to do so with safety! Fastest on the Friday was Rolf Stommelen who turned in a good 1 min 29.2 sec with his Alfa.

On the Friday the Gulf 917s appeared with a lip running across the nose, rather like that adopted on the works Ferrari 512S cars in 1970, in an effort to keep the front of the cars more firmly glued to the track. Once again practice was dominated by the red cars, Ickx turned in a fine lap in 1 min 28.2 sec (bettering Amon's pole position practice time in 1970 by two-fifths of a second), but Stommelen then improved on this with a lap in 1 min 27.8 sec before spinning off (which gave a good indication of how hard he was trying). Later Regazzoni snatched pole position with a lap in 1 min 27.4 sec and Siffert and Rodriguez were third and fourth fastest. To achieve a lap in 1 min 28.4 sec 'Seppi' was trying really hard and then turning on the pressure even more he lost control at Stirlings, spun and smacked the tail of the 917 into the Armco. With damage to the rear chassis tubing and lights, the car was still driveable and he cruised back to the pits to report his misdemeanour to David Yorke.

Fastest in practice were:

1.	Ickx/Regazzoni (Ferrari 312P 3-litre)	1 min 27.4 sec
2.	Stommelen/Hezemans (Alfa Romeo Tipo 33/3 3-litre)	1 min 27.8 sec
3.	Siffert/Bell (Porsche 917 5-litre)	1 min 28.4 sec
4.	Rodriguez/Oliver (Porsche 917 5-litre)	1 min 29.4 sec
5.	de Adamich/Pescarolo (Alfa Romeo Tipo 33/3 3-litre) Elford/Redman (Porsche 917 5-litre)	1 min 29.6 sec
7.	van Lennep/Larrousse (Porsche 917 5-litre)	1 min 31.2 sec
8.	Hobbs/Juncadella (Ferrari 512M 5-litre)	1 min 31.6 sec
9.	Miles/Birrell (Chevron B19-Cosworth 1.8-litre)	1 min 32.0 sec
10.	Bonnier/Westbury (Lola T212-Cosworth 1.8-litre)	1 min 32.2 sec

THE RACE

Race day dawned wet and cold and during unofficial pre-race practice Miles lost control of his Chevron on the very slippery track as he accelerated away from the pits road and into Paddock bend, spun into the bank and shattered the rear suspension on the right-hand side. The team's spare car was cannibalised to repair the Chevron which just made the grid in time for the start. Instead of the three-by-two grid used in previous years, the cars were lined up two-by-two and released in a rolling start after a lap of the circuit.

At the time the flag fell slight rain was still falling and the track was very wet. Despite these conditions the Martini 917s and the Autodelta cars started the race on intermediate tyres.

When the pack moved off, Stommelen's Alfa went ahead initially, but Ickx pushed the Ferrari through on the inside and into the lead at Paddock Bend and began to pull away from Rodriguez, Stommelen, Siffert, de Adamich and Miles who was going magnificently with the blue Chevron. Siffert soon passed Stommelen, both the Martini cars were handling atrociously on their intermediate tyres and Jöst forged by them into seventh place with the Usdau Porsche. Out in front Ickx was driving magnificently with the Ferrari, but Pedro was chasing him hard with the 917. The first five cars had pulled well clear of Miles in sixth place who was being harried by Jöst with the yellow 917. McGovern with the Dulon had already spun once at Druids and now on lap five he lost control again at Westfields. Ickx was just about to scream past to lap him and had no alternative but to take violent evasive action. The Ferrari spun onto the grass, crunched against the Armco and shattered its nose. A full lap had been lost by the time Ickx had extricated the Ferrari from the mud and he made his way back to the pits for a complete new nose section to be fitted. At the same time a punctured rear tyre was changed and eight laps down Ickx eventually screamed back into the race, the Ferrari's chances of victory sadly diminished.

Rodriguez and Siffert now led the field with the Alfas of Stommelen and de Adamich third and fourth, Jöst was now fifth ahead of the Chevron and then came the two Martini-entered 917s, followed by Müller's Ferrari. With less than a quarter of an hour's racing over, Hans-Dieter Dechent in the Martini pit called his two 917s in for wet-weather tyres to be fitted and they rejoined the race well down the field. Ickx, in last place, caught up with Rodriguez' 917 on the road and sat behind the Mexican for a number of laps. Several times he tried to get by the race leader without success and then, as the track began to dry out, Siffert pushed his 917 in front of the Ferrari and closed up behind his team-mate. When the Gulf cars stopped to refuel, Siffert's pit stop was around seven seconds faster and he took the lead from Rodriguez.

The domination of the race by the two Gulf cars lasted until lap fifty-eight when Siffert came round alone. Rodriguez' car had died on him out at Dingle Dell because of a fuel blockage. He managed to partially clear the blockage and made his way back to the pits where the mechanics investigated the trouble. After a couple of minutes Pedro was back in the race, now in fourth place, When the two-hour mark came up Siffert still led from the two Alfas the

Kauhsen/Jöst 917 was fifth and Miles was still sixth with the Chevron. Ickx had now brought the 312P Ferrari through to tenth place and was still racing on the limit in his efforts to regain lost ground. On lap seventy-nine Rodriguez again stopped out at Dingle Dell, but this time he was forced to abandon the Gulf 917.

Miles was now travelling very slowly with the Chevron because the oil level was low and causing the pressure to fluctuate on corners, but after the eightieth lap he could stop to take on more oil and then began to motor as fast as ever. Siffert stopped to hand his 917 over to Bell and reported that the handling of the car was just as bad as it had been in practice, except that it now had a pronounced oversteer instead of understeer. Regazzoni was now at the wheel of the 312P, but the visor had blown completely off his Bell Star helmet and so he tucked himself down in the cockpit as far as possible and just pressed on. With a hundred laps completed, the order was: 1st, Siffert/Bell, 2 hr 48 min 24 sec; 2nd, Stommelen/Hezemans; 3rd, de Adamich/Pescarolo; 4th, Müller/Herzog; 5th, Ickx/Regazzoni; 6th, Elford/Redman. Miles, now in eighth place and overcome by more of the heavy machinery as the track dried out, was six laps behind the leading 917 and still going magnificently. The Usdau 917 had dropped back to twelfth place because of trouble caused by the tyres rubbing against the bodywork.

The Elford/Redman Porsche had developed a leaking fuel bag and petrol working its way on to the back tyres had made the handling worse than ever. The car was checked over in the pits several times, but when it came in to the pits just before half-distance, the leaking fuel ignited, Redman jumped out of the car, tripped as his foot caught in the safety harness and pressed the fire extinguisher button which extinguished the blaze in a matter of seconds. Elford then took over without anyone bothering to clear the extinguisher powder off the car and shortly afterwards Dechent, under some pressure from the scrutineers, decided that the car should be called in and retired. Despite considerable pain from the wind Regazzoni pressed on at the wheel of the works Ferrari until lap 114 when Ickx took the car out and continued the chase while Regazzoni was taken to the first aid centre for attention to his badly cut and bruised face.

Out in front Hezemans with the second-place Alfa was now very close behind Bell with the leading 917. After 3 hours 20 minutes at the wheel (ten minutes under the permitted maximum) Miles brought the DART-entered Chevron in for Birrell to take over and the car rejoined the race fitted with new brake pads and still comfortably leading its class. Not long after Ickx had relieved Regazzoni, the 312P Ferrari developed a sticking throttle and 4 minutes 20 seconds were lost in the pits while the trouble was sorted out. When Bell brought the leading 917 in at 4 pm for a routine refuelling stop and tyre change and for Siffert to take over, one of the front wheels would not come off because the alloy hub had expanded. After a great deal of struggling the wheel was eventually removed and Siffert rejoined the race after a stop lasting six minutes. Then more trouble struck on 'Seppi's' first lap back at the wheel and the car shed its 'space-saver' spare wheel at Paddock bend. The wheel disappeared into the undergrowth, a spare wheel was compulsory under Group 5 Regulations and the Porsche was black-flagged. There was no spare 'space-saver' wheel in the pits, Yorke placed an ordinary wheel on the passenger seat, but the scrutineers would not accept this and so it was necessary to deflate the tyre and force the wheel into the space usually occupied by the 'space-saver'. All this messing about lasted 6 min 12 sec and the 917 rejoined the race in fifth place. The Alfas were now five laps ahead of the van Lennep/Larrousse Porsche and when this lost time because the undertray had come adrift, it seemed that Autodelta had the race in the bag.

Just after five o'clock, the Autodelta chances of victory were reduced by half when the leading car of Hezemans crawled down the hill from Druids in a cloud of white smoke with a con-rod through the side of the engine. Regazzoni now relieved Ickx again at the wheel of the Ferrari 312P and renewed the chase. The Ferrari was now in second place, four laps behind the leader, all Pescarolo with the Alfa had to do was to keep going steadily and the race was in the bag. In his efforts to cut down the Alfa's lead Regazzoni lost more time by spinning at Druids and in a collision with Siffert's 917 which was now in third place, and at the chequered flag the Maranello car was still three laps in arrears. Without doubt the Ferrari, that had been driven on the limit throughout the 6 hours 24 minutes of racing was the hero at Brands Hatch and the favourite with the crowd, but for Alfa the race represented a magnificent triumph. It was Alfa's first World Championship race victory since Juan Fangio won the 1951 Spanish Grand Prix with a Tipo 159M Formula One car and it was a well deserved win for Chiti and the Autodelta team after two years of hard work developing the Tipo 33/3 since its disastrous debut at Sebring in 1969.

Results:

1st, A. de Adamich/H. Pescarolo (Alfa Romeo Tipo 33/3 3-litre), 6 hours 24 min 32.2 sec (97.17 mph),*
2nd, J. Ickx/C. Regazzoni (Ferrari 312P 3-litre), 232 laps,
3rd, J. Siffert/D. Bell (Porsche 917 5-litre), 229 laps,*

4th, H. Müller/R. Herzog (Ferrari 512M 5-litre), 228 laps,
5th, D. Hobbs/J. Juncadella (Ferrari 512M 5-litre), 227 laps,
6th, R. Jöst/W. Kauhsen (Porsche 917 5-litre), 221 laps,
7th, J. Miles/G. Birrell (Chevron B19-Cosworth 1.8-litre), 219 laps,*
8th, J. Bonnier/P. Westbury (Lola T212-Cosworth 1.8-litre), 218 laps,
9th, G. van Lennep/G. Larrousse (Porsche 917 5-litre), 216 laps,
10th, H.-D. Weigel/D. Spoerry (Porsche 908 3-litre), 210 laps,
11th, D. Farnell/P. Crossley (Lola T210-Cosworth 1.8-litre), 209 laps,
12th, A. Fletcher/W. Tuckett (Chevron B16-Cosworth 1.8 litre), 205 laps,*
13th, B. Robinson/B. Maskell (Chevron B16-Cosworth), 202 laps,
14th, D. Weir/M. Walton (Lola T210-Cosworth 1.8-litre), 199 laps,
15th, K. Walker/J. Bridges (Chevron B16-Cosworth 1.8-litre), 185 laps.

*Class winners.

Fastest lap not issued by the organisers.

1970 winners: P. Rodriguez/L. Kinnunen (Porsche 917 4.5-litre), 92.15 mph.

Principal retirements: Rodriguez/Oliver (Porsche 917 5-litre), fuel line blockage; Elford/Redman (Porsche 917 5-litre), leaking fuel tank; Stommelen/Hezemans (Alfa Romeo Tipo 33/3 3-litre), engine trouble.

ROUND FIVE

MONZA 1,000 KILOMETRES RACE

Monza Road Circuit (Circuit length: 3.915 miles) 25th April, 1971
Weather: warm and dry

Prior to the 1970 race the Monza 1,000 Kilometres 'blind' had always been held on the combined road and banked track circuit, but the banking is now in such a state of disrepair that it cannot be used again until someone finds the money for it to be completely resurfaced and during 1968–9 it was in such rough state that it gave suspensions and drivers alike a very severe pounding. The 1970 race had seen a close battle between the Gulf-sponsored Porsche 917s and the works Ferrari 512S cars and although Maranello was no longer interested in the 5-litre cars and was concentrating on the flat-12 Prototype, a strong and varied entry was received for the 1971 race.

THE ENTRY

Group 5 Sports Cars:

J W Automotive Engineering Ltd:

Porsche 917 5-litre cars driven by Jo Siffert/Derek Bell and Pedro Rodriguez/Jack Oliver. Both of the Wyer cars had the longer tails with vertical fins and were running with 4-speed gearboxes. To speed up refuelling, the Wyer team was using a twenty-foot refuelling tower with the petrol dropping by gravity (Alfa Romeo and Ferrari had to make do with fifteen-foot towers!), this permitted 120 litres to enter the tanks in four seconds, automatic cut-off nozzles were used and the drivers did not even get out of the cars during refuelling.

Martini Racing Team:

Porsche 917 5-litre cars driven by Vic Elford/Gerard Larrousse and Helmut Marko/Gijs van Lennep. The Martini cars, which had been given a much-needed repaint, were to the same specification as the Gulf cars. During practice the team tried out the ram-type high air intakes used on one of the cars at Brands Hatch, but in the very wet practice sessions vast quantities of water were sucked in and it was decided to abandon these.

Zitro Racing Cars:

Porsche 917 4.5-litre driven by Dominique Martin and Gerard Pillon. This car was fitted with the normal tail. *Kurz*

Team Auto Usdau:

Porsche 917 4.5-litre driven by Willi Kauhsen/Reinhold Jöst. The yellow car was fitted with the longer tail with tail-fins.

Scuderia Filipinetti:

Ferrari 512S with 512M engine, suspension and brakes driven by Mike Parks/Joakim Bonnier and Ferrari 512M driven by Corrado Manfredini/Giancarlo Gagliardi. This was in fact Manfredini's private car being looked after by the Filipinetti team.

Herbert Müller Racing:

Originally Müller had entered a grand total of three 5-litre Ferraris, but among the drivers were several who were very inexperienced and were in fact only nominated because of their financial interest in the entries. Under pressure from the organisers Müller scratched one of his cars, Teodoro Zeccoli was borrowed from the Autodelta team to co-drive with Moretti and the third car was as usual driven by Müller/René Herzog.

Escuderia Montjuich:

Ferrari 512M 5-litre driven by José Juncadella/Arturo Merzario.

An additional Ferrari entry had come from David Weir who planned to field an ex-North American Racing Team car which was being flown over 'fully race prepared'. When the car arrived, it was clearly in no fit state to run in a race and instead of appearing at Monza was dispatched to Maranello for a complete rebuild.

Group 6 Prototypes:

S.p.a. Ferrari SEFAC:

Ferrari 312P 3-litre (now with two small tail-fins) driven by Jacky Ickx/Clay Regazzoni.

Autodelta:

Alfa Romeo Tipo 33/3 3-litre cars driven by Andrea de Adamich/Henri Pescarolo, Rolf Stommelen/'Nanni' Galli and Toine Hezemans/Nino Vaccarella. Sicilian Vaccarella was driving a Tipo 33/3 for the first time since 1969. Originally Autodelta had entered a fourth car, but this had been scratched. The Alfas featured slightly longer tails.

André Wicky Racing Team:

Porsche 908 Spyder 3-litre driven by André Wicky/P. Mattli. This was the ex-Richard Brostrom car driven by Masten Gregory in 1969 and the early part of 1970.

Team Auto Usdau:

Porsche 908 Spyder 3-litre driven by Hans-Dieter Weigel/Dieter Spoerry.

Bosch Racing Team:

Porsche 908 Spyder 3-litre driven by Otto Stuppacher/Kurt Rieder.

Scuderia Brescia Corse:

Porsche 908 Spyder 3-litre driven by 'Noris'/Oddone Sigala.

Although four Lolas and four Chevrons had been entered in the

2-litre class, only one Lola, driven by Antonio Zadra and 'Gap' and two Chevrons, the B19 of Alberti/Casoni and the B16 of Noe/Dupont made the starting line. Also running were three 2-litre Abarths and as usual the GT class consisted of a host of Porsche 911s, joined at this race by the Chevrolet Corvette of Tuerlinx/Grauls.

PRACTICE

Both practice sessions at Monza were completely ruined by heavy rain. On the Friday afternoon the rain stopped for a short while and it was then, on a very wet track, that the best practice times were set. On the Saturday practice was stopped an hour early because of the weather. The organisers ran a qualifying system based on the three fastest times which resulted in a minimum lap time to qualify of 2 min 2 sec. On the Saturday Galli collided with an Italian 'special' powered by a Fiat Dino engine and completely wrecked his Alfa Tipo 33/3. The young Italian injured a hand and was unable to drive in the race, but Ing. Carlo Chiti took the damaged car away, ostensibly to repair it over-night, but re-appeared on race day with a new car, a breach of the race regulations to which the organisers turned a blind eye. Despite the atrocious conditions many of the drivers were really trying hard and the fastest laps were very brave efforts indeed.

Fastest in practice were:

1st, Elford/Larrousse (Porsche 917 5-litre) .	1 min 32.93 sec (a little over 137 mph)
2nd, Ickx/Regazzoni (Ferrari 312P 3-litre) .	1 min 33.91 sec
3rd, Stommelen/Galli (Alfa Romeo Tipo 33/3 3-litre)	91 1 min 35.15 sec
4th, Parkes/Bonnier (Ferrari 512S 5-litre) .	1 min 35.17 sec
5th { Rodriguez/Oliver (Porsche 917 5-litre) de Adamich/Pescarolo (Alfa Romeo Tipo 33/3-litre) }	1 min 35.74 sec
7th, Siffert/Bell (Porsche 917 5-litre) . .	1 min 36.40 sec
8th, Hezemans/Vaccarella (Alfa Romeo Tipo 33/3 3-litre)	1 min 36.98 sec
9th, Manfredini/Gagliardi (Ferrari 512M 5-litre)	1 min 37.71 sec
10th, Müller/Herzog (Ferrari 512M 5-litre) .	1 min 38.30 sec

Because Galli was unable to drive in the race, it was necessary for Autodelta to play 'musical chairs' with their drivers. De Adamich and Pescarolo were to partner each other as usual, but Hezemans would start with one car and Stommelen with the third car;

Vaccarella would relieve Hezemans, Stommelen would drive for the maximum period permitted by the regulations, then Hezemans would relieve Stommelen and then after he was rested, Stommelen would relieve Vaccarella.

Race day dawned fine, much to everyone's relief, and it was decided to hold a further thirty minutes of untimed practice so that the drivers could acclimatise themselves to the dry track. During this session the Porsche 908 of Stuppacher/Rieder blew up its engine and reduced the number of starters to twenty-nine.

THE RACE

The Monza race was one of the few in 1971 at which a rolling start was not used and when the flag fell at 11.20, Parkes out-dragged the rest of the grid with the Filipinetti Ferrari and led from the 917s and the works Ferrari. Müller's Ferrari was left on the grid because the engine refused to fire, he was given a push-start and then, in accordance with the regulations, stopped, switched off the engine and restarted it on the starter motor. Eventually the Swiss driver joined the race half-a-lap or so behind the rest of the field. Parkes still led at the end of the first lap, but by the end of lap two the two Gulf 917s were in first and second places and Parkes was being harried by Elford with his silver and blue 917. Ickx was in fifth place, sixth was de Adamich with the first of the Alfas and then came Merzario and Stommelen.

As the race progressed, de Adamich was passed by the much more powerful Ferrari of Moretti and Porsche of Marko, on lap six he missed a gear and was passed by team-mates Stommelen and Hezemans and then he dropped further back still when he spun at Parabolica. Ickx had forced the 312P ahead of Parkes on lap four and was battling to maintain contact with the 917s. Siffert moved into a position close behind Rodriguez and the two Gulf 917s had soon pulled out a ten-second lead over Elford. Merzario had been pushing the Montjuich Ferrari along really well (he had been second fastest with a works car in practice at Monza in 1970) and succeeded in passing both Parkes and Ickx with the works Ferrari. On lap twelve Meier's Porsche 907 crossed Merzario's line at Lesmo, the two cars collided, the German car was pushed into the guard-rail and wrecked and Ickx, right on Merzario's tail, was unable to avoid the spinning yellow Ferrari. Both Maranello cars were badly damaged and out of the race; Merzario's car had caught fire, but the flames were soon extinguished. Herzemans' Alfa caught fire while being driven through the scene of the accident, but this blaze, too, was soon put out and the Autodelta driver rejoined the race a lap in arrears. Less lucky was Weigel who smashed the front of his 908 against some of the debris and was out of the race.

While frantic efforts were being made to sort the mess caused by the wrecked cars, Siffert slipped in front of team-mate Rodriguez on lap fourteen but a marshall inadvertently squirted extinguisher fluid over the 917's windscreen as it passed the scene of the accident. With his vision seriously impaired, Siffert began to ease off and he was passed by both Rodriguez and Elford, and Moretti moved up into third place on lap twenty. Eventually Siffert decided to make a premature pit stop and while the car was having its windscreen cleaned, the opportunity was taken to refuel. A battle for fourth place between Marko, Parkes and Stommelen was resolved in favour of the German driver when Parkes retired the Filipinetti car with a con-rod through the side and Marko stopped to complain about low oil pressure. And the other Filipinetti entry was out because of a broken petrol pump drive-belt. Siffert was forced to make another pit stop because of a punctured rear tyre—debris from the accident was the probable cause—and then began to pick up places.

By lap forty Rodriguez was a clear lap ahead of the rest of the field and the Martini challenge was fading rapidly. On lap forty-four Elford stopped at the pits to complain that the engine of his 917 would not rev above 7,000 rpm. He rejoined the race, but the car sounded as bad as ever and he retired soon afterwards. The second Martini 917 driven by Marko developed the same symptoms, but staggered on until broken throttle linkage caused its eventual retirement. The third-place Ferrari of Moretti and Zeccoli dropped from third place to sixth when a lot of time was lost in the pits because the clutch refused to disengage and at half-distance the order was: 1st, Rodriguez/Oliver (two laps ahead of the rest of the entry); 2nd, Siffert/Bell; 3rd, Stommelen/Hezemans; 4th, de Adamich/Pescarolo; 5th, Moretti/Zeccoli (having regained one place since their long pit stop); 6th, Hezemans/Vaccarella; 7th, Müller/Herzog; 8th, Kauhsen/Jöst.

During the next twenty laps the Ferrari of Moretti/Zeccoli pulled back to third place ahead of the Autodelta team, but then lost time again while a clutch line was changed and fell back to ninth place. By now the race was a rather boring procession, dominated overall by the two Gulf 917s, and in the Prototype class, by the trio of very reliable Alfa Romeo Tipo 33/3s. Behind these five cars at the chequered flag was the Ferrari of Müller and Herzog, the epitome of reliability, fast when Müller was at the wheel and much slower, but still running very steadily, when driven by the inexperienced Herzog. The Monza race was not one of the year's more exciting events, but it provided a display of the superb team organisation of the John Wyer organisation, the brilliant driving of Jo Siffert who pulled right back through the field after two set-backs early in the race and the remarkable reliability of the Alfas which two seasons previously had the most hopeless and unreliable of all the Prototypes. After this race Porsche led the Sports Car Championship with 40 points to the 23 of Alfa Romeo and 16 of Ferrari.

Results:

1st, P. Rodriguez/J. Oliver (Porsche 917 5-litre), 4 hours 14 min 32.6 sec (147.396 mph), 174 laps,*
2nd, J. Siffert/D. Bell (Porsche 917 5-litre), 171 laps,
3rd, A. de Adamich/H. Pescarolo (Alfa Romeo Tipo 33/3 3-litre), 168 laps,*
4th, R. Stommelen/T. Hezemans (Alfa Romeo Tipo 33/3 3-litre), 167 laps,
5th, N. Vaccarella/T. Hezemans/R. Stommelen (Alfa Romeo Tipo 33/3 3-litre), 166 laps,
6th, H. Müller/R. Herzog (Ferrari 512M 5-litre), 164 laps,
7th, R. Jöst/W. Kauhsen (Porsche 917 4.5-litre), 164 laps,
8th, G. Moretti/T. Zeccoli (Ferrari 512M 5-litre), 157 laps,
9th , D. Martin/G. Pillon (Porsche 917 4.5-litre), 154 laps,
10th, A. Wicky/ P. Mattli (Porsche 908 3-litre), 144 laps,
11th, 'Pal Joe'/M. Becchetti (Fiat-Abarth 2,000), 139 laps,*
12th, E. Kremer/G. Huber (Porsche 911S 2.2-litre), 134 laps,*
13th, Seiler/P. Ettmuller (Porsche 914/6 2.0-litre), 132 laps,
14th, F. Noel M. Dupond (Chevron B16-Cosworth 1.8-litre), 128 laps,
15th, C. Tuerlinx/I. Grauls (Chevrolet Corvette 7-litre), 127 laps.

*Class winner.

Fastest lap: P. Rodriguez, 1 min 24.0 sec (153.123 mph—new lap record).

Previous lap record: V. Elford (Porsche 917 5-litre), 1 min 24.8 sec (151.68 mph—set in 1970 race).
1970 winners: P. Rodriguez/L. Kinnunen (Porsche 917 4.5-litre), 144.56 mph.

Principal retirements: Ickx/Regazzoni (Ferrari 312P 3-litre), accident; Juncadella/Merzario (Ferrari 512M 5-litre); Parkes/Bonnier (Ferrari 512S 5-litre), engine trougle; Manfredini/Gagliardi (Ferrari 512M 5-litre), sheared fuel pump drive; Elford/Larrousse (Porsche 917 5-litre), engine trouble; Marko/van Lennep (Porsche 917 5-litre), broken throttle linkage.

ROUND SIX

SPA 1,000 KILOMETRES RACE

Spa-Francorchamps (Circuit length: 8.76 miles) 9th May, 1971
Weather: dry and warm

The speed of the difficult Circuit National de Francorchamps and the power of the 5-litre Porsche 917s provided a motor racing spectacle that was unique. This very testing and allegedly dangerous circuit with the high-speed Masta straight, the many difficult corners including the notorious Stavelot and the tight La Source hairpin before the pits (at which the faster cars look as though they are going to crunch the Armco) brings out the best in the more adventurous drivers and the worst in the more timid. As the big 917s swooped round the course, power-sliding through the faster corners, their drivers having to work every inch of the way, spectators witnessed in the 1971 race the last of the true high-speed road races. 1971 was the last year in which the 5-litre cars were permitted to run in World Championship races (and the 3-litre Prototypes are inevitably going to lap much slower on circuits where top-end flat-out performance matters) and the days of the circuit are surely numbered. Spa-Francorchamps was last used for a Formula 1 race in 1970 when a silly chicane was inserted at Malmedy to slow the cars and its use has now been banned by the Grand Prix Drivers' Association. Although there is still a great deal of local enthusiasm for the circuit and it is a favourite circuit with many of the Sports Car drivers, a new Grand Prix circuit has been built, this will inevitably become the focal-point of motor racing interest in Belgium and local residents will not tolerate for many more years the closure of public roads necessary for the running of races at Spa. Although only a small entry was received for the 1971 race—there were only twenty-eight starters—what it lacked in quantity was made up in quality with entries from the Gulf, Martini, Ferrari and Autodelta teams.

THE ENTRY

Group 5 Sports Cars:

J W Automotive Engineering Ltd:

Porsche 917 5-litre cars driven by Jo Siffert/Derek Bell and Pedro Rodriguez. These were both normal short-tail cars with 4-speed gearboxes (at Spa the 917 uses top gear all the way round the course except for La Source hairpin bend). As a spare the Gulf team had brought along one of the Daytona cars (with the perspex panel

In the Targa Florio the Porsche 908/3s were out of luck and victory went to the Autodelta team. This Martini-entered Porsche driven by Elford and Larrousse retired with suspension damaged by a collision with a kerb. (Nigel Snowdon)

For Autodelta the Targa Florio provided a well deserved and long awaited triumph for the Autodelta team. This is the winning Tipo 33/3 car driven by Vaccarella and Hezemans. (Nigel Snowdon)

in the roof for use on the banking) with the slightly longer tail surmounted by tail fins and 5-speed gearbox—this was also the spare car at Monza. Although the longer tail gave slightly greater speed along the straights, the Gulf team found that on Spa's weather-eroded surfaces stability was much better with the standard *Kurz* tail.

Martini Racing Team:

Porsche 917 5-litre cars driven by Vic Elford/Gerard Larrousse and Gijs van Lennep/Helmut Marko. Both of the Martini cars were fitted on factory recommendation with the longer tails, but quite obviously the cars were not handling as well as their Gulf rivals and this, together with the fact that the team reckoned that the engines supplied by the works were down on power compared with those used by Gulf, meant that the drivers were none too happy.

Team Auto Usdau:

Porsche 917 4.5-litre driven by Willi Kauhsen/Reinhold Jöst. Like the Martini cars, this 917 was fitted with the longer tail.

Zitro Racing Cars:

Porsche 917 4.5-litre driven by Dominique Martin/Gerard Pillon. Like the Gulf cars this white-painted car was fitted with the *Kurz* tail.

Scuderia Filipinetti:

Ferrari 512M 5-litre driven by Corrado Manfredini/Giancarlo Gagliardi. As at Monza this was Manfredini's own car being managed for him by Filipinetti.

Herbert Müller Racing:

Ferrari 512M 5-litre driven by Herbert Müller/René Herzog and Ferrari 512S 5-litre driven by Wisendanger/Kocher.

Racing Team VDS:

Lola T70 Mk. 3B-Morand-Chevrolet 5-litre driven by Teddy Pilette/Taf Gosselin.

Bahamas Racing Organisation:

Lola T70 Mk.3B-Chevrolet 5-litre driven by Mike Coombe/Paul Vestey.

Group 6 Prototypes:

S.p.a. Ferrari SEFAC:

Ferrari 312P 3-litre driven by Jackie Ickx/Clay Regazzoni. Since its Monza accident this car had been completely rebuilt.

Autodelta:

Alfa Romeo Tipo 33/3 3-litre driven by Andrea de Adamich/Henri Pescarolo. The team had entered only one car because of concentrating on preparations for the Targo Florio the following weekend.

Ecurie Sonauto:

Porsche 908/2 Spyder 3-litre driven by Claude Ballot-Lena/Guy Chasseuil.

The rest of the field consisted of the Redex-Chevron B6 of Goodwin/Cowin, the Chevron B8-BMW of Birchenhough/Jocelyn, the Dulon-Porsche of Ridelagh/Taylor and the usual collection of Porsche 911s joined in the GT class by a brace of Chevrolet Corvettes. Two of the Group 6 Huron cars with Cosworth engines were entered, but eventually only one car, minus engine, arrived too late for practice and was not allowed to start. As this entry was heavily sponsored by Camel filters who had brought along a caravan and helicopter, the cigarette company was none too pleased!

PRACTICE

Because the *Daily Express* Trophy race was held at Silverstone the same weekend, the organisers had the practice sessions at Spa on the Thursday and Friday, leaving Saturday free for those drivers competing in the British race. During the Thursday session none of the Gulf drivers was able to approach the fantastic lap record of 3 min 16.5 sec set by Rodriguez in the 1970 race, although practice was once again dominated by the Gulf cars. Rodriguez turned in a lap in 3 min 19.2 sec and the best Siffert could manage was 3 min 20.1 sec—which made Marko's lap of 3 min 20.4 sec with a supposedly inferior car a very remarkable performance. That the Ferrari was outclassed on this high-speed circuit soon became apparent and its fastest lap was a 3 min 24.8 sec by Ickx.

On the Friday it was Elford who set the pace and the Martini driver wound up with a lap in 3 min 18.2 and it looked as though this had secured him pole position on the grid. Then in the last fifteen minutes of practice Derek Bell flew round in 3 min 16.0 sec (160.92 mph) making the fastest lap ever recorded at Spa.

Fastest in practice were:

1.	Siffert/Bell (Porsche 917 5-litre) . .	3 min 16.0 sec
2.	Elford/Larrousse (Porsche 917 5-litre) .	3 min 18.2 sec
3.	Rodriguez/Oliver (Porsche 917 5-litre) .	3 min 19.2 sec
4.	Marko/van Lennep (Porsche 917 5-litre) .	3 min 20.4 sec
5.	Ickx/Regazzoni (Ferrari 312B 3-litre) .	3 min 22.2 sec
6.	Manfredini/Gagliardi (Ferrari 512M 5-litre)	*3 min 24.4 sec
7.	Kauhsen/Jöst (Porsche 917 4.5-litre) .	3 min 26.2 sec
8.	de Adamich/Pescarolo (Alfa Romeo Tipo 33/3 3-litre)	3 min 27.1 sec
9.	Müller/Herzog (Ferrari 512M 5-litre) .	3 min 28.3 sec
10.	Wisendanger/Kocher (Ferrari 512S 5-litre)	3 min 36.8 sec

*This time was in fact set by Filipinetti technical chief Mike Parkes and it was improbable that either of the car's drivers could match it.

Although it had been intended that the 130% qualifying rule should be applied, this would have meant the exclusion of fourteen of the twenty-eight cars that appeared in practice and so they were all allowed to start. The slowest car in practice was the 2.2-litre Porsche 911 of Dechamel/Parot which lapped in 4 min 50.0 sec!

THE RACE

Just before the warming-up lap there was a rumour circulating that rain was falling out at Masta and Stavelot and this news resulted in a frantic rush while many of the cars were changed to wet-weather tyres. The JW team, however, was content to leave their 917s on intermediate tyres and their decision was justified when the drivers returned to report that the track was dry all the way round! So all the cars on wet-weather tyres changed back to drys again except for the Elford/Larrousse 917 and the Filipinetti Ferrari. It was then that light rain began to fall, but it stopped very quickly leaving the track in a damp condition. By not getting flapped into making unnecessary tyre changes and remaining calm while the other teams had panicked, the JW boys had already seized a moral advantage!

When the flag fell, Siffert accelerated into the lead from pole position on the grid followed by Elford, Rodriguez, Ickx, Marko and Pescarolo. One car, the Wiesendanger/Kocher 512S, had failed to leave the grid because the engine refused to fire, although the team gave out the reason that a hub had stripped during tyre-changing. Rodriguez soon slipped by Elford whose efforts were marred by starting the race on wet-weather tyres and as the leading 917s screamed up to around 215 mph on the Masta straight they pulled out a clear lead over the rest of the field. At the end of the first lap the order was Siffert (leading by two hundred yards) – Rodriguez – Ickx – Marko – Pescarolo – Kauhsen – Müller. Elford stopped at the pits at the end of the lap to have intermediate tyres fitted – he left the pits half-a-lap down on the leaders – and for reasons best known to the Zitro team Martin brought his 917 in for wet-weather tyres to be fitted! And after only another couple of laps Martin was back in the pits for dry tyres to be fitted and Pillon now took the car over!

By the end of lap two Siffert had pulled out a lead of ten seconds over Rodriguez and the Gulf team was now in complete command of the race. However, the Mexican soon closed the gap and by the end of lap five the two 917s were nose to tail and the third-place Ferrari, completely out-paced, had fallen twenty-seven seconds in arrears. On the next lap the Martini challenge almost completely evaporated when Marko's car expired out on the circuit. The engine had died completely on the Masta straight; initially Marko thought the trouble was a fuel-feed blockage, but in fact it had run out of fuel because of a leaking tank. Marko eventually obtained some petrol to get the car going and when the race was more than half-way over, he brought the car back to the pits to retire. Pilette made two stops with the maroon Lola, for work on the lubrication system and to change a punctured tyre and then Elford, who had climbed back to seventh place with the surviving Martini 917 came into the pits with a very rough engine and complaining about the handling. The car rejoined the race in fifteenth spot, climbed back to eighth place, stopped again, then started in nineteenth place and finally the team retired the car when it was back in eighth place with a suspected cracked chassis.

Mike Coombe retired his Lola on lap nine with a broken rocker arm. The Gulf 917s were lapping faster and faster and on lap ten Rodriguez turned in the fastest ever time at Spa of 3 min 15.5 sec and took the lead from Siffert. Two laps later 'Seppi' stopped for his first routine refuelling stop which lasted a mere twelve seconds, Rodriguez stopped next time round, he was stationary for fifteen seconds and rejoined the race without losing the lead. The two Gulf cars, lapping in formation, were making it look all too easy and what should have been a closely fought race as in 1970 had turned into an impressive and over-whelming demonstration of Gulf-Porsche power. The Ferrari 312P, lapping in 3 min 22/23 sec, stopped at the end of lap seventeen and carried on in third place. Kauhsen and Müller were battling for fourth place, Pescarolo was unable to maintain the pace set by the Sports Cars and trailed in sixth spot, and Gagliardi was seventh with the Filipinetti-entered car.

Still the two leading cars lapped nose-to-tail and on lap twenty-one Siffert was timed in 3 min 14.6 sec (160.09 mph) which stands as the Spa outright lap record. Müller handed over to Herzog who began to lose ground and Pescarolo, who had made a brief pit stop for the glass-fibre passenger door to be patched up, moved up into sixth place. On lap twenty-seven Pillon had lost control of the Zitro 917 under braking for Eau Rouge corner just past the pits and the car was retired with a crumpled nose. On lap thirty-three Ickx handed the 312P Ferrari over to Regazzoni, Pescarolo took fourth place when Kauhsen stopped at the pits, Siffert handed over to Bell at the end of lap thirty-five and Oliver relieved Rodriguez two laps later. When de Adamich relieved Pescarolo, it soon became obvious that the Italian was having an 'off' day, he began to fall back rapidly and after only ten laps he was called in for Pescarolo to take over again.

Although the Ferrari had been completely out-paced by the 917s, it had been going well for a 3-litre car and seemed all set for victory in the Prototype category. But it was not to be and the model's ill luck continued. On lap fifty-five Ridelagh with the Dulon-Porsche (the car that had put Ickx off the course at Brands Hatch) pulled out in front of Regazzoni at Stavelot, the Ferrari ran up the back of the Dulon and the two cars skidded down the course for around 300 yards and crumpled themselves against the Armco. Already the Müller/Herzog and Manfredini/Gagliardi Ferraris had retired with engine trouble and the order behind the two Gulf 917s was now Kauhsen – Pescarolo – Ballot-Lena with the Sonauto Porsche – Pilette with the VDS Lola. Shortly afterwards Kauhsen's 917 blew a tyre at Stavelot when travelling at close to 200 mph, for the moment the driver thought he was going to write himself and the car off, but he succeeded in bringing the yellow Porsche under control; driving on the grass to prevent damage to the suspension he motored slowly back to the pits for a new wheel to be fitted and for the bodywork, damaged by the flailing rubber, to be patched.

In the closing stages of the race the two leading 917s were slowed by the Gulf pit, Oliver and Bell remained at the wheel and when the chequered flag fell after just four hours of spectacular high-speed driving, the two blue and orange cars crossed the line four laps ahead of the Alfa Romeo Tipo 33/3. This was the Wyer team's fourth victory of the season, and eleventh Championship race victory since the start of the collaboration between Zuffenhausen and Slough. Alfa Romeo, too, had cause for satisfaction for the third place gained on this high-speed circuit gave the team its fifth successive Prototype class win.

Results:

1st, P. Rodriguez/J. Oliver (Porsche 917 5-litre), 4 hours 1 min 9.7 sec, (154.772 mph), 71 laps,*
2nd, J. Siffert/D. Bell (Porsche 917 5-litre), 4 hours 1 min 10.1 sec,
3rd, H. Pescarolo/A. de Adamich (Alfa Romeo Tipo 33/3 3-litre), 67 laps,*
4th, W. Kauhsen/R. Jöst (Porsche 917 4.5-litre), 66 laps,
5th, C. Ballot-Lena/G. Chasseuil (Porsche 908 3-litre), 60 laps,
6th, T. Pilette/T. Gosselin (Lola T70-Chevrolet 5-litre), 58 laps,
7th, E. Kremer/G. Huber (Porsche 911S 2.4-litre), 55 laps,*
8th, J. Ickx/C. Regazzoni (Ferrari 312P 3-litre), 54 laps, not running at the finish,
9th, G. Quist/D. Krumm (Porsche 914/6 2-litre), 53 laps,
10th, K. Simonson/R. Larsson (Porsche 911S 2.4-litre), 53 laps,
11th, P. Greub/J-C. Gueri (Porsche 911S 2.4-litre), 52 laps,
12th, T. Birchenhough/B. Joscelyne (Chevron B8-BMW 2-litre), 52 laps,*
13th, C. Manfredini/G. Gagliardi (Ferrari 512M 5-litre), 51 laps, not running at the finish,
14th, S. Gaban/W. Braillard (Porsche 911S 2.4-litre), 51 laps,
15th, H. Müller/R. Herzog (Ferrari 512M 5-litre), 50 laps, not running at the finish.

*Class winners.

Fastest lap: J. Siffert, 3 min 14.6 sec (162.087 mph – record).
Previous lap record: P. Rodriguez (Porsche 917 5-litre), 3 min 16.5 sec (160.53 mph – set in 1970 race).
1970 winners: J. Siffert/B. Redman (Porsche 917 5-litre), 149.42 mph.

Principal retirements: Elford/Larrousse (Porsche 917 5-litre), cracked chassis; Marko/van Lennep (Porsche 917 5-litre), split fuel tank; Manfredini/Gagliardi (Ferrari 512M 5-litre), engine trouble; Müller/Herzog (Ferrari 512M 5-litre), engine trouble.

ROUND SEVEN

TARGA FLORIO

Little Madonie (Circuit length: 44.7 miles) 16th May, 1971
Race length: 491.7 miles (11 laps) Weather: dry and very hot

Although it had been thought that new legislation in Italy would result in all races and hill climbs held on public roads being banned, and it seemed that the days of the Targa Florio, the last survivor of the great road races, were numbered, there was an exception for races established longer than thirty years and so the Palermo Automobile Club carries on organising what is now the most arduous of all the races in the Sports Car Championship. It is a sad fact that the number of serious contenders entering the race gets smaller each year and in 1971 Ferrari missed the Targa Florio – just as he had in 1969 – despite having a car that was ideally suited to the conditions in which the race is run.

THE ENTRY

Group 6 Prototypes:
JW Automotive Engineering Ltd:

Porsche 908/3 3-litre cars driven by Pedro Rodriguez/Herbert Müller and Jo Siffert/Brian Redman. As usual the two Gulf cars were distinguishable by distinctively different colour finishes. Because of their lack of Targa experience both Bell and Oliver had been dropped for this race and their places taken by Targa experts.

Martini Racing Team:

Porsche 908/3 3-litre driven by Vic Elford/Gerard Larrousse. A second car had been entered for van Lennep/Kinnunen, but it could not be got ready in time and so these drivers were released and appeared for the Autodelta team.

As in 1970 the cars were looked after at this race by Porsche factory personnel. The 1971 908/3s were lighter than those raced the previous year and were fitted with tail-fins similar to those seen on the 917s at Monza and Spa. The effect of the fins was to cause a break-up of turbulence and even on short straights allowed the engine to pull an extra 200 rpm.

Autodelta:

Alfa Romeo Tipo 33/3 3-litre cars driven by Andrea de Adamich/ Gijs van Lennep, Nino Vaccarella/Toine Hezemans and Rolf Stommelen/Leo Kinnunen. Because of Pescarolo's lack of familiarity with the Little Madonie course and because Galli was still unable to drive following his Monza accident, Autodelta were only too glad to take on the services of the two drivers not needed by Porsche and both had proved their worth in the 1970 race (Kinnunen was the circuit record holder). Autodelta had also brought a fourth car to the race, the new Tipo 33/TT/3 car, based on Porsche 908/3 design practice, much shorter, lower, narrower and lighter than the existing model and with the gearbox ahead of the rear axle. The car was nominally entered for Carlo Facetti/Teodoro Zeccoli, but there was never any intention of it actually running in the race and in training it was mainly driven by Rolf Stommelen.

Scuderia Brescia Corse:

Alfa Romeo Tipo 33/3 3-litre driven by Nino Todaro/'Cordones' and Lola T212-Cosworth 1.8-litre driven by Antonio Zadra/'Gap'.

Scuderia Filipinetti:

Lola T212-Cosworth 1.8-litre driven by Jo Bonnier/Richard Attwood and Mike Parkes/Peter Westbury.

David Weir:

Lola T212-Cosworth 1.8-litre driven by David Weir and Alain de Cadenet.

Antonio Nicodemi:

Lola T212-Cosworth 1.8-litre driven by Nicodemi and Jonathan Williams.

This class was completed by two Abarth 2000SP cars, a Chevron B19, a Ferrari Dino (now rather outdated) and the AMS powered by a Cosworth FVA 1.6-litre engine. In the small Prototype class there were four entries: the British Jerboa, an AMS with an Alfa Romeo engine, a Gilberti and a Daf. The 1,000 cc Prototype class was made up of Abarth Spyders plus the British-built Daren.

Group 5 Sports Cars:

At this race no large capacity Sports Cars were entered. The 2,000 cc class consisted of an aged Porsche 906 'Carrera,' an Abarth 2,000S and a pair of British-entered and rather elderly Chevron B8-BMW coupés. In the 1,300 cc Group 5 class there were two entries, a Matra Djet and an Abarth and, as usual, the Group 4 GT classes were largely composed of Porsche 911s with engines of 2 litres and above.

Even before practice began, it was obvious that the race was to prove a straight fight between the three Porsche 908/3s and the three Alfa Romeo Tipo 33/3s, with the Lolas scrapping for the lower places and finishing in the first six if any of the fastest cars fell by the wayside.

PRACTICE

In fact practice at the Targa Florio means very little, for few drivers get the chance to do more than a single lap in their race car.

The Porsche drivers were strictly limited to a lap apiece and had to do the rest of their practice in one of the Porsche 914/6 production cars the team had brought to the circuit.

Once again, as in 1970, practice was on the Thursday before the race and this allowed entrants two clear days before the race to repair battered bodies and chassis. The Porsche team had a thoroughly miserable practice session, but everything went smoothly for Alfa Romeo's and Autodelta's drivers dominated the practice times. Although Rodriguez managed to complete his full lap without problems, when Müller did his lap, he scraped a wall and lost a lot of time while he stopped to inspect the car. Redman had a tyre puncture and it took three-quarters of an hour before he could get the car going again; when Siffert went out with this 908/3, he lost control on a corner and damaged the left-hand side of the chassis and body against a wall. Finally, to complete this session of misery, after Larrousse's trouble-free lap, Elford took over the third car and broke a radius arm when he hit a wall. All this while the Alfas were circulating almost completely without trouble and despite jumping about badly on parts of the circuit, the Lolas were going well and recording good times. Although the first thirty kilometres of the course had been resurfaced since the 1970 race, the rest of the circuit had suffered badly during a hard winter, it was even bumpier than usual and caught out a number of drivers both during practice and in the race.

Fastest in practice were:

1st, Vaccarella*/Hezemans (Alfa Romeo Tipo 33/3 3-litre	34 min 14.2 sec
2nd, de Adamich*/van Lennep (Alfa Romeo Tipo 33/3 3-litre)	34 min 36.9 sec
3rd, Stommelen*/Kinnunen (Alfa Romeo Tipo 33/3 3-litre)	34 min 49.3 sec
4th, Larrousse*/Elford (Porsche 908/3 3-litre)	35 min 22.4 sec
5th, Rodriguez*/Müller (Porsche 908/3 3-litre)	35 min 48.1 sec
6th, Bonnier*/Attwood (Lola T212 1.8-litre)	37 min 20.3 sec
7th, Stommelen*/Vaccarella (Alfa Romeo Tipo 33/TT/3 3-litre)	37 min 26.7 sec
8th, Parkes/Westbury (Lola T212 1.8-litre)	37 min 44.6 sec
9th, Nicodemi/Williams (Lola T212 1.8-litre)	39 min 19.4 sec
10th, Todaro/'Codones' (Alfa Romeo Tipo 33/3 3-litre)	39 min 35.2 sec

NOTE: * indicates driver who set fastest lap
The first named driver started the race.
The Tipo 33/TT/3 car which did not start the race.

Although the regulations prescribed that the start would be in ascending numerical order, this was varied to ascending order of practice times in each class which meant that Vaccarella was away first with a clear road in front of him. The cars left at fifteen-second intervals.

Lap 1: Before all the field had left the start line, disaster had already struck for several of the leading contenders. Only seventeen kilometres from the start Stommelen, who had gone so well in practice, slid off the road and was out of the race with a buckled wheel and smashed suspension. Redman's 908/3, not handling properly following Siffert's practice crash, understeered off the road, hit a wall and caught fire. Despite the fact that the 908/3s had been fitted with fire extinguishers for the 1971 race, when the car burst into flames, Redman suffered bad burns on his face and neck. And Rodriguez hit a kerb near Collesano, wrecking two wheels and putting himself out of the race. So, with one lap gone, three of the likely winners were out of the race and Vaccarella led on the road by forty seconds from de Adamich, with Larrousse third and Bonnier fourth. On time Larrousse led from Vaccarella. Long after the faster cars had gone by, Parkes crawled into the Filipinetti pit. He had been delayed by loss of fuel pressure on the Lola, had jammed the pressure release valve with a piece of wood and the second Filipinetti car was now in forty-fourth place. Peter Westbury then took the car over, leaving the pits in sixty-seventh place!

Lap 2: Now a pattern was emerging among the three fastest cars. The Alfas were faster along the straights, the Porsche nippier through the twistier parts. Vaccarella covered his second lap in 34 min 6.7. sec and this put him in the lead on time. For much of the lap Larrousse had hounded de Adamich, passed the Italian when the Alfa spun and then de Adamich had forced his way past again along a straight stretch. At the end of the lap Larrousse stopped to refuel and to hand over to Elford. On this lap the Alpine of Fulvio Tandoy went off the road, and the driver sustained injuries from which he later died.

Lap 3: At the end of this lap Vaccarella stopped to refuel and to hand over to Hezemans and de Adamich was relieved by van Lennep. After these refuelling stops Vaccarella/Hezemans still led the race by 1 min 20 sec, Elford was second and de Adamich/van Lennep third. Zadra retired his Lola on this lap with a broken rear wishbone.

Lap 4: Elford now had the 908/3 really wound up, on this lap he set fastest lap in 33 min 45.6 sec and by the end of the lap he was in the lead by a margin of eighteen seconds. The Alfas were still second and third and very much in the hunt and in fourth place was the Lola of Bonnier/Attwood. De Cadenet crashed his Lola, but was lucky to escape with minor injuries.

Lap 5: Now Elford was right behind Hezemans on the road and trying everything he knew to get by. Eventually, when the Alfa was baulked by a Porsche 911, Elford swished by both cars to lead on the road as well as on time. Todaro, at the wheel of the Scuderia Brescia Corse Alfa, had been running steadily, although never in contention for the lead, but he crashed into a parked car when a front tyre deflated. At the end of the lap Elford stopped to hand over to Larrousse and just as the Frenchman was rejoining the race, Hezemans went by the pits to re-take the lead on the road.

Lap 6: By the end of this lap Larrousse had pulled out a lead of nearly a minute over the two Alfas, both of which stopped at the pits for driver changes. Unfortunately both of the Autodelta cars needed new rear tyres and for a minute or so sheer panic and confusion reigned while the Sicilian crowd, seeing that the Porsche was pulling out an ever-increasing lead, whistled and cat-called in the direction of the Alfa pit. By the time the Alfas had left the pits, they were around fifty seconds in arrears and it seemed as though Autodelta had lost the race.

Lap 7: On this lap disaster struck at Porsche's hopes; Larrousse had a rear tyre puncture near Cerda, he stopped to fit the 'space-saver' spare, but a little further on the other rear tyre punctured. On two tyres proper, a rim and the 'space-saver' Larrousse limped on until he reached the Gulf service depot at Bivio Polizzi, some thirty kilometres further on. Here new tyres were fitted and at the end of the lap, having misunderstood advice that he should stop at the pits for the suspension to be checked, Larrousse went roaring past instead of stopping to hand over to Elford.

Lap 8: Having tried so hard to make up lost ground, poor Larrousse retired on this lap out at Cerda with broken suspension after contact with a kerb. Whether he hit the kerb and the suspension broke or the suspension broke first is far from clear. Now the two Autodelta entries were completely unchallenged.

Laps 9 to 11: At the end of lap nine both of the Alfa 33/3s stopped at the pits again so that Hezemans and Van Lennep could take over for the last two laps and they completed these without incident. At the finish the only car not to be lapped by the two Autodelta entries was the very well driven Lola of Attwood and Bonnier which finished in third place. By this stage Parkes and Westbury had worked marvels with their Lola after the time lost on the first lap and they finished fifth, having completed ten laps, behind the Porsche 911S of Pucci and Schmid.

The 1971 Targa Florio was not a great race, but it delighted the Sicilian crowd to see an Italian victory and for Autodelta and Vaccarella it was a great triumph, for the Milan team had been trying to break the Porsche strangle-hold on the race since they ran the first 2-litre Alfa 33s in 1967 and the Sicilian lawyer had been hoping to repeat a victory in the race ever since his win with a Ferrari in 1965. Porsche had won the race every year since 1966, a defeat after this record of five successive wins cannot have come as too much of a disappointment, but it must be remembered that it is the efforts of Porsche that have kept the race alive in recent years.

Results:

1st, N. Vaccarella/T. Hezemans (Alfa Romeo Tipo 33/3 3-litre), 6 hours 35 min 46.2 sec (74.60 mph),*
2nd, A. de Adamich/G. van Lennep (Alfa Romeo Tipo 33/3 3-litre), 6 hours 36 min 57.9 sec,
3rd, J. Bonnier/R. Attwood (Lola T212-Cosworth 1.8-litre), 7 hours 0 min 0.5 sec,*
4th, B. Chenevière/P. Keller (Porsche 911S 2.4-litre), 10 laps,*
5th, M. Parkes/P. Westbury (Lola T212-Cosworth 1.8-litre), 10 laps,
6th, G. Pucci/D. Schmid (Porsche 911S 2.4-litre), 10 laps,
7th, A. Nicodemi/J. Williams (Lola T212-Cosworth 1.8-litre), 10 laps,
8th, P. Greub/S. Garant (Porsche 911S 2.4-litre), 10 laps,
9th, S. Calascibetta/P. Monti (Opel GT 2-litre), 9 laps,*
10th, G. Schon/ G. Bertoni (Porsche 911S 2-litre), 9 laps,
11th, W. Kauhsen/G. Steckonnig (Porsche 914/6 2-litre), 9 laps,
12th, M. Zanetti/R. Rospa (Alfa Romeo GTA 1.6-litre), 9 laps,*
13th, E. Bologna/G. Spatafora (Lancia Fulvia 1.6-litre), 9 laps,
14th, M. Barone/M. Campanini (Abarth 1-litre), 9 laps,*
15th, F. Berruto/A. Mola (Porsche 906 2-litre), 9 laps.*

*Class winners.

Fastest lap: V. Elford (Porsche 908/3 3-litre), 33 min 45.6 sec (79.51 mph)

Existing lap record: L. Kinnunen (Porsche 908/3 3-litre), 33 min 36.0 sec (79.90 mph – set in 1970 race).

1970 winners: J. Siffert/B. Redman (Porsche 908/3 3-litre), 74.66 mph.

Principal retirements: Stommelen/Kinnunen (Alfa Romeo Tipo 33/3 3-litre), accident; Siffert/Redman (Porsche 908/3 3-litre), accident; Rodriguez/Müller (Porsche 908/3 3-litre), accident; N. Todaro 'Cordones' (Alfa Romeo Tipo 33/3 3 litre), accident.

ROUND EIGHT

NÜRBURGRING 1,000 KILOMETRES RACE

Nürburgring (Circuit length: 14.17 miles) 30th May, 1971
Weather: dry and warm

Since the last 1,000 Km race at the Nürburgring, the circuit had been extensively altered to meet the demands of the members of the Grand Prix Drivers' Association who had refused to race at the circuit in 1970 and whose action had resulted in the transfer of the German Grand Prix to Hockenheim. Thousands of trees had been removed, mile upon mile of Armco barriers had been installed, the jumps had been levelled off and many of the familiar recognition points had disappeared so that some drivers had difficulty in familiarising themselves with the 'Ring' in its new form. At this race the section running down to Adenau was unchanged, the straight was still lined by hedges and a large number of changes were still to be made before the Grand Prix at the beginning of August. These drastic alterations to the circuit meant that there would be very little comparison between the circuit in its old and new forms and the best guide to likely lap times came from the Formula 2 Eifelrennen which had been run on the revised circuit earlier in May. At this race fastest lap was set by Ronnie Peterson in 7 min 57.1 sec (107.06 mph), six seconds faster than the old Formula 2 record. As in 1970 the Nürburgring race was dominated by 3-litre Prototypes and very few of the 5-litre Sports Cars were entered.

THE ENTRY

Group 6 Prototypes:

JW Automotive Engineering Ltd:

Porsche 908/3 3-litre cars driven by Jo Siffert/Derek Bell and Pedro Rodriguez/Jack Oliver. For this race the Slough team had been supplied with two new cars with additional strengthening to the chassis and front suspension and with larger oil tanks because of the very high oil consumption experienced by this team in the 1970 race. No. 1, the Rodriguez/Oliver entry had a broad orange line running from the rear of the car and fanning out to full-width across the nose and extending along the sides. No. 2, the car for Siffert/Bell, had a broad orange arrow running along the left hand side of the upper bodywork.

Martini Racing Team:

Porsche 908/3 3-litre cars driven by Vic Elford/Gerard Larrousse and Helmut Marko/Gijs van Lennep. The first pair drove the car they had handled in the Targa Florio and the latter pair were provided with the car which Rodriguez had crashed in the Sicilian race. The Martini team was in receipt of full works support and while the JW team controlled their own race, Zuffenhausen ran the show for Martini. All four 908/3s were identical, but, of course, the JW cars were on Firestone tyres and the Martini cars on Goodyears and the latter were to prove an advantage in both practice and the race.

Autodelta:

Alfa Romeo Tipo 33/3 3-litre cars driven by Andrea de Adamich/Henri Pescarolo, Rolf Stommelen/'Nanni' Galli and Nino Vaccarella/Toine Hezemans. These cars were in identical trim to the Targa winners and the team had also brought along the Tipo 33/TT/3 lightweight car for Carlo Facetti/Teodoro Zeccoli, but once again there was no intention that it should be raced.

S.p.a. Ferrari SEFAC:

Ferrari 312P 3-litre driven by Jackie Ickx/Clay Regazzoni. Once again the car had been rebuilt, this time because of the accident at Spa.

Private Porsche 908s:

A total of five of these now outdated cars were entered. The Martini team fielded their 908/2 for Prince Hohenzollern/Prince Bayern, but the former crashed on his first practice lap and the car was too badly damaged to run. The other cars were driven by Hans-Dieter Weigel/Dieter Spoerry (entered by Team Auto Usdau), Ernst Kraus/Dieter Basche, Claude Ballot-Lena/Guy Chasseuil (Sonauto entry) and André Wicky/Mario Cabral.

In the 2,000 cc Prototype class there were the familiar and almost notorious Dulon with Porsche 910 engine driven by Ridehalgh/Garton, a Chevron B19, two B16s (including the Mazda rotary-engined car driven by Deprez/Vernaeve), the Chevron-Redex Spyder and two Darens, the latter both works entries and one fitted with a Lotus-Vauxhall 2-litre engine.

The 1,600 cc Prototype class was headed by two Cosworth FVA-powered Martins, the Lola of Edwards and Franey with a similar engine and several lesser vehicles brought the number in the class up to seven.

Group 5 Sports Cars:

Herbert Müller Racing:

Ferrari 512M 5-litre driven by Müller/Herzog and 512S 5-litre driven by Wiesendanger/Kocher (the latter pair having failed to leave the grid at Spa with the same car). This team had also brought along another 512M as a spare car.

Gelo Racing:

Ferrari 512M 5-litre driven by Georg Loos/Helmut Kelleners. This pair were also racing a Porsche 911 which they shared with Franz Pesch, a confusing arrangement permitted under Nürburgring regulations.

Team Auto Usdau:

Porsche 917 4.5-litre driven by Willi Kauhsen/Reinhold Jöst. This car was still in Spa trim and running with tail-fins.

Racing Team VDS:

Lola T70 Mk 3B-Chevrolet 5-litre driven by Teddy Pilette/Taf Gosselin.

The only cars running in the 2,000 cc Group 5 class were a Porsche 910, a Porsche 906 and the Chevron B8-BMW of Birchenhough/Joscelyne. As usual there were hordes of 911 Porsches running in the GT class, plus a privately entered Ferrari Dino and a trio of Alpine-Renaults.

PRACTICE

After the Porsche débâcle in the Targa Florio, it was expected that Zuffenhausen would make a special effort at the Nürburgring, but in fact the JW cars were barely ready in time for practice and were not properly sorted out. Both cars were handling badly and the gearbox and drive-shafts were changed on the Siffert/Bell car in an effort to cure a bad vibration. Nor was the Martini team in a much happier state. During the first day's practice on the Friday a bolt dropped out of the front suspension of Elford's car causing a tyre to puncture and the Marko/van Lennep car spent most of the day in front of the pits with the mechanics working furiously.

In contrast the Ferrari and the Alfas were running without any troubles and motoring very quickly. Regazzoni was fastest on the first day in 7 min 59.8 sec and this time was achieved on a very wet and treacherous track. On the Saturday, in much improved weather, the Ferrari dominated practice once again. Although Ickx turned in a lap in 7 min 45.0 sec early in the session, both of the Maranello drivers subsequently improved on this time, Reggazzoni with a lap in 7 min 42.3 sec and Ickx in 7 min 36.1 sec and the latter time was nine seconds faster than any of the opposition could manage. Both of the Martini cars were now running well, although unable to match the time set by the Galli/Stommelen Alfa, but the JW cars were still handling badly and were never really in the picture.

Fastest in practice were:

1. Ickx/Regazzoni (Ferrari 312P 3-litre) .	7 min 36.1 sec
2. Stommelen/Galli (Alfa Romeo Tipo 33/3 3-litre)	7 min 45.1 sec
3. Elford/Larrousse (Porsche 908/3 3-litre) .	7 min 46.9 sec
4. Marko/van Lennep (Porsche 908/3 3-litre)	7 min 47.9 sec
5. Siffert/Bell (Porsche 908/3 3-litre) . .	7 min 52.7 sec
6. Rodriguez/Oliver (Porsche 908/3 3-litre) .	7 min 54.6 sec
7. de Adamich/Pescarolo (Alfa Romeo Tipo 33/3 3-litre)	7 min 55.8 sec
8. Hezemans/Vaccarella (Alfa Romeo Tipo 33/3 3-litre)	8 min 1.2 sec
9. Wiesendanger/Kocher (Ferrari 512M 5-litre)*	8 min 16.0 sec
10. Jöst/Kauhsen (Porsche 917 4.5-litre) .	8 min 18.8 sec

*This time was in fact set by Herbert Müller.

THE RACE

A total of fifty-one cars formed behind the Mercedes 350SL pace car – one of the smallest fields in the history of the race – and when the flag was lowered, Ickx with the 312P seared into the lead. By the end of the first lap he had pulled out a lead of 4.5 seconds and behind him came Stommelen, Elford, Siffert, van Lennep, de Adamich and Rodriguez. On the next lap Rodriguez and de Adamich passed van Lennep. That the 312P was the fastest of all the Prototypes was beyond doubt, after three laps Ickx had a lead of 16.5 sec, after four laps he had extended it to 27.1 sec and on the fifth lap he set a new circuit record of 7 min 40.8 sec (110.86 mph) and increased his lead to 40.7 sec. But so far in its career the 312P had completed only one race and the big question mark at the Nürburgring was whether the car could possibly last the distance.

It seemed that this question had been answered when Ickx pulled into the pits at the end of lap six with the engine boiling furiously. The team concluded that there was a leak, but could not trace it and so the water was topped up and the car sent back into the race in the faint hope that the trouble would cure itself. While Ickx was stationary in the pits, Stommelen, Elford and Siffert went past, the Wyer car still handling badly and 'Seppi' far from happy with his mount. On lap seven, however, came the first of the retirements among the fast boys. The sub-frame at the rear of

Siffert's 908/3 – the one supporting the engine and gearbox – broke and the car careered along in a shower of sparks as the metal ground on the track. Siffert succeeded in retaining control and brought the car back round to the pits to retire. David Yorke decided to partner Siffert with Rodriguez and so neither Oliver nor Bell had a drive at this race. Jöst had been battling with Müller's Ferrari for eighth place, but he was forced to stop at the pits because the 917 had been grounding on the track and worn a hole through the floor. A new floor was riveted in and the car eventually rejoined the race.

On lap eight Elford caught up with Stommelen's Alfa, but had difficulty in finding a way past the well-driven Autodelta entry. On lap eleven, just before the cars made the first of their three routine pits stops, Elford slipped ahead and came into the pits first. However, at this race, Autodelta pit work was slicker and Galli (relieving Stommelen) was back in the race slightly ahead of Larrousse (who had taken over from Elford). Ickx was now back in third place, Siffert relieved Rodriguez (but valuable seconds were lost while the seat was adjusted), de Adamich handed fifth place to Pescarolo and Hezemans passed his car over to Vaccarella with the warning that it was handling oddly and that he had spun unexpectedly.

Ickx caught up with the two leaders on lap twelve, on the next lap he passed Larrousse at the North Turn and Galli at Adenau and at the end of the lap came round with an incredible 25.5-second lead. The next car in trouble was Galli's Alfa and at the end of lap fourteen he coasted into the pits to retire with oil all over the engine which had serious internal damage. Now Ickx led by fifty-one seconds from Larrousse and the Ferrari, for the time being at least, was going better than ever. Siffert was third and then came Pescarolo and Marko. A tyre punctured on Herzog's Ferrari and the flailing tread damaged the front wing. He stopped at the pits where the shattered glass-fibre was patched and Müller took the car over. However, the repairs were a rather bodged mess and the Ferrari was black-flagged. It rejoined the race with the nose from the team's spare car, but the incident had damaged the front suspension and the car was retired. Vaccarella, pressing on too energetically with the ill-handling Alfa, had a rather frightening spin and at the end of the lap stopped at the pits. The steering and suspension were checked over, but nothing wrong was found and the car rejoined the race over a lap behind the leaders.

The leading Ferrari's first routine stop was at the end of lap fifteen (extra fuel had been added when the car stopped the first time). Now Regazzoni resumed at the wheel and although the car was only 18.5 sec ahead of the Porsche of Larrousse when it rejoined the race, the Swiss driver had no difficulty in maintaining his advantage. However, the Maranello car began to run too hot again, its pace noticeably slowed, it began to trail an ominous cloud of smoke and finally, on lap twenty-one, Regazzoni pulled into the pits. The engine was now completely dry, when water was poured in, it ran straight out again through the exhausts and the 312P was pushed away into retirement. When the second round of routine fuel stops had been completed Elford, back at the wheel of the leading car, was 22.5 seconds ahead of Rodriguez and then came van Lennep and de Adamich (the leading Alfa had dropped to fourth place as a result of a slow pit stop).

Now Rodriguez was trying hard to catch Elford, but the Wyer car was still handling badly and the Mexican was unable to reduce the gap below twenty seconds. When the third and final round of routine stops came, Rodriguez stayed at the wheel and new front tyres were fitted. No tyres were changed on the Elford/Larrousse car, but the *rear* tyres were changed on third-place 908/3 of Marko/van Lennep. During the last phase of the race Rodriguez was struggling with his Porsche which was handling worse than ever, Marko closed right up on the blue and orange car and Pedro ensured that the Gulf car was as 'wide' as possible and using most of the road. At the chequered flag Larrousse/Elford were 1 min 44 sec ahead of Rodriguez/Siffert and the Gulf car was chased across the line by the second Martini entry. The only other car on the same lap as the leader was the first of the Alfas driven by de Adamich/Pescarolo.

Results:

1st, G. Larrousse/V. Elford (Porsche 908/3 3-litre), 5 hours 51 min 49.3 sec (106.51 mph),*
2nd, P. Rodriguez/J. Siffert (Porsche 908/3 3-litre), 5 hours 53 min 33.4 sec,
3rd, H. Marko/G. van Lennep (Porsche 908/3 3-litre), 5 hours 53 min 33.5 sec,
4th, A. de Adamich/H. Pescarolo (Alfa Romeo Tipo 33/3 3-litre), 5 hours 56 min 20.0 sec,
5th, T. Hezemans/N. Vaccarella (Alfa Romeo Tipo 33/3 3-litre), 42 laps,
6th, R. Jöst/W. Kauhsen (Porsche 917 4.5-litre), 40 laps,*
7th, C. Ballot-Lena/G. Chasseuil (Porsche 908/2 3-litre), 40 laps,
8th, D. Basche/H. Kraus (Porsche 908/2 3-litre), 40 laps,
9th, G. Loos/F. Pesch (Ferrari 512M 5-litre), 40 laps,
10th, A. Wicky/M. Cabral (Porsche 908/2 3-litre), 38 laps,
11th, S. Greger/R. Lins (Porsche 910 2-litre), 37 laps,*

12th, E. Kremer/J. Neuhaus (Porsche 911 2.4-litre), 37 laps,*
13th, C. Haldi/P. Keller (Porsche 911 2.4-litre), 37 laps,
14th, G. Quist/D. Krumm (Porsche 914/6 2-litre), 36 laps,*
15th, G. Stekkonig/D. Schmid (Porsche 914/6 2-litre), 36 laps.

*Class winners.

Fastest lap: J. Ickx (Ferrari 312P 3-litre), 7 min 40.8 sec (110.86 mph – outright circuit record).

Previous lap record: J. Ickx (Brabham BT26-Cosworth F1), 7 min 43.8 sec (110.13 mph – set in 1969 German Grand Prix)

Previous Prototype lap record: P. Rodriguez (Porsche 908/3 3-litre), 7 min 50.4 sec (108.62 mph – set in 1970 race)

1970 winners: V. Elford/K. Ahrens (Porsche 908/3 3-litre), 102.59 mph.

Principal retirements: Siffert/Bell (Porsche 908/3 3-litre), chassis breakage; Stommelen/Galli (Alfa Romeo Tipo 33/3 3-litre), engine trouble; Müller/Herzog (Ferrari 512M 5-litre), suspension failure; Ickx/Regazzoni (Ferrari 312P 3-litre), overheating.

ROUND NINE

LE MANS 24 HOURS RACE

La Sarthe (Circuit length: 8.34 miles) 12th–13th June, 1971
Weather: dry and cool

Although still an event of nation-wide importance in France and attracting as enormous crowds as ever, Le Mans has degenerated into a long, tedious marathon of attrition, with most of the faster cars retiring and with very little interest or drama except in the first few hours. The 1971 race attracted the worst entry for many years, neither Autodelta nor Ferrari sent cars and in the original entry list thirty-one of the seventy-four entries were Porsche 911s. However, there was the usual very strong entry of Porsche 917s, the only likely challenger was the Sunoco-Ferrari entered by Penske and it seemed highly unlikely that any car but a Porsche could win the race.

No.	*Car and Practice Time*	*Drivers and Entrant*
1.	Chevrolet Corvette, 6998 cc (4 min 9.5 sec)	J-C. Aubriet/J-P. Rouget (Ecurie Leopard)
2.	Chevrolet Corvette, 6998 cc (4 min 12.6 sec)	H. Greder/Mlle. M-C. Beaumont (Greder Racing)

Mlle. Beaumont is a leading French rally driver and this was the first occasion since 1952 that a woman had been allowed to drive in the race.

5.	Lola T70 mk 3B-Chevrolet, 4995 cc (3 min 45.0 sec)	T. Pilette/T. Gosselin (Racing Team VDS)
6.	Ferrari 512M, 4994 cc (3 min 27.7 sec)	C. Manfredini/G. Gagliardi (Scuderia Filipinetti)
7.	Ferrari 512M, 4994 cc (3 min 21.1 sec)	M. Parkes/H. Pescarolo (Scuderia Filipinetti)

This was the special Filipinetti car which had been prepared under Mike Parkes' supervision and was known informally as the '512F'. Originally Bonnier was to have co-driven with Parkes, but he withdrew from the race after an accident had happened to his son.

9.	Ferrari 512M, 4994 cc (3 min 21.6 sec)	H. de Fierlandt/A. de Cadenet (Ecurie Francorchamps)
10.	Ferrari 512M, 4994 cc (3 min 26.7 sec)	G. Loos/F. Pesch (Gelo Racing Team)
11.	Ferrari 512M, 4994 cc (3 min 18.5 sec)	M. Donohue/D. Hobbs (North American Racing Team)

This was the Sunoco car prepared by Penske who had taken over one of NART's entries. The car was fourth fastest in practice and its only weakness was that it lacked the speed of the Porsche 917s along the Mulsanne straight.

12.	Ferrari 512M, 4994 cc (3 min 26.5 sec)	S. Posey/T. Adamowicz (North American Racing Team)
14.	Ferrari 512S, 4994 cc (3 min 29.7 sec)	M. Gregory/G. Eaton (North American Racing Team)

This was a rather elderly Ferrari with the open Spyder body.

15.	Ferrari 512M, 4994 cc (3 min 18.7 sec)	J. Juncadella/N. Vaccarella (Escuderia Montjuich)

16. Ferrari 512M, 4994 cc (3 min 21.3 sec) — D. Weir/C. Craft (David Piper)

Weir had taken over Piper's entry for his ex-NART Ferrari which had been completely rebuilt at the factory.

17. Porsche 917, 4907 cc (3 min 17.6 sec) — J. Siffert/D. Bell (JW Automotive Engineering Ltd)

This was a brand-new long-tail car of the type that Oliver had driven at the Test Weekend. It was third fastest in practice.

18. Porsche 917, 4907 cc (3 min 13.9 sec) — P. Rodriguez/J. Oliver (JW Automotive Engineering Ltd)

This was the actual long-tail car that Oliver had driven at the Test Weekend.

19. Porsche 917, 4907 cc (3 min 22.2 sec) — R. Attwood/H. Müller (JW Automotive Engineering Ltd)

This was one of the team's usual cars fitted with the longer tail with tail-fins. All the Wyer and Martini cars were fitted with 4907 cc engines (as opposed to the 4999 cc units used at Monza and Spa) and 5-speed gearboxes.

21. Porsche 917, 4907 cc (3 min 14.9 sec) — V. Elford/G. Larrousse (Martini Racing Team)

This was a long-tail car similar to those entered by Wyer and it was the only one of the three Martini entries finished in the team's usual silver and blue colours. It was second fastest in practice.

22. Porsche 917, 4907 cc (3 min 18.7 sec) — H. Marko/G. van Lennep (Martini Racing Team)

This was a standard car with the longer tail with tail-fins loaned to Martini by the works. It was brand new and untested when it arrived at the circuit and painted plain white (later some Martini 'decorations' were added).

23. Porsche 917, 4907 cc (3 min 21.0 sec) — W. Kauhsen/R. Jöst (Martini Racing Team)

This was the short, fat 917 that had appeared at the Test Weekend and had been nick-named the 'pig'. The car had now been painted pink and dotted lines indicated the different joints formed by a pig's anatomy!

24. Ligier JS3, 2993 cc (3 min 39.8 sec) — J. Ligier/P. Depailler (Automobiles Ligier)

27. Porsche 910 (with 907 2195 cc engine) (4 min 11.9 sec) — C. Poirot (entrant)/J-C. Andruet

28.	Porsche 908 Spyder, 2997 cc (3 min 45.5 sec)	C. Ballot-Lena/G. Chasseuil (Auguste Veuillet)
29.	Porsche 908 Spyder, 2997 cc (4 min 7.5 sec)	A. Wicky/M. Cohen-Olivar) (André Wicky Racing Team
30.	Porsche 908 Spyder, 2997 cc (3 min 56.2 sec)	L. Cosson (entrant)/H. Leuze
32.	Matra-Simca MS660, 2999 cc (3 min 31.9 sec)	C. Amon/J-P. Beltoise (Equipe Matra)
49.	Porsche 907, 1981 cc (4 min 6.0 sec)	P. Mattli/W. Brun (André Wicky Racing)
50.	Lola T212-Cosworth, 1798 cc (4 min 2.8 sec)	G. Edwards/R. Enever (Camel Filters-Team Huron)
57.	Porsche 917, 4494 cc (3 min 43.3 sec)	D. Martin/G. Pillon (Zitro Racing Cars)

This was the standard short-tail car raced by this team all season and in practice it was the slowest of the 917s.

58.	Ferrari 365 GTB 4 'Daytona', 4390 cc (4 min 21.3 sec)	R. Grossmann/L. Chinetti, jnr. (North American Racing Team)

This was a standard 'Daytona' (running complete with air conditioning) and apart from the exhaust system it had few modifications. Because the model was not homologated as a GT car, it had to run in Group 5.

60.	Porsche 908 Spyder, 2997 cc (3 min 50.0 sec)	C. Haldi/H-D. Weigel (Although entered in Haldi's name, this was in fact the Team Auto Usdau car).

Making up the field were the usual collection of Porsche 911s ranging from 2 litres to 2.4 litres in capacity, together with two 914/6s – in all a total of twenty of these cars. The latest 'stretched' version of the 911 engine allowed these cars to attain around 160 mph on the Mulsanne straight, almost 70 mph slower than the speeds achieved by the 917 *Lang* cars. Because of the very fast lap speeds achieved by the 917s certain of the GT cars had difficulty in qualifying under the rule that each driver of each car must lap within 140 per cent of the average of the three fastest lap times. So another three 911s failed to qualify, as did a GT Alpine.

The only serious accident in practice was when Wicky's Porsche 908 had its rear suspension collapse on the Mulsanne straight (it was travelling at around 180 mph at the time) and the car scraped along the tarmac for almost a kilometre before coming to rest. It was repaired in time to run in the race. A serious incident, however, occurred on the Thursday when Tuckett at the wheel of a 911 (one of those that failed to qualify) pulled across the front of Siffert at the curves before White House and in avoiding a collision 'Seppi' went into a wild spin, the 917 gyrating several times down the road at high speed. It scraped the Armco barrier, but the damage was negligible.

THE RACE

Because of the introduction of an Armco barrier along the outer edge of the pits road, the traditional Le Mans line-up of the cars in front of the pits had to be abandoned and instead the cars completed a paced lap behind a Porsche 911 and were released in a rolling start. Right at the start two of the Ferraris were in trouble. Craft's car was suffering from low fuel pressure and Gregory pulled into the pits before the fall of the flag with the old NART 512S. On this car the trouble was a fuel blockage, the car did not complete a single lap until the rest of the field had completed half an hour's racing and after more than three hours' abortive work and with a total of seven laps to its credit it was finally retired.

Rodriguez, Larrousse and Siffert with the three 917 *Lang* cars led away at the start and at the end of the first lap these cars were still in the first three places with Vaccarella (Ferrari) fourth, Donohue (Ferrari) fifth and Marko (917) sixth). With two laps gone Rodriguez led by five seconds and at the end of that lap Posey brought his Ferrari into the pits to complain about low oil pressure – but was immediately sent on his way again. After the first round of refuelling stops at about 4.45 pm, Rodriguez still led and slicker pit work by the Gulf team had put Siffert into second place ahead of Larrousse and Penske efficiency did the same thing for Donohue who now led Vaccarella. After one hour's racing the order behind these five cars was Parkes, Attwood, Marko, Kauhsen, de Fierlandt (already a lap in arrears) and then the Matra which led the 3-litre Prototype category. The first retirement came just after five o'clock when Pilette brought the VDS Lola in with piston failure. Soon afterwards Poirot hit the bank at Arnage and brought his Porsche 910 into the pits to retire with shattered suspension and bodywork.

During the second round of refuelling stops the Gulf drivers stayed strapped in their cars, but Elford replaced Larrousse. Rodriguez lost time because of a faulty fuel filler and rejoined the race in second place. Craft lost twenty minutes while the fuel pump was changed on Weir's Ferrari and Weigel brought the Usdau 908 in with gearbox trouble. The mechanics spent three hours repairing the 'box, but it was still defective and the car was retired. Pedro soon made up the time lost in the pits and took up station behind Siffert once more. During the third round of stops the Siffert/Bell car lost time while a loose condenser was repaired and at the end of the first three hours, the order was: 1st, Rodriguez/Oliver; 2nd, Larrousse/Elford; 3rd, Donohue/Hobbs; 4th, Siffert/Bell; 5th, Marko/van Lennep; 6th, Vaccarella/Juncadella. Not long after the three-hour mark the Edwards/Enever Lola retired out at Tertre Rouge with a detached flywheel. Both of the Filipinetti Ferraris were in trouble; Parkes made a short stop for the mechanical fuel pump-drive belt to be changed and the Manfredini/Gagliardi car was stationary for two and a half hours while the clutch was rebuilt. The Posey/Adamowicz Ferrari had run out of petrol twice, flattened its battery and the oil pressure was still low!

As darkness began to envelope the circuit the Rodriguez/Oliver Porsche was still led, but the Sunoco-Ferrari of Donohue and Hobbs had climbed through to second place. Unfortunately the blue Ferrari's fine run came to an end at 8.15 pm when Donohue came slowly into the pits to report that the engine had tightened up. For nearly half an hour the mechanics worked on the car, trying to locate the trouble, and the car was eventually pushed away into retirement with suspected transmission trouble. Now the Elford/Larrousse 917 was back in second place with Siffert/Bell third and Vaccarella/Juncadella fourth. While the Ferrari was stationary in the pits, the second-place Porsche lost its cooling fan, the engine over-heated and the car was pushed away into retirement. Another retirement came when the Loos/Pesch Ferrari broke a piston. The Zitro 917 lost over an hour in the pits while the gearbox was sorted out and just before 10 pm the Marko/van Lennep 917 lost ten minutes while the alternator belt was changed. So at 10 pm the Gulf 917s were in the first three places in the order, Rodriguez/Oliver, Siffert/Bell and Attwood/Müller and they were followed by Vaccarella/Juncadella, Kauhsen/Jöst, Beltoise/Amon and Marko/van Lennep.

Now Siffert came into the pits to complain about the handling of his second-place 917; the trouble was a broken damper and damaged suspension upright and after seventy minutes' work, the car rejoined the race in fourteenth place, twenty-eight laps in arrears. Similar troubles struck the Ligier which lost an hour and a half while broken rear suspension mountings on the gearbox were welded. The Manfredini/Gagliardi 512M which had rejoined the race after its clutch repairs had to stop again while the battery was changed and the transistor box replaced. As 1 pm approached Parkes lost the other Filipinetti Ferrari at White House and spun into the barrier. He arrived at the pits with all four wheels broken, the body shattered and a hole in the monocoque. Although the car rejoined the race after an hour and three quarters, it was soon back in the pits again for further repairs and it was eventually retired at a little after 3 am.

It was close to 3 pm when the Gulf domination disintegrated. Oliver brought the leading 917 in complaining about the handling and the trouble was found to be the same as on the Siffert/Bell car. The car eventually rejoined the race in fourth place. Now the Attwood/Müller 917 led, but on this, fifth gear, indispensable at Le Mans, failed and the mechanics started to strip the gearbox. The 'pig' 917 lost thirteen minutes in the pits while a broken throttle cable was replaced and not long after Jöst had rejoined the race, he went off the road at Arnage and damaged the car badly enough for retirement. So, after all these troubles, the order at 4 am was: 1st, Vaccarella/Juncadella; 2nd, Marko/van Lennep; 3rd, Rodriguez/Oliver; 4th, Beltoise/Amon; 5th, Attwood/Müller; 6th, Posey/Adamowicz.

At one minute past four the Spanish-entered Ferrari's unexpected lead came to an end when Vaccarella stopped at the pits to report about clutch slip. The clutch was adjusted and Juncadella took the car out – but only ten minutes later the clutch failed altogether and the Spaniard was forced to abandon the car out on the circuit. Now more trouble struck the Gulf team; an oil pipe burst on Rodriguez' 917 and flooded the cockpit with hot oil. Pedro managed to retain control and brought the car back to the pits where fresh oil was added. When the car was started up, the engine was very rough and another 917 joined the list of retirements.

By 7 am the Müller/Attwood 917 was back into second place ahead of the Matra which had now developed a mis-fire that the pit staff were unable to locate. The Siffert/Bell 917 had developed a crankcase oil leak, sealing the crankcase with compound had only a temporary effect and the car circulated ahead of large clouds of oil smoke until it was finally retired. The Zitro 917 stopped at the pits again with gearbox trouble and although it rejoined the race, it was retired at 11 am when the selectors failed yet again. Both the de Fierlandt/de Cadenet and Craft/Weir Ferraris had clutch trouble and were stationary in the pits, but the latter car eventually rejoined the race. At 9.40 am the Matra expired out at Mulsanne corner with failure of the fuel injection metering unit. On Wicky's 908, the gearbox jammed in fourth, it staggered away from the pits only to expire before it reached the circuit proper and the Ligier developed gearbox trouble which resulted in a three-and-a-half-hour pit stop and the loss of too much ground for it to be classified as a finisher.

As midday approached the Marko/van Lennep Porsche still led

comfortably from Attwood/Müller and these positions remained unchanged until the finish at 4 o'clock, although the Wyer car climbed back to two laps behind the winner. Despite the whole host of troubles that had afflicted it, the Posey/Adamowicz Ferrari was third ahead of the similar car of Craft/Weir and NART's 'Daytona' Ferrari took fifth place. The 1971 Le Mans was probably one of the least exciting since the inception of the race in 1923, but it was remarkable for a phenomenally high rate of clutch and gearbox failures for which there seemed to be no obvious explanation.

Results:

1st, H. Marko/G. van Lennep (Porsche 917 5-litre), 396 laps, 3315.36 miles (138.11 mph),*
2nd, R. Attwood/H. Müller (Porsche 917 5-litre), 394 laps,
3rd, S. Posey/A. Adamowicz (Ferrari 512M 5-litre), 365 laps,
4th, C. Craft/D. Weir (Ferrari 512M 5-litre), 354 laps,
5th, L. Chinetti, jnr./R. Grossmann (Ferrari 365 GTB 4.4-litre), 313 laps,
6th, R. Tourol/A. Anselme (Porsche 911S 2.4-litre), 305 laps,*
7th, W. Brun/P. Mattli (Porsche 907 2-litre), 305 laps,*
8th, R. Mazzia/J. Barth (Porsche 911S 2.4-litre), 302 laps,
9th, J. Mesange/'Gedehem' (Porsche 911S 2.2-litre), 297 laps,
10th, N. Koob/E. Kremer (Porsche 911S 2.2-litre), 291 laps,
11th, G. Verrier/G. Foucault (Porsche 911S 2.2-litre), 289 laps,
12th, P. Vestey/R. Bond (Porsche 911S 2.2-litre), 285 laps,
13th, B. Waldegard/B. Chenevière (Porsche 911S 2.4-litre), 262 laps
– G. Ligier/P. Depailler (Ligier JS3-Cosworth 3-litre), 269 laps, but spent more than three hours in pits and unclassified.

*Class winners.

Fastest lap: P. Rodriguez (Porsche 917 5-litre), 3 min 18.7 sec (151.81 mph – record).

Previous lap record: V. Elford, (Porsche 917 5-litre), 3 min 21.0 sec (149.68 mph – set in 1970 race)

1970 winners: R. Attwood/H. Herrmann (Porsche 917 4.5-litre), 119.29 mph.

Principal retirements: M. Gregory/G. Eaton (Ferrari), fuel pump blockage M. Donohue/D. Hobbs (Ferrari), suspected transmission trouble; G. Loos/F. Pesch (Ferrari), engine trouble; V. Elford/G. Larrousse (Porsche), engine trouble; M. Parkes/H. Pescarolo (Ferrari), accident damage; W. Kauhsen/R. Jöst (Porsche), accident; J. Juncadella/N. Vaccarella (Ferrari), clutch failure;

P. Rodriguez/J. Oliver (Porsche), engine trouble; C. Manfredini/G. Gagliardi (Ferrari), gearbox trouble; J. Siffert/D. Bell (Porsche), engine trouble; C. Amon/J-P. Beltoise (Matra), broken fuel injection metering unit; H. de Fierlant/A. de Cadenet (Ferrari), gearbox trouble; D. Martin/G. Pillon (Porsche), gearbox trouble.

ROUND TEN

AUSTRIAN 1,000 KILOMETRES RACE

Osterreichring (Circuit length: 3,673 miles) 27th June, 1971
Weather: dull and wet.

In 1969 and 1970 the Austrian 1,000 Km races had been amongst the most successful in the World Championship series and although neither race had attracted a large entry, it was more than made up for in quality and this pattern repeated itself in 1971 when entries were received from the Wyer, Martini, Ferrari and Autodelta teams.

THE ENTRY

Group 5 Sports Cars:

JW Automotive Engineering Ltd:

Porsche 917 5-litre cars driven by Jo Siffert/Derek Bell and Pedro Rodriguez/Dickie Attwood. Attwood had come into the team to replace Oliver who, faced with the choice of letting down John Wyer or his entrant at the Can-Am race the same weekend, had chosen to break his Gulf contract. As a result he had been dismissed from the team. Both of the 917s were the usual short-tail cars and a similar spare car had also been brought along. This was fitted with Girling front twin-disc brakes as tried on the Formula 1 Tyrrells, but the discs used on the Porsche were rather larger. The spare car was mainly driven in practice by Attwood and Bell. The Rodriguez/Attwood 917 was fitted with wide front rims which necessitated adding strips to widen the front wings. The Siffert/Bell car was tried in practice with the 'Monza' tail with tail-fins, but it was decided to use the standard tail in the race.

Martini Racing Team:

Porsche 917 5-litre driven by Helmut Marko/Gerard Larrousse. The Martini team cars had now been returned to the works and instead there appeared a works car with 'Monza' tail, painted in

Martini colours, and with a full complement of works mechanics. This was primarily because the car was fitted with an experimental transistorised brake anti-locking system. Although the team would not reveal details of this, it was clear that neither driver was very happy with the system, although it did allow them to brake much deeper into corners. Originally the team had asked the works to supply a second car, but this idea was abandoned when Elford asked to be released so that he could drive in the Can-Am race the same weekend.

Escuderia Montjuich:

Ferrari 512M 5-litre driven by José Juncadella/Alex Soler-Roig.

Scuderia Brescia Corse:

Ferrari 512M 5-litre driven by 'Pam' (Marsilio Pasotti)/Mario Casoni.

Herbert Müller Racing:

Ferrari 512M 5-litre driven by Herbert Müller/René Herzog and Ferrari 512S 5-litre driven by Heinrich Wiesendanger/Masten Gregory.

The Sports Car class was completed by a Porsche 910 with Spyder bodywork and a brace of ancient Porsche 906 Carreras.

Group 6 Prototypes:

S.p.a. Ferrari SEFAC:

Ferrari 312P 3-litre driven by Jackie Ickx/Clay Regazzoni. The car now had modified suspension to suit low profile Firestone tyres.

Autodelta:

Alfa Romeo Tipo 33/3 3-litre cars driven by Rolf Stommelen/'Nanni' Galli, Henri Pescarolo/Andrea de Adamich and Toine Hezemans/Nino Vaccarella. The team had also brought along the Tipo 33/TT/3 light-weight car, but there was still no serious intention of racing it.

Hubert Ascher:

Alfa Romeo Tipo 33/3 3-litre car driven by Claus Reisch/Carlo Facetti.

Apart from these five cars, the only other Prototype entered was the 1.8-litre Lola T212 driven by Guy Edwards/Roger Enever. As usual the GT category was all Porsche 911s and 914/6s, plus, on this occasion, a single Lotus Europa that was not likely to do well (in fact it failed to qualify as a starter).

PRACTICE

Autodelta visited the circuit early for an unofficial session on the Wednesday and so the cars were well sorted when practice proper started on the Friday. However, practice went sadly awry for the Milan team. On the Friday the engines of both the Pescarolo/de Adamich car and the lightweight car blew up and on the Saturday 'Nanni' Galli succeeded in rendering three cars temporarily *hors de combat.* He was lapping really quickly with the 33/TT/3 when he lost control and damaged the offside of the car, fortunately not too badly. Immediately he went out again in his normal team car, but when he tried to pass team-mate Vaccarella at the Jochen Rindt curve, the two cars collided, Vaccarella rammed the guard-rail damaging the front of his car and Galli spun off, wrecking the right-hand rear suspension. Although the team contemplated running the lightweight car (which was the easiest to repair), Autodelta succeeded in getting the carnage sorted out in time for the start. None of the Gulf drivers was particularly happy with the handling of their cars, but there was nothing obviously wrong with either. Just before practice finished on the Saturday the Müller 512S put a rod through the side of the engine and this became a non-starter.

Fastest in practice were:

1.	Rodriguez/Attwood (Porsche 917 5-litre)	1 min 39.49 sec
2.	Ickx/Regazzoni (Ferrari 312P 3-litre)	1 min 40.10 sec
3.	Marko/Larrousse (Porsche 917 5-litre)	1 min 41.61 sec
4.	Siffert/Bell (Porsche 917 5-litre)	1 min 42.22 sec
5.	Müller/Herzog (Ferrari 512M 5-litre)	1 min 42.55 sec
6.	Stommelen/Galli (Alfa Romeo Tipo 33/3 3-litre)	1 min 42.92 sec
7.	de Adamich/Pescarolo (Alfa Romeo Tipo 33/3 3-litre)	1 min 43.29 sec
8.	Hezemans/Vaccarella (Alfa Romeo Tipo 33/3 3-litre)	1 min 43.44 sec
9.	Juncadella/Soler-Roig (Ferrari 512M 5-litre)	1 min 44.33 sec
10.	Galli/Pescarolo (Alfa Romeo Tipo 33/TT/3 3-litre)*	1 min 44.78 sec
11.	Reisch/Facetti (Alfa Romeo Tipo 33/3 3-litre)	1 min 47.46 sec
12.	Wiesendanger/Gregory (Ferrari 512S 5-litre)*	1 min 47.52 sec

*Non-starters.

At the Osterreichring the cars form up on the grid and with only twenty-four of them lined up for the start, the track looked almost empty. Slight drizzle was falling and while Rodriguez roared away, Siffert muffed his start, almost burnt out the clutch and set off already trailing badly. With one lap gone the order was Rodriguez, Ickx, Müller, de Adamich, Marko, Hezemans and Siffert. While Rodriguez gradually pulled out a useful lead over the flat-12 Ferrari, Siffert was struggling to make up ground and by lap six he was in fifth place and the Alfas of de Adamich and Hezemans had been pushed back to sixth and seventh places. Stommelen was eighth and then came Pasotti, Reisch and Juncadella. On lap thirteen Juncadella pulled over to let Stommelen pass, but then was forced to brake heavily, the Spaniard lost control, hit the Armco and the Ferrari rolled over down the track and out of the race. Fortunately the driver suffered only slight injuries.

Marko took third place from Müller on lap fourteen and only three laps later the front suspension of Müller's well-driven Ferrari collapsed as he braked for a corner, the car swerved to the left and collided with a Porsche 911. Both cars were out of the race, but neither driver was hurt. Not long afterwards Reisch retired his private Alfa Tipo 33/3 with engine failure. By lap twenty-six Rodriguez had pulled out a lead of twenty-five seconds over Ickx' Ferrari and was motoring magnificently. Then, on lap thirty, just as the Gulf staff were preparing for Rodriguez to come into the pits to refuel, he shot in sooner than expected. The trouble was a drop-off in fuel pressure caused by a flat battery. The battery was changed, the fuel tanks filled and Rodriguez rejoined the race in seventh place and three laps behind the now-leading Ferrari. Marko stopped to refuel on lap thirty-four, Siffert on lap thirty-six and when the Sports Cars had completed their pit stops, Ickx led by forty-five seconds with Siffert eleven seconds behind Marko and the Alfas, in the next three places, shortly to be lapped.

It was at this point that the Gulf pit began to pull out all the stops in an effort to retrieve the race. For although Siffert retired shortly before the leading Ferrari made its first pit stop because the 917's clutch would not take the strain of the start from the pits and gave up altogether two laps later, Rodriguez had been speeded up and was lapping faster and faster. Marko took the lead from Regazzoni on lap fifty while the Swiss driver was getting accustomed to the handling of the Ferrari with full tanks, but then Clay began to close up again, and swept back into the lead on lap sixty-one. Rodriguez had reduced the lap record to 1 min 39.9 sec and now that heavy rain had begun to fall, he was catching the cars in front even quicker. By lap sixty he had recovered one of the lost laps and by lap eighty-five he was in third place ahead of the Alfas, about a lap and a half behind the Ferrari. Larrousse relieved Marko with the second-place 917, but the Frenchman did not seem at all happy and Regazzoni had soon extended his lead to a full lap. Regazzoni made the second stop with the Ferrari at the end of lap eighty-eight, all four wheels were changed – and so were Ferrari tactics; because of the threat of the Gulf 917 which was drawing nearer and nearer Ickx took over the 312P again to try and extend the team's lead. By the time the Ferrari was back in the race its lead over Larrousse's 917 had diminished to fourteen seconds, but, rather more important, Rodriguez was now on the same lap.

Just as Rodriguez' maximum spell of three and a half hours at the wheel came up, he pulled into the pits to hand over to Attwood. Dickie was allowed only twelve laps at the wheel, during which he gained about forty-five seconds on Larrousse, and then he was back in the pits again for Pedro to resume the battle. By the time this change-over had been completed the Ferrari's lead was over a lap. Pescarolo coasted into the pits to retire his Alfa with loss of oil pressure, but the other two Autodelta entries were still going strongly although tyre wear on all three cars had been heavier than expected. On lap 123 a tyre deflated on Larrousse's Porsche, the car spun and clouted its tail against the guard-rail; the Martini 917 made it back to the pits, and although the car rejoined the race, the suspension had been damaged and it was retired after only another lap.

The Ferrari made its final pit stop on lap 132 and Regazzoni went out for the final spell at the wheel. While the Maranello car was stationary, the Porsche got on to the same lap, but then Rodriguez made a fifteen-second stop for fuel. The 917 had only been going again for ten laps when Rodriguez whistled past the Ferrari to put himself back on the same lap and soon disappeared into the distance. Rodriguez had to make up a 100 seconds in twenty-five laps, he was catching Regazzoni at the rate of three seconds a lap and it looked as though the Ferrari would be in front at the finish. But still the 312P was plagued by atrocious luck and on lap 148 (twenty-two before the finish), Regazzoni lost control under braking and wrote the front of the car off against the Armco. Although Regazzoni said afterwards that the brakes had played up, it looked as though something in the suspension had broken.

Now Rodriguez was unchallenged leader and eased off to finish two laps ahead of the Alfas of Hezemans/Vaccarella and Stommelen/Galli which had performed with their usual fine reliability. This was the Gulf-Porsche team's fifth victory of the season and it was probably Rodriguez' finest drive at the wheel of a 917 since he started driving these cars in 1970.

Results:

1st, P. Rodriguez/R. Attwood (Porsche 917 5-litre), 170 laps, 5 hours 4 min 26.01 sec (123.07 mph),*
2nd, T. Hezemans/N. Vaccarella (Alfa Romeo Tipo 33/3 3-litre), 168 laps,*
3rd, R. Stommelen/N. Galli (Alfa Romeo Tipo 33/3 3-litre), 168 laps,
4th, M. Pasotti/M. Casoni (Ferrari 512M 5-litre), 159 laps,
5th, 'Pooky'/E. Bonomelli (Porsche 910 2-litre), 140 laps,
6th, C. Schickentanz/P. Kersten (Porsche 911S 2.4-litre), 139 laps,*
7th, C. Haldi/P. Keller (Porsche 911S 2.4-litre), 139 laps,
8th, A. Trummer/D. Sessitch (Porsche 906 2-litre), 139 laps,
9th, G. Stekkonig/D. Schmid (Porsche 914/6 2-litre), 136 laps,
10th, E. Kremer/R. Lins (Porsche 911S 2.4-litre), 133 laps,
11th, P. Greub/J.-C. Guerie (Porsche 911S 2.4-litre), 133 laps.
* Class winners.

Fastest lap: P. Rodriguez, 1 min 39.35 sec (132.90 mph – record).
Previous lap record: J. Ickx (Ferrari 512S 5-litre), 1 min 40.0 sec (132.34 mph – set in 1970 race).
1970 winners: J. Siffert/B. Redman (Porsche 917 5-litre), 121.49 mph.

Principal retirements: J. Juncadella/A. Soler-Roig (Ferrari), accident; H. Müller/R. Herzog (Ferrari), suspension failure/accident; J. Siffert/D. Bell (Porsche 917 5-litre), clutch failure; A. de Adamich/H. Pescarolo (Alfa Romeo), loss of oil pressure; H. Marko/G. Larrousse (Porsche 917 5-litre), accident; J. Ickx/C. Regazzoni (Ferrari), accident.

ROUND ELEVEN

WATKINS GLEN 6 HOURS RACE

Watkins Glen (Circuit length: 2.428 miles) 24th July, 1971
Weather: dry at start, rain later

Since the last race at the circuit in New York State, the organisers had completed the first stage of an extensive rebuild of Watkins Glen that was not to be completed until the United States Grand Prix when an additional .94-mile stretch of road was incorporated. By July the length of the circuit had been marginally increased to

Most likely challenger to Porsche at Le Mans was this Roger Penske-prepared Ferrari 512M driven by Mark Donohue and David Hobbs. Unfortunately it retired early in the race with transmission trouble. (Nigel Snowdon)

This Matra MS660 driven by Amon and Beltoise was in third place at Le Mans when mechanical trouble caused its retirement on the Sunday morning. (Nigel Snowdon)

Victory at Le Mans went to this Martini-entered Porsche 917 driven by Helmut Marko and Gijs van Lennep. (Nigel Snowdon)

2.428 miles from 2.35 miles, it had been increased to a uniform width of thirty-six feet throughout, it had been extensively resurfaced, the former Fast bend had been replaced by a chicane (a left-hand bend followed by a right-hand) and the final corner was much tighter and banked. In certain places it was felt that the Armco was too close to the edge of the circuit and there were criticisms of the lack of run-off space, but generally the circuit in its new form received the approval of the drivers. A good entry was received, but with the notable absence of the Martini team and Matra who had competed in only two races thus far during the season.

THE ENTRY

Group 5 Sports Cars:

J W Automotive Engineering Ltd:

Porsche 917 5-litre cars driven by Jo Siffert/Gijs van Lennep and Derek Bell/Dickie Attwood. Van Lennep had been brought into the team following the death of Pedro Rodriguez at the wheel of a Müller Ferrari in the Nuremberg 200 Interserie race. Both 917s were the normal short-tail cars.

David Piper:

Porsche 917 5-litre driven by Mario Cabral and Tony Adamowicz.

Roger Penske Racing:

Sunoco-Ferrari 512M 5-litre driven by Mark Donohue and David Hobbs.

North American Racing Team:

Ferrari 512M 5-litre driven by Sam Posey/Ronnie Bucknum.

Herbert Müller Racing:

Ferrari 512M driven by Herbert Müller and George Eaton.

Ecurie Evergreen:

Ferrari 512M 5-litre driven by Alain de Cadenet/Lothar Motschenbacher. This ex-Francorchamps car had a bulge in the roof to accommodate Motschenbacher's height.

Young American:

Ferrari 512M 5-litre driven by Gregg Young/Jim Adams.

Bahamas Racing Organisation:

Lola T70 Mk 3-Chevrolet 5-litre driven by Robin Ormes/R. Brown/R. Bondurant.

Group 6 Prototypes:

S.p.a. Ferrari SEFAC:

Ferrari 312P 3-litre driven by Jackie Ickx/Mario Andretti.

Autodelta:

Alfa Romeo Tipo 33/3 3-litre cars driven by Henri Pescarolo/Rolf Stommelen, 'Nanni' Galli/Vic Elford and Andrea de Adamich/Ronnie Peterson. The team had also brought along the Tipo 33/TT/3 lightweight which it was hoped to race for the first time and a 4-litre version of the V-8 engine intended for use in the Can-Am race the following day. Vic Elford had signed up to drive for Autodelta in 1972 and appeared at this race to familiarise himself with the Autodelta set-up.

Making up the rest of the field were the usual Porsche 911s, four Chevrolet Corvettes and a rather mixed bag of Lolas.

Practice:

On the Monday and Tuesday before the race there were unofficial practice sessions and most of the teams took advantage of these. Qualifying for the race took place on the Friday and Donohue took pole position with the Penske Ferrari in 1 min 7.74 sec (129.035 mph) and Siffert was eight-tenths of a second slower. During this session Galli had yet another prang when he collided the 'Tubolare Telaio' car with a Porsche 911. The lightweight Alfa was too badly damaged to run in the race and so the Autodelta team had to remove the 4-litre engine from one of the Tipo 33/3 cars and fit a 3-litre unit. During practice the Sunoco-Ferrari was timed on the straight at 184.6 mph, the 917s at around 175 mph and the 312P Ferrari at 165 mph.

Fastest in practice were:

1. Donohue/Hobbs (Ferrari 512M 5-litre)	1 min 7.74 sec
2. Siffert/van Lennep (Porsche 917 5-litre)	1 min 8.51 sec
3. Ickx/Andretti (Ferrari 312P 3-litre)	1 min 8.64 sec
4. Bell/Attwood (Porsche 917 5-litre)	1 min 8.97 sec
5. Posey/Bucknum (Ferrari 512M 5-litre)	1 min 9.10 sec
6. de Adamich/Peterson (Alfa Romeo Tipo 33/3 3-litre)	1 min 9.22 sec

7. Stommelen/Pescarolo (Alfa Romeo Tipo 33/3 3-litre)	1 min 9.80 sec
8. Elford/Galli (Alfa Romeo Tipo 33/TT/3 3-litre)*	1 min 11.00 sec
9. Müller/Eaton (Ferrari 512M 5-litre) .	1 min 11.51 sec
10. de Cadenet/Motschenbacher (Ferrari 512M 5-litre)	1 min 12.73 sec
11. Cabral/Adamowicz (Porsche 917 5-litre) .	1 min 15.38 sec
12. Young/Adams (Ferrari 512M 5-litre)* .	1 min 15.58 sec

* Non-starters.

THE RACE

The Young/Adams Ferrari developed a fuel leak on the morning of the race and became a non-starter and this with the elimination of some of the slower starters under the 130 per cent qualifying rule reduced the number of cars that formed up for the rolling start to a mere twenty-six. The slow Lola T70 joined the race late and retired after only a couple of laps because of a broken throttle cable.

After two paced laps, the field was released and Donohue took an immediate lead with the Penske Ferrari, heading Siffert, Bell, Ickx and Müller. While Donohue drew away in the lead, Ickx was harrying the two Gulf 917s and by the end of lap thirteen he was through into second place. It was on this lap that Siffert slowed off and two laps later he came into the pits to have a flat tyre changed. 'Seppi' rejoined the race in ninth place and almost a complete lap behind Donohue. An early retirement came when Müller collided with a Porsche 911 and, locked together, the two cars slid into the guard-rail and bounced off again. The Ferrari's fuel tanks were punctured and fuel streamed down the track.

On lap thirty-six Bell set fastest lap of the race in 1 min 8.297 sec (127.98 mph), but then the 917's throttle broke and the car came to rest out on the circuit. Bell got out of the car, lifted the engine cover and rummaged around, but then realised that there was still enough movement in the collapsed pedal assembly for him to be able to nurse the car back to the pits. At the pits the pedal was replaced, Attwood took over and rejoined the race with the car in nineteenth place. When Donohue stopped to refuel on lap fifty, he was only passed by Ickx while the Sunoco car was stationary in the pits and on lap fifty-two the blue 512M went back into the lead. But on the next lap the bolt connecting the steering tie rod to the left-hand front suspension collapsed. So the 512M was out of the race and the 312P was firmly in the lead.

Ickx brought the leading red Ferrari into the pits to refuel on lap fifty-six, but the engine refused to fire again because the starter motor had jammed at the beginning of the race and was now completely burnt out. For fifteen minutes the mechanics worked on the car and then it was pushed away into retirement. Now Peterson led the race for Autodelta, Siffert had nosed into second place ahead of Stommelen's Alfa and when the two Tipo 33/3s made their routine pit stops, the Gulf 917 led from Posey's Ferrari. Attwood climbed back to eleventh place with the second of the two Gulf 917s, only to suffer another puncture. Siffert continued to lead until lap 104 when he made his second routine pit stop, fuel was added and new tyres were fitted, but the mechanics had difficulty in removing the rear wheels and three minutes had been lost by the time the car rejoined the race with van Lennep at the wheel. The de Adamich/Peterson Alfa now led by two laps and third – and close behind the Porsche – was the Alfa of Elford/Galli. The Pescarolo/Stommelen Alfa collided with a Porsche 911 and was eliminated from the race.

Another car in trouble was the NART 512M of Posey/Bucknum which was withdrawn from the race with a broken starter motor and David Piper's Porsche 917 was delayed so long by a faulty alternator and a series of flat batteries that it fell too far behind to be classified as a finisher. Now increasingly heavy rain began to fall, the Gulf 917s and the Autodelta Alfas stopped to change to wet-weather tyres and it was in these conditions, with visibility almost non-existent that Elford ran into the back of a Lola T212 driven by Skip Barber. Both cars were out of the race, but neither driver was hurt. All hopes of the 917s getting back on level terms with the surviving Alfa had now disappeared, both cars were mis-firing badly because of wet ignition leads and the Bell/Attwood car developed a crankcase oil leak. At the chequered flag, after the winning Alfa had completed 279 laps of the short Watkins Glen course, the 917s were in second and third places, two and twenty laps behind the winner and with the de Cadenet/Motschenbacher Ferrari in fourth place. This was Alfa's third and last World Championship race victory of the season and the team's prospects in 1972 when there was a capacity limit of 3 litres for both Sports Cars and Prototypes could hardly be better.

Results:

1st, R. Peterson/A. de Adamich (Alfa Romeo Tipo 33/3 3-litre), 279 laps, 112.77 mph,*

2nd, J. Siffert/G. van Lennep (Porsche 917 5-litre), 277 laps,*

3rd, R. Attwood/D. Bell (Porsche 917 5-litre), 259 laps,

4th, A. de Cadenet/L. Motschenbacher (Ferrari 512M 5-litre), 253 laps,

5th, J. Greenwood/R. Johnson (Chevrolet Corvette 7-litre), 229 laps,*
6th, P. Gregg/H. Haywood (Porsche 916 2.0-litre), 228 laps,*
7th, D. Heinz/D. Yenko (Chevrolet Corvette 7-litre), 221 laps,
8th, W. Schumacher/R. McLure/R. Keifer (Chevrolet Corvette 7-litre), 210 laps,
9th, R. Everett/R. Beasely (Porsche 911T 2.2-litre), 168 laps,
10th, P. Keating/L. Pentecost/A. Togersen (Porsche 911S 2-litre), 162 laps.
*Class winners

Fastest lap: D. Bell, 1 min 8.30 sec (127.98 mph).
Existing race record: P. Rodriguez (Porsche 917 5-litre), 1 min 4.9 sec (127.58 mph – set in 1970 race over different circuit).
1970 winners: P. Rodriguez/L. Kinnunen (Porsche 917 5-litre), 117.81 mph.

Principal retirements: H. Müller/G. Eaton (Ferrari), accident; M. Donohue/D. Hobbs (Ferrari), steering failure; J. Ickx/M. Andretti (Ferrari), starter motor failure; R. Stommelen/H. Pescarolo (Alfa Romeo), accident; S. Posey/R. Bucknum (Ferrari), starter motor failure; N. Galli/V. Elford (Alfa Romeo), accident; A. Adamowicz/M. Cabral (Porsche), alternator failure.

8 Sports Car Manufacturers' Championship Results

Points are awarded on the basis of 9, 6, 4, 3, 2 and 1 point for the first six places. Only the highest placed car of each make is eligible for points. In the 1971 Championship the best eight results counted towards each make's total.

	Points
1st, Porsche	72
(85 points actually gained)	
2nd, Alfa Romeo	51
(54 points actually gained)	
3rd, Ferrari	26
4th, Lola	5
4th, Chevrolet	5

9 European 2-litre Constructors' Championship

The second year of this new and very successful Championship witnessed yet another battle between the rival British marques, Chevron and Lola, and with the works Fiat-Abarth team as a good also-ran. A strong team of two of the latest Lola T212 cars with Cosworth FVC 1.8-litre engines was fielded under the Scuderia Filipinetti banner by Joakim Bonnier for himself and Vic Elford. In addition Bonnier also looked after the two cars belonging to the German entrant Karl von Wendt. Von Wendt fielded one car regularly for Austrian driver Helmut Marko and a second car at some races for Gijs van Lennep and Jean-Pierre Jabouille. Karl von Wendt drove at the first of the season's races before retiring for business reasons.

Chevron fielded a works B19 Spyder (also with Cosworth engine) for Chris Craft, but this was largely out of luck and most of the make's successes were gained by private teams. The leading private teams were the Red Rose Racing Team fielding cars for Chevron director John Bridges and for John Hine (and Niki Lauda scored a victory for this team at Salzburg), the DART team (Dobie Auto Racing Team) who entered cars with Castrol sponsorship for ex-Lotus driver John Miles and Toine Hezemans, and the Canon Cameras team. This last team consisted of Dutchman Ed Swart and John Burton, who used to race under the banner of the Worcestershire Racing Association.

Although the Abarth team started the season as a full works organisation directly controlled by Carlo Abarth, by the Nürburgring race in September the company had been acquired by Fiat and the works team was taken over by Abarth agent Enzo Osella.

Results

Round 1 TROPHÉE PAUL RICARD 18th April, 1971

Paul Ricard Circuit, Castellet 140 laps (272 miles)

1st, H. Marko/J-P. Jabouille (Lola T212-Cosworth 1.8-litre), 3 hours 9 min 16.9 sec (speed not issued by the organisers),
2nd, V. Elford (Lola T212-Cosworth 1.8-litre), 3 hours 9 min 29.0 sec,
3rd, J. Miles/T. Hezemans (Chevron B19-Cosworth 1.8-litre), 3 hours 10 min 14.8 sec,
4th, E. Swart/T. Hezemans (Chevron B19-Cosworth 1.8-litre), 3 laps in arrears,
5th, K. von Wendt/J-P. Jabouille (Lola T212-Cosworth 1.8-litre), 4 laps in arrears,
6th, G. Birrell/J. Miles (Chevron B19-Cosworth 1.8-litre), 4 laps in arrears.

Fastest lap: J-P. Jabouille, 1 min 18.8 sec (92.65 mph).

Round 2 SALZBURGRING RACE 23rd May, 1971

Salzburgring, Austria

Aggregate of two 45-lap heats (237 miles)

1st, N. Lauda (Chevron B19-Cosworth 1.8-litre), 1 hour 54 min 40.4 sec (124.03 mph),
2nd, A. Merzario (Fiat-Abarth 2000SP 2-litre), 1 hour 54 min 41.8 sec,
3rd, J. Hine (Chevron B19-Cosworth 1.8-litre), 1 hour 54 min 54.1 sec,
4th, V. Elford (Lola T212-Cosworth 1.8-litre), 1 hour 55 min 0.3 sec,
5th, J. Burton (Chevron B19-Cosworth 1.8-litre), 1 hour 55 min 25.2 sec,
6th, G. van Lennep (Lola T212-Cosworth 1.8-litre), 1 hour 56 min 4.3 sec.

Fastest lap: N. Lauda, 1 min 14.5 sec (127.03 mph).

Round 3 MARTINI INTERNATIONAL TROPHY RACE 5th June, 1971

Silverstone, England

Aggregate of two 40-lap heats (234.7 miles)

1st, T. Hezemans (Chevron B19-Cosworth 1.8-litre), 1 hour 56 min 25.8 sec (120.67 mph),

2nd, R. Peterson (Lola T212-Cosworth 1.8-litre), 1 hour 56 min 42.8 sec,
3rd, J. Lepp (Chevron B19-Cosworth 1.8-litre), 1 lap in arrears,
4th, G. Edwards (Lola T212-Cosworth 1.8-litre), 1 lap in arrears,
5th, J. Bridges (Chevron B19-Cosworth 1.8-litre), 2 laps in arrears,
6th, P. Hanson (Taydec-Cosworth 1.8-litre), 4 laps in arrears.

Fastest lap: G. Larrousse (Lola) and C. Craft (Chevron), 1 min 25.2 sec (123.68 mph).

Round 4 HOCKENHEIM RACE 4th July, 1971

Hockenheim Motordrom, Germany

Aggregate of two 25-lap heats (211 miles)

1st, H. Marko (Lola T212-Cosworth 1.8-litre), 1 hour 48 min 6.7 sec (117.04 mph),
2nd, V. Elford (Lola T212-Cosworth 1.8-litre), 1 hour 48 min 38.0 sec,
3rd, A. Merzario (Fiat-Abarth 2000SP 2-litre), 1 hour 49 min 51.3 sec,
4th, J. Bonnier (Lola T212-Cosworth 1.8-litre), 1 lap in arrears,
5th, J. Lepp (Chevron B19-Cosworth 1.8-litre), 1 lap in arrears,
6th, T. Croker (Lola T210-Cosworth 1.8-litre), 2 laps in arrears.

Fastest lap: H. Marko, 2 min 7.0 sec (119.57 mph).

Round 5 BOLOGNA A.C. CUP RACE 25th July, 1971

Imola, Italy

Aggregate of two 28-lap heats (175 miles)

1st, H. Marko (Lola T212-Cosworth 1.8-litre), 1 hour 31 min 31.2 sec (114.47 mph),
2nd, J-P. Jabouille (Fiat-Abarth 2000SP 2-litre), 1 hour 32 min 4.9 sec,
3rd, M. Casoni (Lola T212-Cosworth 1.8-litre), 1 hour 33 min 21.0 sec,
4th, E. Swart (Chevron B19-Cosworth 1.8-litre), 1 lap in arrears,

5th, J. Burton (Chevron B19-Cosworth 1.8-litre), 1 lap in arrears,
6th, G. Moretti (Lola T212-Cosworth 1.8-litre), 2 laps in arrears.

Fastest lap: H. Marko, 1 min 36.1 sec (116.76 mph).

Round 6 NÜRBURGRING 500 5th September, 1971

Nürburgring, Germany 22 laps (311 miles)

1st, V. Elford (Lola T212-Cosworth 1.8-litre), 2 hour 57 min 13.8 sec (105.70 mph),
2nd, C. Craft (Chevron B19-Cosworth 1.8-litre), 3 hours 0 min 54.8 sec,
3rd, J. Burton/P. Gaydon (Chevron B19-Cosworth 1.8-litre), 3 hours 2 min 45.2 sec,
4th, J. Lepp (Chevron B19-Cosworth 1.8-litre), 3 hours 4 min 11.5 sec,
5th, J-P. Jabouille (Lola T212-Cosworth 1.8-litre), 3 hours 4 min 28.6 sec,
6th, J. Bamford (Chevron B19-Cosworth 1.8-litre), 1 lap in arrears.

Fastest lap: V. Elford, 7 min 52.5 sec (108.12 mph).

Round 7 TROPHY OF THE DUNES 26th September, 1971

Zandvoort, Holland

Aggregate of two 40-lap heats (208 miles)

1st, J. Hine (Chevron B19-Cosworth 1.8-litre), 1 hour 54 min 15.3 sec (speed not issued by the organisers),
2nd, E. Swart (Chevron B19-Cosworth 1 8-litre), 1 hour 54 min 53.9 sec,
3rd, J. Burton (Chevron B19-Cosworth 1.8-litre), 1 hour 55 min 10.7 sec,
4th, H. Marko (Lola T212-Cosworth 1.8-litre), 1 hour 55 min 33.6 sec,
5th, J. Bonnier (Lola T212-Cosworth 1.8-litre), 2 laps in arrears,
6th, P. Hanson (Lola T210-Cosworth 1.8-litre), 3 laps in arrears.

Fastest lap: J. Burton, 1 min 23.2 sec (112.73 mph).

Round 8 COPPA IGNAZIO GIUNTI 31st October, 1971

Vallelunga Circuit, Rome

Aggregate of two 40-lap heats (159 miles)

1st, A. Merzario (Fiat-Abarth 2000SP 2-litre), 1 hour 41 min 26.0 sec (94.08 mph),
2nd, H. Marko (Lola T212-Cosworth 1.8-litre), 1 hour 42 min 55.6 sec,
3rd, V. Elford (Lola T212-Cosworth 1.8-litre), 1 lap in arrears,*
4th, M. Casoni/J. Bonnier (Lola T212-Cosworth 1.8-litre), 2 laps in arrears,
5th, A. Zadra (Lola T212-Cosworth 1.8-litre), 6 laps in arrears,
6th, E. Bonomelli (Porsche 910 2-litre), 7 laps in arrears,
7th, G. Alberti (Chevron B19-Cosworth 1.8-litre), 8 laps in arrears.

* Disqualified for leaving pits while red light was showing.

Fastest lap: V. Elford, 1 min 14.6 sec (95.95 mph).

Round 9 JARAMA TWO HOURS RACE 7th November, 1971

1st, J. Bonnier (Lola T212-Cosworth 1.8-litre), 78 laps (83.51 mph),
2nd, J. Juncadella (Chevron B19-Cosworth 1.8-litre), 78 laps,
3rd, A. Zadra (Lola T212-Cosworth 1.8-litre), 72 laps,
4th, J. Bridges (Chevron B19-Cosworth 1.8-litre), 71 laps,
5th, H. Le Guellec (Dulon LD11-Porsche 2-litre), 68 laps,*
6th, A. Fletcher (Chevron B19-Cosworth 1.8-litre), 68 laps,*

* Running at the finish but not classified as 90 per cent of the race distance had not been covered.

Fastest lap: J. Bonnier, 1 min 23.4 sec (88.15 mph).

CHAMPIONSHIP RESULTS

	Points
1st, Lola	57
2nd, Chevron	46
3rd, Fiat-Abarth	25
4th, Porsche	2
5th, Taydec	1

10 Interserie Championship

This Championship, first introduced in 1970, is intended as a sort of European equivalent of the Can-Am series of races and to encourage interest in large capacity Sports Cars. The Championship is open to Group 5 Competition Sports Cars, Group 6 Prototypes and Group 7 two-seater Racing Cars without any capacity limit for the last of these categories. In the 1971 Championship the main contenders were the latest Porsche 917 5000 Can-Am Spyder cars – open, lighter conversions of the normal 917 coupé – and these were driven by Leo Kinnunen (entered by the Finnish AAW Racing Team), Jürgen Neuhaus and Michel Weber (entered with a 4.5-litre version by the Gesipa Racing Team). Other serious contenders were the McLaren M8E-Chevrolet Can-Am cars entered by Ecurie Evergreen for Chris Craft, and by Sid Taylor for Peter Gethin and Derek Bell, and McLaren M8C and M8E cars of the VDS team for Teddy Pilette. At the first round of the Championship at Imola Ferrari entered a very special, lightweight version of the Ferrari 512M for Arturo Merzario and it was strongly rumoured that this car was fitted with a 7-litre engine as a try-out for the Can-Am races. Helmut Kelleners ran a March 717 Can-Am car fitted with an 8.3-litre Chaparral-developed engine. Pedro Rodriguez appeared with the new BRM P167-Chevrolet car at Zolder, but failed to start because of engine trouble in practice, and the car re-appeared in the hands of Brian Redman (entered by Sid Taylor) in the sixth round at Imola and the final round at Hockenheim. Joakim Bonnier drove a Lola T222 Can-Am car with 7.6 and 8.1-litre Chevrolet engines. It was at the fourth round of the Championship at the Norisring that Pedro Rodriguez, at the wheel of a Ferrari 512M entered by Herbert Müller, so tragically crashed and lost his life.

Although the Interserie shows tremendous promise as an exciting series of races, it lacks starting or expense money, prize money is low, there is little sponsorship and the cars are among the most expensive to run (Porsche were charging £7,000 for a Spyder conversion and £10,000 for a full 4,999 cc engine developing something over 600 bhp). It is understood that the works Porsche team will be competing in the 1972 Championship and although this will give the series a much needed publicity boost, it will also push the less affluent private teams out of the picture.

Round 1 COPPA SHELL DI IMOLA (ITALY) 2nd May, 1971

60 laps (aggregate of two 30-lap heats – each of 151.8 km)

1st, A. Merzario (Ferrari 512M 5-litre), 1 hour 35 min 34.0 sec (117.45 mph),
2nd, C. Craft (McLaren M8E-Chevrolet 7.6-litre), 1 hour 36 min 10.1 sec,
3rd, L. Kinnunen (Porsche 917 Spyder 5-litre), 1 hour 36 min 10.6 sec,
4th, T. Zeccoli (Alfa Romeo Tipo 33/3 3-litre), 1 hour 37 min 54.6 sec,
5th, J. Juncadella (Ferrari 512M 5-litre), 59 laps,
6th, M. Weber (Porsche 917 Spyder 4.5-litre), 59 laps.

Fastest lap: C. Craft, 1 min 32.8 sec (120.96 mph – circuit record).
Fastest practice lap: A. Merzario, 1 min 33.42 sec.

Round 2 KENT 300 RACE, ZOLDER (BELGIUM) 6th June, 1971

72 laps (aggregate of two 36-lap heats – each of 83.6 miles)

1st, P. Gethin (McLaren M8E-Chevrolet 8.1-litre), 1 hour 43 min 23.5 sec (108.63 mph),
2nd, L. Kinnunen (Porsche 917 Spyder 5-litre), 1 hour 44 min 27.7 sec,
3rd, T. Hezemans (Alfa Romeo Tipo 33/3 3-litre), 71 laps,
4th, J. Neuhaus (Porsche 917 Spyder 5-litre), 70 laps,
5th, M. Weber (Porsche 917 Spyder 4.5-litre), 70 laps,
6th, R. Stommelen (Alfa Romeo Tipo 33/3 3-litre), 68 laps.

Fastest lap: P. Gethin, 1 min 24.2 sec (111.15 mph – circuit record).
Fastest practice lap: P. Gethin, 1 min 23.7 sec.

Round 3 SOLITUDENRENNEN, HOCKENHEIM (GERMANY) 4th July, 1971

30 laps (126.55 miles)

1st, D. Bell (McLaren M8E-Chevrolet 8.1-litre), 1 hour 1 min 44.6 sec (122.97 mph),

2nd, L. Kinnunen (Porsche 917 Spyder 5-litre), 1 hour 2 min 8.4 sec,
3rd, V. Elford (Lola T222-Chevrolet 7.6-litre), 1 hour 2 min 34.8 sec,
4th, M. Weber (Porsche 917 Spyder 5-litre), 1 hour 2 min 40.7 sec,
5th, J. Neuhaus (Porsche 917 Spyder 5-litre), 1 hour 2 min 41.4 sec,
6th, E. Kraus (Porsche 908 Spyder 3-litre), 28 laps.

Fastest lap: D. Bell, 2 min 1.6 sec (124.88 mph).
Fastest practice lap: D. Bell, 1 min 59.8 sec.

Round 4 NUREMBERG 200 RACE, NORISRING (GERMANY) 11th July, 1971

52 laps (aggregate of two heats – 204.88 km). NOTE: each heat should have been of 26 heats, but following Rodriguez' accident the first heat was stopped on lap 12, i.e. with eleven laps completed.

The second heat was extended to 41 laps, but the first fifteen laps counted as part of the first heat and the positions were taken at that stage, and calculated on aggregate with the remaining 26 laps.
1st, C. Craft (McLaren M8E-Chevrolet 7.6-litre), 1 hour 6 min 52.9 sec (114.21 mph),
2nd, P. Gethin (McLaren M8E-Chevrolet 8.1-litre), 1 hour 7 min 54.0 sec,
3rd, J. Bonnier (Lola T222-Chevrolet 7.6-litre), 1 hour 7 min 54.6 sec,
4th, G. Loos (McLaren M8E-Chevrolet 8.1-litre), 1 hour 8 min 17.5 sec,
5th, 'Pam' (Ferrari 512M 5-litre), 51 laps,
6th, F. Pesch (Ferrari 512M 5-litre), 51 laps.

Fastest lap: P. Gethin, 1 min 13.8 sec (119.43 mph–circuit record).
Fastest practice lap: C. Craft, 1 min 15.1 sec.

Round 5 KEIMOLA RACE, HELSINKI (FINLAND) 22nd August, 1971

70 laps (aggregate of two 35-lap heats – 231 km)

1st, L. Kinnunen (Porsche 917 Spyder 5-litre), 1 hour 26 min 7.19 sec,

2nd, P. Gethin (McLaren M8E-Chevrolet 8.1-litre), 1 hour 26 min 59.94 sec,
3rd, H. Kelleners (March 717-Chevrolet 8.3-litre), 1 hour 27 min 48.50 sec,
4th, M. Weber (Porsche 917 Spyder 5-litre), 69 laps,
5th, J. Neuhaus (Porsche 917 Spyder 5-litre), 69 laps,
6th, A. Nolte (Porsche 908 Spyder 3-litre), 64 laps.

Fastest lap: L. Kinnunen, 1 min 12.64 sec (101.90 mph – circuit record).
Fastest practice lap: L. Kinnunen, 1 min 12.78 sec.

Round 6 IMOLA 500 KILOMETRES RACE (ITALY) 12th September, 1971

40 laps (aggregate of two 30-lap heats – there were separate heats for cars under and over 3 litres – and 10-lap final – 351.98 km). NOTE: The final should also have been of 30 laps, but because of delays the race would have finished in the dark, so it was shortened to 10 laps.

1st, B. Redman (BRM P167-Chevrolet 7.6-litre), 1 hour 23 min 30.4 sec (89.61 mph),
2nd, C. Facetti (Alfa Romeo Tipo 33/3 3-litre), 39 laps,
3rd, A. Merzario (Abarth 2000 Prototype 2-litre), 39 laps,
4th, L. Kinnunen (Porsche 917 Spyder 5-litre), 39 laps,
5th, M. Casoni (Porsche 917 5-litre), 39 laps,
6th, M. Weber (Porsche 917 Spyder 5-litre), 39 laps.

Fastest lap: C. Regazzoni (Ferrari 312P 3-litre), 1 min 41.6 sec (110.48 mph).
Fastest practice lap: P. Gethin (McLaren M8E-Chevrolet 8.1-litre), 1 min 29.35 sec.

Round 7 HOCKENHEIM INTERSERIE RACE (GERMANY) 3rd October, 1971

40 laps (168.72 miles)

1st, B. Redman (BRM P167-Chevrolet 8.1-litre), 1 hour 21 min 0.4 sec (124.96 mph),
2nd, M. Weber (Porsche 917 Spyder 5-litre), 1 hour 23 min 2.0 sec,
3rd, L. Kinnunen (Porsche 917 Spyder 5-litre), 39 laps,

4th, J. Neuhaus (Porsche 917 Spyder 5-litre), 39 laps,
5th, G. Loos (McLaren M8E-Chevrolet 7.6-litre), 38 laps,
6th, F. Pesch (Ferrari 512M 5-litre), 38 laps.

Fastest lap: B. Redman, 1 min 59.3 sec (204.85 kph).
Fastest practice lap: B. Redman, 1 min 58.4 sec.

INTERSERIE CHAMPIONSHIP

1st, L. Kinnunen, 81,000 Swiss Francs
2nd, P. Gethin, 59,600 Swiss Francs
3rd, M. Weber, 48,800 Swiss Francs
4th, B. Redman, 43,000 Swiss Francs
5th, C. Craft 40,000 Swiss Francs
6th, J. Neuhaus, 38,600 Swiss Francs

The front row of the grid at the Formula 2 race at Mallory Park in March. Nearest the camera is Ronnie Peterson (March 712M), no. 31 is Pescarolo with a similar car and the third car is Gerry Birrell's Lotus 69. Peterson crashed when the steering on the March failed. (Nigel Snowdon)

Seen at Thruxton on Easter Monday is Tim Schenken's Brabham BT36 entered by Rondel Racing. He finished fifth. (Nigel Snowdon)

McLaren once again dominated the 1971 Can-Am races with the latest M8F cars. Denis Hulme is seen in the Mosport race which he won. (Pete Lyons, *Autosport*)

Strongest challenger to McLaren supremacy was the Lola T260 driven by Jackie Stewart and sponsored by L & M cigarettes. The car was fast on smooth tracks and achieved a fair measure of success. (Pete Lyons, *Autosport*)

11 Non-Championship Sports Car Races

With a total of three different European Championship series, plus the Springbok series at the end of the year (not reported in this book), there was precious little time left in the racing calendar for other long-distance Sports Car races, but two of those held, the Paris 1000 Kilometres race and the Kyalami Nine Hours race, were events of long standing and attracted entries from a number of leading teams. For 2-litre cars the Kyalami race was also the first round in the Springbok series.

3 HEURES DU MANS — 18th April, 1971

Le Mans

This race was held on the Sunday afternoon of the Le Mans and apart from a brace of private Ferrari 512M cars, the only really fast car entered was the works Porsche 917 'pig' with very stubby bodywork. This car appeared under the banner of the Martini Racing Team and was driven by Kauhsen/van Lennep. It led the race until eliminated by electrical trouble, Juncadella retired his Ferrari with a damaged gearbox and the lead was then taken by the Ferrari of George Loos/Franz Pesch which ran out of fuel in the closing minutes of the race.

Results:

1st, G. Chasseuil/C. Ballot-Lena (Porsche 908/2 Spyder), 46 laps (383.64 miles), 128.67 mph,
2nd, G. Ligier (Ligier JS3-Cosworth 3-litre), 45 laps,
3rd, B. Barnes (Porsche 906 2-litre), 41 laps,
4th, P. Mauroy/J. Lagniez (Porsche 911S 2.4-litre), 40 laps,
5th, J-C. Aubriet (Chevrolet Corvette 7-litre), 40 laps,
6th, J. Cochet/J. Selz (Porsche 911S 2-litre), 39 laps.

Fastest lap: not issued by the organisers.

VILA REAL GRAND PRIX 4th July, 1971

Vila Real (Portugal)

International races have been held on the Vila Real circuit since 1931 and in recent years this event held over a true road circuit at this very pleasant town situated in the mountains between Porto and the Spanish border has attracted a strong overseas entry. Perhaps because the race had been reduced in length from seventy-three laps (500 km) to thirty-five laps (242 km) the foreign entry was rather smaller in 1971. However, David Piper entered his Porsche 917 for Portuguese driver Mario Cabral, René Herzog drove one of the Herbert Müller Racing Ferrari 512Ms, three works-assisted Abarth cars were there (including a brand-new 3-litre V-8 model for Spanish driver Bonjoch) and there were several small capacity British cars. Cabral and Herzog battled for the lead until lap eighteen when the Porsche driver stopped at the pits to complain of low oil pressure – he rejoined the race in third place. Herzog now led and he stayed in front until lap twenty-eight when a rear tyre deflated and the Ferrari spun into a barrier.

Results:

1st, J. de Bagration (Porsche 908 Spyder 3-litre), 1 hour 28 min 33.54 sec (102.04 mph),
2nd, M. Cabral (Porsche 917 4.5-litre), 1 hour 29 min 18.57 sec,
3rd, J. Bamford (Chevron B19-Cosworth 1.8-litre), 34 laps,
4th, C. Santos (Porsche 906 2-litre), 33 laps,
5th, E. Negus (Martin BM7-Cosworth 1.6-litre), 32 laps,
6th, R. Knight (Chevron B8-BMW 2-litre), 32 laps.

Fastest lap: M. Cabral, 2 min 27.42 sec (105.08 mph – circuit record).

TROPHÉE D'AUVERGNE 20th June, 1971

Clermont-Ferrand (France)

This race was originally intended to be a round in the 2-litre Sports Car Championship, but this was cancelled and the race was opened to larger capacity cars. Heading the entry list was the works Matra MS660 that had run at Le Mans, now driven by Gerard Larrousse, and the other main contenders were Helmut Marko at the wheel of a Lola T212 entered by Karl von Wendt Racing, Vic Elford and Jo Bonnier with Scuderia Filipinetti T212s, the Canon Racing Team Chevron B19s of Ed Swart and John Burton and the similar Red Rose Racing cars driven by John Bridges and John Hine. Larrousse made a perfect start at the fall of the flag and led comfortably until lap eleven when he stopped at the pits with a punctured tyre. Larrousse rejoined the race in fourth place and the remaining laps were Lola-dominated. The race was held over a distance of thirty-eight laps (300 km).

Results:

1st, H. Marko (Lola T212-Cosworth 1.8-litre), 2 hours 3 min 58.7 sec (92.05 mph),
2nd, J. Bonnier (Lola T212-Cosworth 1.8-litre), 2 hours 5 min 19.1 sec,
3rd, G. Larrousse (Matra MS660 3-litre), 2 hours 5 min 54.60 sec,
4th, C. Swietlik (Lola T210-Cosworth 1.8-litre), 37 laps,
5th, G. Edwards (Lola T212-Cosworth 1.8-litre), 37 laps,
6th, T. Croker (Lola T210-Cosworth 1.8-litre), 37 laps.

Fastest lap: G. Larrousse, 3 min 10.8 sec (94.44 mph).

BARCELONA 1000 KM RACE 12th October, 1971 (264 laps)

Montjuich Park (Spain)

Heading the entry list at this tortuous and testing circuit was the sole remaining Gulf-Porsche 917 (all the other cars had been returned to the factory) and this was driven by Derek Bell/Gijs van Lennep. Clearly the Gulf drivers would have preferred to be at the wheel of one of the 908/3 cars and it was all the more galling that the first of these to pass into private hands (allegedly for a price of £20,000) and still painted in Gulf colours was being rather indifferently driven by the brothers Fernandez, José and Juan. The most serious opponent to the 917 was the Scuderia Filipinetti Lola T212 of Jo Bonnier and Ronnie Peterson and there were two other Lolas and several Chevrons entered. The Gulf car gradually came through to take the lead from the Chevron-Abarth of Hezemans and Soler-Roig. The Chevron was eliminated after catching fire twice, the Bonnier/Peterson Lola moved up to second place and took the lead and victory when the 917 was delayed by brake trouble.

Results:

1st, J. Bonnier/R. Peterson (Lola T212-Cosworth 1.8-litre), 7 hours 23 min 23.5 sec (84.01 mph),
2nd, D. Bell/G. van Lennep (Porsche 917 5-litre), 259 laps,

3rd, J. Juncadella/J. Hine (Chevron B19-Cosworth 1.8-litre), 249 laps,
4th, J. de Bagration/J. Pla (Porsche 908 Spyder 3-litre), 242 laps,
5th, J. Fernandez/J. Fernandez (Porsche 908/3 3-litre), 240 laps,
6th, P. Hanson/R. Howlings (Lola T210-Cosworth 1.6-litre), 236 laps.

Fastest lap: R. Peterson, 1 min 31.1 sec (93.08 mph).

PARIS 1000 KM RACE 17th October, 1971
(128 laps)

Montlhéry (France)

The John Wyer team travelled straight on from Barcelona to Paris to compete at Montlhéry with the same car and the same pair of drivers. The Montlhéry course was much more suited to the speed and handling characteristics of the 917, but the team faced strong opposition. Two of the Porsche 917 Spyders that had competed in the Interserie races were entered for Leo Kinnunen/Gerard Larrousse and Michel Weber/Helmut Marko and a trio of Ferrari 512Ms were fielded. From Matra came the familiar MS660, making only its fourth outing of the season, in the hands of Beltoise/Amon. Originally two of the new Alfa Romeo Tipo 33/TT/3 cars were entered, but only one appeared and this non-started after Pescarolo had crashed on the warming-up lap. The Matra led until just before the second round of refuelling stops when Marko took the lead with his 917 Spyder, but the Matra went back in front when this Porsche retired with a broken con-rod. As the race progressed, rain, which had been falling at the start, soaked the circuit once more and Beltoise, plagued by gearbox trouble, lost control of the Matra and crashed. The Gulf 917 now had an unassailable lead and finished five laps ahead of the second-place Spyder of Larrousse and Kinnunen.

Results:
1st, D. Bell/G. van Lennep (Porsche 917 5-litre), 6 hours 14 min 22.8 sec (100.15 mph),
2nd, G. Larrousse/L. Kinnunen (Porsche 917 Spyder 5-litre), 123 laps,
3rd, J-C. Andruet/C. Ballot-Lena (Ferrari 365 GTB 4 Daytona 4.4-litre), 112 laps,

4th, C. Swietlik/G. Salles (Lola T210-Cosworth 1.8-litre), 110 laps,
5th, E. Kremer/G. Huber (Porsche 911S 2.2-litre), 109 laps,
6th, P. Mauroy/B. Waldegaard (Porsche 911S 2.2-litre), 109 laps.

Fastest lap: H. Marko (Porsche 917 Spyder 5-litre), 1 min 30.3 sec (116.93 mph – circuit record).

KYALAMI NINE HOURS RACE 6th November, 1971

Kyalami (South Africa)

In 1970 Ferrari had won the South African race with the then new 512M 5-litre and the following year the Maranello team returned in force with both the original 312P car driven by Brian Redman/Clay Regazzoni and a brand new car with a more compact body, low profile wheels and lower weight for Jackie Ickx/Mario Andretti. Facing these two fleet Prototypes was a strong entry that included two Porsche 917s entered by David Piper for Richard Attwood/Dave Charlton and Mario Casoni/Tony Adamowicz and a whole host of Chevrons and Lolas in the 2-litre class. Regazzoni went straight into the lead at the start of the race, but Andretti's car cut out and he lost a lot of ground before he managed to get going again. During the second hour Regazzoni lost time in the pits having the bodywork patched after a collision with the 917 driven by Adamowicz and Andretti's car expired out on the course, losing forty-five minutes before it rejoined the race. The Regazzoni/Redman car, despite being penalised two laps because five mechanics had worked on the car, soon pulled back into the lead and as the race progressed the second works Ferrari gradually worked its way back to second place. Both of the Piper-entered Porsche 917s ran into trouble and the Adamowicz/Casoni car lost second place because of a misfiring engine caused by a flat battery.

Results:
1st, C. Regazzoni/B. Redman (Ferrari 312P 3-litre), 355 laps (905.30 miles), 100.58 mph,
2nd, J. Ickx/M. Andretti (Ferrari 312P 3-litre), 340 laps,
3rd, H. Ganley/P. Driver/M. Hailwood (Chevron B19-Cosworth 1.8-litre), 336 laps,
4th, T. Adamowicz/M. Cabral (Porsche 917 5-litre), 333 laps,
5th, H. Marko/J. Love (Lola T212-Cosworth 1.8-litre), 324 laps,
6th, J. Hine/P. de Klerk (Chevron B19-Cosworth 1.8-litre), 323 laps.

Fastest lap: M. Andretti, 1 min 20.1 sec.

Part Three
Racing Round the World

12 The Formula 2 Year

The end of the 1971 season marked the end of five successful seasons of 1,600 cc Formula 2 racing (there is a 2,000 cc capacity limit from 1972 onwards). Throughout these five years the most consistently successful marque was Brabham, while both Matra and Tecno enjoyed runs of success and the dominant make in 1971 was the March. During the year the Bicester concern reached a total production of twenty-one of their simple, but effective cars with monocoque chassis using the engine as a semi-stressed member and with suspension similar to that of the 1970 701 Grand Prix car. Like almost every other contender since the Formula started, March used the Cosworth FVA unit developing around 240 bhp at 9,500 rpm. After a patch of unreliability early in the season, the March team ironed out all the faults on their 712 model and works driver Ronnie Peterson enjoyed a run of success that brought him victories at Rouen, Mantorp Park, Tulln-Langenlebarn and Vallelunga and in the Formula 2 Championship. In addition to fielding the Smog (Vick in Sweden)-sponsored car for Peterson, March ran a number of other sponsored cars for drivers who had succeeded in raising their own finance.

Second in the Championship was Argentinian Carlos Reutemann (who drives as number two in the Formula 1 Brabham team in 1972) and he appeared at the wheel of a Brabham BT30/2 and subsequently a new BT36 fielded by the ACA/YPF team. It was estimated that this team had approximately £100,000 at its disposal to cover the cost of the season's racing. About half of this money was provided by the Automovil Club Argentina and the rest came from a number of sources that included the state-owned YPF petrol concern. The BT36 was another sound, conventional Brabham design, based on a multi-tubular space-frame, with inboard rear brakes and a larger chassis that would enable it to comply with 1972 regulations. As with the March, the power unit was the Cosworth FVA and transmission was by a Hewland FT200 gearbox. The second driver in the ACA/YPF team was Carlos Ruesch. Another successful entrant of Brabhams was the Rondel Racing team whose immaculate BT36 cars were driven by Tim Schenken (who performed well, but was consistently out of luck), Graham Hill and Bob Wollek. Peter Westbury's private FIRST team continued to field a Brabham, but little success came his way.

Although it had been hoped that there would be a new model from Lotus, this was not proceeded with and teams were forced to rely on the 69 car that had appeared for 1970. This model with a monocoque centre-section and square tubular sections fore and aft was slightly modified for 1971 and these changes appeared to have affected the handling adversely. The Fittipaldi brothers, Emerson and Wilson, drove a brace of these cars under the Team Bardahl banner, but Wilson was far from happy with his and switched to a March. Another Lotus user was the LIRA team whose cars were driven by Reine Wisell and Francois Migault, but the team had financial difficulties, there were problems about obtaining parts for the 69s and then a series of legal actions finally disrupted the team.

Following Regazzoni's success in 1970, the Italian Tecno team persevered with what was basically a 1968 model. This simple, short-wheelbase, space-frame car retained the split-radiator wide-nose that had been introduced in mid-1970, but was now fitted with inboard rear brakes. These cars were powered by the team's own Tecno-BDA engine which was more powerful, but less reliable than its Cosworth rival. These cars, with Elf backing, were driven by Francois Cevert and Jean-Pierre Jabouille. The 1970 Tecnos were sold off to the Ceramiche-Iris team, but this team's standards of preparation were poor indeed and although these cars showed a considerable turn of speed in the hands of 'Nanni' Galli, Claudio Francisci and others, they were hopelessly unreliable and achieved no success.

Frank Williams fielded a total of three private March 712 cars with Motul sponsorship, but this proved too much for the team to cope with and although Pescarolo won at Mallory Park, very little other success came the team's way. Another and very interesting March was the BMW-powered car entered for Dieter Quester by Eifelland Caravans. In their last season of racing in 1970 before retiring, the BMWs had displayed a tremendous turn of speed, the March-BMW went very well on the faster circuits and Quester finished third overall in the Championship. The French Pygmée team produced a much improved car (but suffered from inadequate preparation) which went well with Beltoise at the wheel, Chevron started the season well and then faded out and the new Lola T240 fielded by Joakim Bonnier for Austrian driver Helmut Marko failed to impress.

1971 was one of the best seasons since the Formula's inception with plenty of races, a plethora of competitors and some very close racing. That March and Brabham came out on top was not unexpected.

Formula 2 Regulations (1966–71): maximum capacity of 1,600 cc unsupercharged, engines not to have more than six cylinders and must be derived from a series production car of which not less than 500 units have been built; minimum weight of 420 kg.

EUROPEAN FORMULA 2 CHAMPIONSHIP

Note: Graded drivers not eligible for points are marked with an asterisk.

Round 1 JIM CLARK TROPHY (HOCKENHEIM) 4th April, 1971

Aggregate of two 20-lap heats (84.4 miles each)

1st, F. Cevert (Tecno 71-Pederzani), 1 hour 27 min 9.8 sec (117.53 mph),
2nd, G. Hill (Brabham BT36-Cosworth), 1 hour 27 min 14.7 sec,*
3rd, C. Reutemann (Brabham BT30-Cosworth), 1 hour 27 min 21.5 sec,
4th, W. Fittipaldi (Lotus 69-Cosworth), 1 hour 27 min 31.7 sec,*
5th, T. Schenken (Brabham BT36-Cosworth), 1 hour 27 min 34.8 sec,
6th, G. Birrell (Lotus 69-Cosworth), 1 hour 28 min 36.1 sec.*

Fastest lap: R. Peterson (March 712M-Cosworth), 2 min 4.40 sec (122.10 mph – record).
Previous Formula 2 record: D. Quester (BMW 70), 2 min 8.7 sec (117.99 mph).

Round 2 JOCHEN RINDT MEMORIAL TROPHY (THRUXTON) 12th April, 1971

Two 28-lap heats and Final of 50 laps (117.8 miles)

1st, G. Hill (Brabham BT36-Cosworth), 1 hour 2 min 36.2 sec (113.1 mph),*
2nd, R. Peterson (March 712M-Cosworth), 1 hour 2 min 36.8 sec,
3rd, D. Bell (March 712M-Cosworth), 1 hour 2 min 56.0 sec,
4th, F. Cevert (Tecno 71-Pederanzi), 1 hour 3 min 15.6 sec,
5th, T. Schenken (Brabham BT36-Cosworth), 1 hour 3 min 16.0 sec,
6th, W. Fittipaldi (Lotus 69-Cosworth), 1 hour 3 min 37.6 sec.

Fastest lap: R. Peterson, 1 min 13.4 sec (115.55 mph – record).
Previous lap record: J. Rindt (Lotus 69-Cosworth), 1 min 14.0 sec (114.62 mph).

Round 3 EIFELRENNEN (NÜRBURGRING) 2nd May, 1971

10 laps (142.62 miles)

1st, F. Cevert (Tecno 71-Pederzani), 1 hour 20 min 19.2 sec (106.00 mph),
2nd, E. Fittipaldi (Lotus 69-Cosworth), 1 hour 20 min 37.0 sec,*
3rd, C. Reutemann (Brabham BT30-Cosworth), 1 hour 20 min 42.1 sec,
4th, P. Westbury (Brabham BT36-Cosworth), 1 hour 20 min 48.2 sec,
5th, G. Hill (Brabham BT36-Cosworth), 1 hour 20 min 48.4 sec,*
6th, N. Lauda (March 712M-Cosworth), 1 hour 20 min 48.4 sec.

Fastest lap: R. Peterson (March 712M-Cosworth), 7 min 57.1 sec (107.06 mph – record).
Previous Formula 2 Record: J. Stewart (Matra MS7-Cosworth), 8 min 5.3 sec (105.26 mph).

Round 4 MADRID GRAND PRIX (JARAMA) 16th May, 1971

60 laps (126.9 miles)

1st, E. Fittipaldi (Lotus 69-Cosworth), 1 hour 29 min 42.9 sec (84.88 mph),*
2nd, D. Quester (March 712M-Cosworth), 1 hour 29 min 57.7 sec,
3rd, C. Reutemann (Brabham BT30-Cosworth), 1 hour 30 min 12.3 sec
4th, J. Cannon (March 712M-Cosworth), 1 hour 30 min 17.0 sec,
5th, J-P. Jaussaud (March 712M-Cosworth), 1 hour 30 min 37.4 sec,
6th, W. Fittipaldi (Lotus 69-Cosworth), 1 hour 30 min 42.9 sec.

Fastest lap: T. Schenken (Brabham BT36-Cosworth), 1 min 28.2 sec (86.34 mph – equals record).
Formula 2 Record: J-P. Beltoise (Matra MS7-Cosworth).

Round 5 HILTON TRANSPORT TROPHY (CRYSTAL PALACE) 31st May, 1971

Two 45-lap heats and Final of 50 laps (69.5 miles)

1st, E. Fittipaldi (Lotus 69-Cosworth), 42 min 3.0 sec (99.17 mph),*
2nd, T. Schenken (Brabham BT36-Cosworth), 42 min 7.4 sec,
3rd, R. Peterson (March 712M-Cosworth), 42 min 8.2 sec,
4th, J-P. Jaussaud (March 712M-Cosworth), 42 min 8.8 sec,
5th, C. Reutemann (Brabham BT30-Cosworth), 1 lap in arrears,
6th, G. Birrell (Lotus 69-Cosworth), 1 lap in arrears.

Fastest lap: First four drivers equalled record held by J. Stewart (Brabham BT30-Cosworth), 49.6 sec (100.89 mph)

Round 6 ROUEN GRAND PRIX 27th June, 1971
(ROUEN)

Two 16-lap heats and Final of 25 laps (101.62 miles)

1st, R. Peterson (March 712M-Cosworth), 55 min 36.3 sec (109.66 mph),
2nd, D. Quester (March 712M-BMW), 55 min 42.0 sec,
3rd, G. Hill (Brabham BT36-Cosworth), 55 min 43.6 sec,*
4th, N. Lauda (March 712M-Cosworth), 56 min 1.1 sec,
5th, F. Migault (Lotus 69-Cosworth), 56 min 41.8 sec,
6th, T. Schenken (Brabham BT36-Cosworth), 3 laps in arrears – did not finish.

Fastest lap: F. Cevert (Tecno 71-Pederanzi), 2 min 11 sec (111.71 mph).
Formula 2 record: T. Schenken (Brabham BT30-Cosworth), 2 min 0.8 sec (121.14 mph).

Round 7 MANTORP PARK GRAND PRIX 8th August, 1971
(MANTORP PARK)

Aggregate of two 36-lap heats (85.4 miles each)

1st, R. Peterson (March 712M-Cosworth), 1 hour 46 min 8.2 sec,
2nd, T. Schenken (Brabham BT36-Cosworth), 1 hour 46 min 43.7 sec,
3rd, C. Reutemann (Brabham BT36-Cosworth), 1 hour 46 min 50.1 sec,
4th, W. Fittipaldi (March 712M-Cosworth), 1 hour 47 min 25.2 sec,
5th, J. Watson (Brabham BT30/36-Cosworth), 1 hour 47 min 50.6 sec,
6th, G. Birrell (Lotus 69-Cosworth), 1 hour 47 min 57.7 sec.

Fastest lap: R. Peterson (1 min 27.1 sec (106.00 mph).
Formula 2 record: C. Regazzoni (Tecno 70/2-Cosworth), 1 min 26.4 sec.

Round 8 FLUGPLATZRENNEN 12th September, 1971
(TULLN-LANGENLEBARN)

Aggregate of two 35-lap heats (62.2 miles each)

1st, R. Peterson (March 712M-Cosworth), 1 hour 24 min 32.26 sec (88.36 mph),
2nd, T. Schenken (Brabham BT36-Cosworth), 1 hour 24 min 59.91 sec,
3rd, D. Quester (March 712M-BMW), 1 hour 25 min 12.94 sec,
4th, W. Fittipaldi (March 712M-Cosworth), 1 hour 25 min 44.29 sec,
5th, J. Watson (Brabham BT30/36-Cosworth), 1 lap in arrears,
6th, R. Wollek (Brabham BT36-Cosworth), 1 lap in arrears,

Fastest lap: T. Schenken, 1 min 10.79 sec (90.27 mph).
Formula 2 record: F. Cevert (Tecno 70-Cosworth), 1 min 1.6 sec (103.84 mph).

Round 9 ALBI GRAND PRIX 26th September, 1971
(ALBI)

63 laps (142.3 miles)

1st, E. Fittipaldi (Lotus 69-Cosworth), 1 hour 16 min 49.1 sec (111.37 mph),*
2nd, C. Reutemann (Brabham BT36-Cosworth), 1 hour 17 min 49.6 sec,
3rd, J-P. Jarier (March 712M-Cosworth), 1 hour 17 min 59.5 sec,
4th, F. Migault (March 712M-Cosworth), 1 lap in arrears,
5th, G. Hill (Brabham BT36-Cosworth), 2 laps in arrears,*
6th, R. Peterson (March 712M-Cosworth), 2 laps in arrears.

Fastest lap: C. Reutemann, 1 min 11.7 sec (113.44 mph – record).
Previous Formula 2 record: J. Rindt (Brabham BT23C-Cosworth), 1 min 12.8 sec (111.73 mph).

Round 10 ROME GRAND PRIX 10th October, 1971
(VALLELUNGA)

Aggregate of two 35-lap heats (68 miles each)

1st, R. Peterson (March 712M-Cosworth), 1 hour 25 min 57.2 sec (97.15 mph),
2nd, D. Quester (March 712M-BMW), 1 hour 26 min 7.0 sec,
3rd, C. Reutemann (Brabham BT36-Cosworth), 1 hour 26 min 38.9 sec,
4th, M. Beuttler (March 712M-Cosworth), 1 hour 26 min 51.2 sec,

5th, G. Birrell (Lotus 69-Cosworth), 1 hour 27 min 7.7 sec,
6th, J. Watson (Brabham BT30/36-Cosworth), 1 hour 27 min 10.0 sec.

Fastest lap: E. Fittipaldi, 1 min 12.8 sec (98.23 mph – record).
Previous Formula 2 record: J. Servoz-Gavin (Matra MS7-Cosworth), 1 min 15.7 sec (92.19 mph).

Round 11 MADUNINA GRAND PRIX (VALLELUNGA) 17th October, 1971

65 laps (124.8 miles)

1st, M. Beuttler (March 712M-Cosworth), 1 hour 19 min 49.1 sec (97.06 mph),
2nd, D. Quester (March 712M-BMW), 1 hour 20 min 0.1 sec,
3rd, J-P. Jarier (March 712M-Cosworth), 1 hour 20 min 45.4 sec,
4th, C. Ruesch (Brabham BT36-Cosworth), 1 hour 20 min 59.6 sec,
5th, V. Brambilla (March 712M-Cosworth), 1 hour 21 min 1.0 sec,
6th, S. Moser (Brabham BT36-Cosworth), 1 lap in arrears.

Fastest lap: D. Quester and M. Beuttler, 1 min 12.5 sec (98.74 mph – record).
Previous Formula 2 record: E. Fittipaldi (Lotus 69-Cosworth), 1 min 12.8 sec (98.23 mph).

EUROPEAN FORMULA 2 CHAMPIONSHIP

Points are awarded to the first six non-graded drivers as follows: first, 9 points; second, 6; third, 4; fourth, 3; fifth, 2; sixth, 1. Points are only awarded to drivers who have covered at least nine-tenths of the number of laps completed by the highest placed non-graded driver.

	Points
1st, R. Peterson	54
2nd, C. Reutemann	40
3rd, D. Quester	31
4th, T. Schenken	27
5th, F. Cevert	22
6th, W. Fittipaldi	16

OTHER FORMULA 2 RACES

COLOMBIAN GRAND PRIX (ROUND 1)

Bogota 7th February, 1971

Aggregate of two 30-lap heats (73.2 miles each)

1st, J. Siffert (Chevron B18-Cosworth), 1 hour 34 min 22.7 sec (92.95 mph),
2nd, G. Hill (Lotus 69-Cosworth), 1 hour 36 min 42.7 sec,
3rd, P. Westbury (Brabham BT30-Cosworth), 1 lap in arrears,
4th, A. Walker (Brabham BT30-Cosworth), 1 lap in arrears,
5th, R. Stommelen (Brabham BT30-Cosworth), 1 lap in arrears,
6th, X. Perrot (Chevron B18-Cosworth), 2 laps in arrears.

Fastest lap: J. Siffert, 1 min 27.6 sec (100.23 mph – record).
No previous record for this circuit.

COLOMBIAN GRAND PRIX (ROUND 2)

Bogota 14th February, 1971

Aggregate of two 30-lap heats (73.2 miles each)

1st, A. Rollinson (Brabham BT30-Cosworth), 1 hour 28 min 05.2 sec (99.67 mph),
2nd, R. Stommelen (Brabham BT30-Cosworth), 1 hour 28 min 13.2 sec,
3rd, D. Bell (March 712M-Cosworth), 1 hour 28 min 14.6 sec,
4th, P. Westbury (Brabham BT30-Cosworth), 1 hour 29 min 9.9 sec
5th, E. Corti (Lotus 69-Cosworth), 1 lap in arrears,
6th, J. Siffert (Chevron B18-Cosworth), 2 laps in arrears.

Fastest lap: J. Siffert, 1 min 25.4 sec (102.81 mph)
Previous Formula 2 record: J. Siffert, 4 min 27.6 sec (100.23 mph).

SPEED INTERNATIONAL

Mallory Park 14th March, 1971

Aggregate of two 40-lap heats (54 miles each)

1st, H. Pescarolo (March 712M-Cosworth), 59 min 57.2 sec (108.08 mph),
2nd, G. Birrell (Lotus 69-Cosworth), 1 hour 0 min 36.0 sec,
3rd, B. Hart (Brabham BT30-Cosworth), 1 lap in arrears,
4th, P. Westbury (Brabham BT30-Cosworth), 2 laps in arrears,
5th, Tetsu Ikuzawa (Lotus 69-Cosworth), 2 laps in arrears,
6th, J. Richardson (Brabham BT30-Cosworth), 2 laps in arrears.

Fastest lap: R. Peterson (March 712M-Cosworth) and H. Pescarolo, 43.2 sec (112.5 mph – record).

PAU GRAND PRIX

Pau — 25th April, 1971

70 laps (120 miles)

1st, R. Wisell (Lotus 69-Cosworth), 1 hour 33 min 23.7 sec (77.12 mph),
2nd, J-P. Jabouille (Tecno 71-Pederzani), 1 hour 33 min 40.4 sec,
3rd, J-P. Jaussaud (March 712M-Cosworth), 1 hour 33 min 54.3 sec,
4th, F. Mazet (Chevron B18-Cosworth), 1 hour 34 min 25.9 sec,
5th, J.-P. Jarier (March 712M-Cosworth), 1 lap in arrears,
6th, P. Depailler (Tecno 71-Cosworth), 1 lap in arrears.

Fastest lap: F. Cevert (Tecno 71-Cosworth), 1 min 18.2 sec (78.95 mph – record).
Previous Formula 2 record: J. Rindt (Lotus 59B-Cosworth), 1 min 18.9 sec (78.24 mph).

MADUNINA GRAND PRIX

Vallelunga — 13th June, 1971

Aggregate of two 35-lap heats (68 miles each)

1st, F. Cevert (Tecno 71-Pederzani), 1 hour 27 min 24.6 sec, (95.42 mph),
2nd, W. Fittipaldi (March 712M-Cosworth), 1 hour 27 min 30.6 sec,
3rd, C. Pace (March 712M-Cosworth), 1 hour 27 min 38.2 sec,
4th, J. Cannon (March 712M-Cosworth), 1 hour 28 min 11.2 sec,
5th, G. Francisci (Tecno-Cosworth), 1 hour 28 min 42.1 sec,
6th, C. Reutemann (Brabham BT30-Cosworth), 1 hour 28 min 47.4 sec.

Fastest lap: F. Cevert, 1 min 13.7 sec (97.13 mph – record).
Previous Formula 2 record: J. Servoz-Gavin (Matra MS7-Cosworth), 1 min 15.7 sec (92.19 mph).

LOTTERY GRAND PRIX

Monza — 20th June, 1971

Aggregate of two 20-lap heats (71.5 miles each)

1st, D. Quester (March 712M-BMW), 1 hour 3 min 15.7 sec (135.55 mph),
2nd, D. Bell (March 712M-Cosworth), 1 hour 3 min 16.52 sec,
3rd, P. Westbury (Brabham BT36-Cosworth), 1 hour 3 min 16.7 sec,
4th, J. Cannon (March 712M-Cosworth), 1 hour 3 min 17.34 sec,
5th, J-P. Jaussaud (March 712M-Cosworth), 1 hour 3 min 18.0 sec,
6th, X. Perrot (March 712M-Cosworth), 1 hour 3 min 18.1 sec.

Fastest lap: B. Hart (Brabham BT30-Cosworth), 1 min 33.0 sec (138.30 mph – record).
Precious Formula 2 record: R. Widdows (Brabham BT23C-Cosworth), 1 min 33.1 sec (138.16 mph).

IMOLA GRAND PRIX

Imola 25th July, 1971

Aggregate of two 28-lap heats (87.2 miles each)

1st, C. Pace (March 712M-Cosworth), 1 hour 30 min 57.6 sec (115.04 mph),
2nd, G. Salvati (March 712M-Cosworth), 1 hour 33 min 22.8 sec,
3rd, X. Perrot (March 712M-Cosworth), 1 hour 33 min 34.3 sec,
4th, W. Fittipaldi (March 712M-Cosworth), 2 laps in arrears,
5th, A. Potocki (Lotus 69-Cosworth), 4 laps in arrears,
6th, D. Quester (March 712M-BMW), 11 laps in arrears.

Fastest lap: F. Cevert (Tecno 71-Cosworth), 1 min 36.0 sec (116.93 mph).
Formula 2 record: J. Ickx (BMW 70), 1 min 35.5 sec (117.51 mph).

SWEDISH GOLD CUP

Kinekulle 22nd August, 1971

Aggregate of two 24-lap heats (31.3 miles each)

1st, R. Peterson (March 712M-Cosworth), 41 min 5.5 sec,
2nd, C. Reutemann (Brabham BT36-Cosworth), 41 min 29.0 sec,
3rd, T. Schenken (Brabham BT36-Cosworth), 41 min 36.0 sec,
4th, R. Wisell (Lotus 69-Cosworth), 41 min 48.0 sec,
5th, G. Birrell (Lotus 69-Cosworth), 41 min 55.4 sec,
6th, N. Lauda (March 712M-Cosworth), 42 min 11.7 sec.

Fastest lap: R. Peterson, 50.2 sec (94.47 mph – record).
No previous Formula 2 record for this circuit.

ROTHMANS INTERNATIONAL TROPHY

Brands Hatch 30th August, 1971

40 laps (106 miles)

1st, R. Peterson (March 712M-Cosworth), 58 min 41.6 sec (108.35 mph),
2nd, G. Hill (Brabham BT36-Cosworth), 58 min 56.4 sec,
3rd, C. Reutemann (Brabham BT36-Cosworth), 58 min 56.8 sec,
4th, P. Westbury (Brabham BT36-Cosworth), 59 min 1.2 sec,

5th, G. Birrell (Lotus 69-Cosworth), 59 min 2.4 sec,
6th, R. Wisell (Lotus 69-Cosworth), 59 min 5.4 sec.

Fastest lap: P. Westbury, 1 min 27.0 sec (109.66 mph – record).

HOCKENHEIM RACE

Hockenheim — 3rd October, 1971

36 laps (152 miles)

1st, C. Reutemann (Brabham BT36-Cosworth), 1 hour 15 min 24.9 sec (117.44 mph),
2nd, D. Quester (March 712M-BMW), 1 hour 15 min 35.0 sec,
3rd, W. Fittipaldi (March 712M-Cosworth), 1 hour 15 min 35.4 sec,
4th, S. Moser (Brabham BT36-Cosworth), 1 hour 16 min 41.3 sec,
5th, J. Watson (Brabham BT30/36-Cosworth), 1 hour 17 min 19.6 sec,
6th, B. Hart (Brabham BT30-Cosworth), 1 lap in arrears.

Fastest lap: C. Reutemann, 2 min 6.9 sec (119.66 mph).
Formula 2 record: R. Peterson (March 712M-Cosworth), 2 min 4.40 sec (122.10 mph).

TORNEIO SERIES (ROUND 1)

Interlagos (Brazil) — 31st October, 1971

Aggregate of two 14-lap heats (70 miles each)

1st, E. Fittipaldi (Lotus 69-Cosworth), 1 hour 17 min 0.52 sec (108.10 mph),
2nd, R. Peterson (March 712M-Cosworth), 1 hour 17 min 0.81 sec,
3rd, W. Fittipaldi (March 712M-Cosworth), 1 hour 18 min 2.22 sec,
4th, C. Reutemann (Brabham BT36-Cosworth), 1 hour 18 min 5.1 sec,
5th, G. Salvati (March 712M-Cosworth), 1 hour 18 min 25.49 sec,
6th, G. Hill (Brabham BT36-Cosworth), 1 hour 18 min 26.29 sec.

Fastest lap: R. Peterson and E. Fittipaldi, 2 min 43.2 sec (109.11 mph – record).
No previous Formula 2 record for this circuit.

TORNEIO SERIES (ROUND 2)

Interlagos — 7th November, 1971

Aggregate of two 14-lap heats (70 miles each)

1st, E. Fittipaldi (Lotus 69-Cosworth), 1 hour 18 min 26.4 sec (105.93 mph),

2nd, C. Reutemann (Brabham BT36-Cosworth), 1 hour 18 min 36.4 sec,
3rd, W. Fittipaldi (March 712M-Cosworth), 1 hour 18 min 41.3 sec,
4th, M. Beuttler (March 712M-Cosworth), 1 hour 19 min 43.0 sec,
5th, G. Hill (Brabham BT36-Cosworth), 1 hour 19 min 45.6 sec,
6th, C. Ruesch (Brabham BT36-Cosworth), 1 hour 19 min 47.0 sec.

Fastest lap: R. Peterson, 2 min 43.0 sec (109.24 mph – record).
Previous Formula 2 record: R. Peterson (March 712M-Cosworth) and E. Fittipaldi (Lotus 69-Cosworth), 2 min 43.2 sec (109.11 mph).

TORNEIO SERIES (ROUND 3)

Porto Alegre (Brazil) 4th November 1971

Aggregate of two 30-lap heats (56 miles each)

1st, C. Reutemann (Brabham BT36-Cosworth), 1 hour 3 min 42.44 sec (108.24 mph),
2nd, E. Fittipaldi (Lotus 69-Cosworth), 1 hour 3 min 45.39 sec,
3rd, C. Pace (March 712M-Cosworth), 1 hour 4 min 50.56 sec,
4th, W. Fittipaldi (March 712M-Cosworth), 1 hour 4 min 59.13 sec,
5th, P. Westbury (Brabham BT36-Cosworth), 1 hour 5 min 18.24 sec,
6th, G. Hill (Brabham BT36-Cosworth), 1 hour 5 min 19.82 sec.

Fastest lap: not issued by the organisers.
No existing Formula 2 record for this circuit.

TORNEIO SERIES (ROUND 4)

Córdoba (Argentina) 21st November, 1971

Aggregate of two 35-lap heats (67.4 miles each)

1st, T. Schenken (Brabham BT36-Cosworth), 1 hour 5 min 24.28 sec (123.73 mph),
2nd, C. Reutemann (Brabham BT36-Cosworth), 1 hour 5 min 44.54 sec,
3rd, C. Ruesch (Brabham BT36-Cosworth), 1 hour 6 min 39.38 sec,
4th, P. Westbury (Brabham BT36-Cosworth), 1 lap in arrears,
5th, L. Bueno (March 712M-Cosworth), 2 laps in arrears,
6th, S. Dini (Tecno 70-Cosworth), 2 laps in arrears.

Fastest lap: T. Schenken, 54.98 sec (126.16 mph – record).
Previous Formula 2 record: P. Courage (Brabham BT23C-Cosworth), 56.90 sec (121.91 mph).

13 The Canadian-American Challenge Cup

For the first time the series was given official recognition in 1971 by the Federation Internationale de l'Automobile. Since 1967 the series has been dominated by the superbly prepared McLarens and this pattern of domination persisted once more in 1971 despite a strong challenge from the Lola T260 driven by Jackie Stewart. This year's works McLaren model was the M8F powered by an 8.1-litre version of the push-rod Chevrolet V-8 engine developed by Gary Knutson to push out 740 bhp. This engine features special alloy blocks developed by McLaren's sponsor, the Reynolds Aluminium Corporation. The M8F had much in common with the very successful 1970 M8D car, but the monocoque had been strengthened, the wheelbase was three inches longer and aerodynamic 'fences' ran the full length of the body on each side to increase stability. Denis Hulme, as usual, drove for the team, but he was now partnered by Peter Revson who had handled the works Lola in the 1970 series. To private purchasers McLaren offered the M8E which had been tested during the 1970 season. The works cars were distinguished, as in 1970, by the bodywork sweeping up into prominent tail-fins bridged by an aerofoil. The production version had a normally mounted aerofoil.

The works Lola T260, entered by Carl Haas and sponsored by L & M Cigarettes, was a much improved monocoque car with very aerodynamic body of the same general style as that used on the Chevron B19 and Porsche 908/3 – and pioneered on the Irving-designed Sunbeam used in the 'twenties by Sir Henry Segrave for attacks on the Land Speed Record. Full monocoque construction in light alloys was used with the fuel bags contained in the sides of the monocoque. The power unit was the ubiquitous Chevrolet, in 8.1-litre form and developed by George Foults to produce 650 bhp. The car had a wheelbase of 8 ft 2 in., front and track of 4 ft 10 in. and an overall length of 11 ft 7 in. Although the car first appeared with a normal rear-mounted aerofoil, during the course of the

Can-Am series a number of changes were made and a front aerofoil projecting well beyond the nose was adopted. The Lola had the speed to match the McLarens and went particularly well on smooth tracks, but it failed to prove the success that Stewart had hoped and in 1972 he will be driving a works McLaren in the Can-Am series.

Two other cars, both of which appeared at Watkins Glen, are worthy of special mention. From Porsche came the 917-10 Spyder with a full 5-litre engine developing some 620 bhp and bodywork that looked rather like a 'blown-up' version of the 908/3. This project was instigated by Jo Siffert and largely financed by the STP Corporation. Despite not competing until the fourth round, without scoring an outright victory and although he lost his life at Brands Hatch before the final round in the series, Siffert was posthumous fourth in the Championship. It is the car that will form the basis of Porsche's Can-Am racing efforts in 1972. The other car to appear at Watkins Glen was the Tipo 712P Ferrari driven by Mario Andretti. This featured a 7-litre V-12 engine in a much modified Tipo 512 Competition Sports Car chassis and neat bodywork of a pronounced wedge shape.

Can-Am rules

The series of races is held for Group 7 two-seater racing cars as defined by the Federation Internationale de l'Automobile. There is no maximum engine capacity limit, but there is a minimum capacity limit of 2,500 cc. Gas-turbine engines are completely banned. Bodywork restrictions can be summarised as follows: there may be no aerodynamic device above the wheel centre-line that is connected to the suspension; no forward-facing gap located in the air-stream may have a roof higher than 80 cm above the bottom of the chassis (this rule affects air scoops and aerofoils); the cockpit opening must be symmetrical and about a centre-line and the windscreen projection must be the same for both driver and passenger positions; the passenger seat must not be faired in; the body sides must not extend more than four inches beyond the outermost sides of the tyres; and behind the rear tyres the bodywork must extend down to the wheel centre-line. All major body components must be maintained in their normal position and, at the discretion of the clerk of the course, a car running minus part of the body, for example after an accident, may be disqualified. All cars must be fitted with a built-in starter system with its own power supply.

The Points System

Points in the Championship are awarded on the basis of 20, 15, 12, 10, 8, 6, 4, 3, 2 and 1 from first to tenth place. Towards his total a driver counts only his best four placings from the first five and the second five races of the series respectively. No points are awarded if drivers share a car in a race, although the entrant still receives his prize money.

CANADIAN-AMERICAN CHALLENGE CUP

Round 1 LABATT'S BLUE TROPHY RACE 13th June, 1971

Mosport Park 80 laps (197 miles)

1st, D. Hulme (McLaren M8F-Chevrolet 8.1-litre), 1 hour 48 min 15.2 sec (109.03 mph),
2nd, P. Revson (McLaren M8F-Chevrolet 8.1-litre), 1 hour 48 min 16.1 sec,
3rd, L. Motschenbacher (McLaren M8D-Chevrolet 8.1-litre), 1 lap in arrears,
4th, R. Bondurant (McLaren M8E-Chevrolet 8.1-litre), 1 lap in arrears,
5th, J. Cordts McLaren M8C-Chevrolet 8.1-litre), 2 laps in arrears,
6th, R. Brown (McLaren M6B-Chevrolet 8.1-litre), 2 laps in arrears.

Fastest lap: D. Hulme, 1 min 18.8 sec.

Round 2 LABATT TROPHY RACE 27th June, 1971

Le Circuit, Mont Tremblant 75 laps (198.75 miles)

1st, J. Stewart (Lola T260-Chevrolet 8.1-litre), 1 hour 59 min 29.1 sec (100.95 mph),
2nd, D. Hulme (McLaren M8F-Chevrolet 8.1-litre), 2 hours 0 min 35.9 sec,
3rd, P. Revson (McLaren M8F-Chevrolet 8.1-litre), 1 lap in arrears,
4th, C. Parsons (McLaren M8D-Chevrolet 7-litre), 2 laps in arrears,
5th, L. Motschenbacher (McLaren M8D-Chevrolet 8.1-litre), 2 laps in arrears,
6th, H. Kazato (Lola T222-Chevrolet 8-litre), 4 laps in arrears.

Fastest lap: D. Hulme, 1 min 33.6 sec.

Round 3 ROAD ATLANTA CAN-AM RACE 11th July, 1971

Hall County, Georgia 75 laps (189 miles)

1st, P. Revson (McLaren M8F-Chevrolet 8.1-litre), 1 hour 42 min 9.0 sec (111.17 mph),
2nd, D. Hulme (McLaren M8F-Chevrolet 8.1-litre), 1 hour 42 min 26.0 sec,

3rd, L. Motschenbacher (McLaren M8D-Chevrolet 8.1-litre), 1 lap in arrears,
4th, T. Adamowicz (McLaren M8B-Chevrolet 8-litre), 3 laps in arrears,
5th, M. Minter (Porsche 917 4.5-litre), 4 laps in arrears,
6th, D. Durant (Lola T163-Chevrolet 8-litre), 7 laps in arrears.

Fastest lap: J. Stewart (Lola T260-Chevrolet 8-litre), 1 min 17.42 sec.

Round 4 WATKINS GLEN CAN-AM RACE 25th July, 1971

Watkins Glen, New York State 82 laps (199.096 miles)

1st, P. Revson (McLaren M8F-Chevrolet 8.35-litre), 1 hour 32 min 54.14 sec (128.58 mph),
2nd, D. Hulme (McLaren M8F-Chevrolet 8.1-litre), 1 hour 33 min 1.15 sec,
3rd, J. Siffert (Porsche 917-10 5-litre), 2 laps in arrears,
4th, M. Andretti (Ferrari 712P 7-litre), 2 laps in arrears,
5th, T. Adamowicz (McLaren M8B-Chevrolet 8-litre), 3 laps in arrears,
6th, S. Posey (Ferrari 512M 5-litre), 3 laps in arrears.

Fastest lap: D. Hulme, 1 min 6.08 sec (132.76 mph).

Round 5 MID-OHIO CAN-AM RACE 22nd August 1971

Lexington, Ohio 80 laps (192 miles)

1st, J. Stewart (Lola T260-Chevrolet 8.1-litre), 2 hours 0 min 16.76 sec (95.78 mph),
2nd, J. Siffert (Porsche 917-10 5-litre), 2 laps in arrears,
3rd, T. Adamowicz (McLaren M8B-Chevrolet 8-litre), 3 laps in arrears,
4th, H. Müller (Ferrari 512M 5-litre), 4 laps in arrears,
5th, C. Parsons (Lola T163-Chevrolet 8-litre), 5 laps in arrears,
6th, M. Minter (Porsche 917 4.5-litre), 5 laps in arrears.

Fastest lap: P. Revson (McLaren M8F-Chevrolet 7.9-litre), 1 min 28.0 sec (98.18 mph).

Round 6 ROAD AMERICA CAN-AM RACE 29th August, 1971

Elkhart Lake, Wisconsin 50 laps (200 miles)

1st, P. Revson (McLaren M8F-Chevrolet 8.35-litre), 1 hour 50 min 4.75 sec (109.01 mph),

2nd, J. Siffert (Porsche 917-10 5-litre), 1 lap in arrears,
3rd, V. Elford (McLaren M8E-Chevrolet 8-litre), 1 lap in arrears,
4th, L. Motschenbacher (McLaren M8D-Chevrolet 8-litre), 1 lap in arrears,
5th, H. Kazato (Lola T222-Chevrolet 8-litre), 3 laps in arrears,
6th, D. Causey (Lola T222-Chevrolet 8-litre), 3 laps in arrears.

Fastest lap: D. Hulme (McLaren-Chevrolet 8.35-litre), 2 min 8.14 sec (112.38 mph).

Round 7 MINNESOTA CAN-AM RACE 12th September, 1971

Donnybrooke Speedway, Brainerd 70 laps (210 miles)

1st, P. Revson (McLaren M8F-Chevrolet 8.1-litre), 1 hour 45 min 45.64 sec (119.14 mph),
2nd, D. Hulme (McLaren M8F-Chevrolet 8.1-litre), 1 hour 46 min 33.02 sec,
3rd, G. Young (McLaren M8E-Chevrolet 8.1-litre), 1 lap in arrears,
4th, V. Elford (McLaren M8E-Chevrolet 8.1-litre), 1 lap in arrears,
5th, J. Siffert (Porsche 917-10 5-litre), 1 lap in arrears,
6th, J. Stewart (Lola T260-Chevrolet 8.1-litre), 2 laps in arrears.

Fastest lap: D. Hulme, 1 min 27.86 sec (122.92 mph).

Round 8 KLONDIKE 200 RACE 26th September, 1971
Edmonton 80 laps (201 miles)

1st, D. Hulme (McLaren M8F-Chevrolet 8.1-litre), 2 hours 7 min 47.1 sec (94.92 mph),
2nd, J. Stewart (Lola T260-Chevrolet 8.1-litre), 2 hours 8 min 47.5 sec,
3rd, J. Oliver (Shadow Mk 2-Chevrolet 8-litre), 2 laps in arrears,
4th, J. Siffert (Porsche 917-10 5-litre), 2 laps in arrears,
5th, M. Minter (Porsche 917 4.5-litre), 3 laps in arrears,
6th, J. Cordts (McLaren M8C-Chevrolet 8.1-litre), 6 laps in arrears.

Fastest lap: D. Hulme, 1 min 26.3 sec.

Round 9 MONTEREY-CASTROL GRAND PRIX 17th October, 1971

Laguna Seca, California 90 laps (171 miles)

1st, P. Revson (McLaren M8F-Chevrolet 8.1-litre), 1 hour 33 min 56.86 sec (109.21 mph),

2nd, J .Stewart (Lola T260-Chevrolet 8.1-litre), 1 hour 34 min 6.59 sec,
3rd, D. Hulme (McLaren M8F-Chevrolet 8.1-litre), 1 hour 34 min 30.85 sec,
4th, B. Redman (BRM P167-Chevrolet 8.1-litre), 1 lap in arrears,
5th, J. Siffert (Porsche 917-10 5-litre), 2 laps in arrears,
6th, L. Motschenbacher (McLaren M8D-Chevrolet 8-litre), 3 laps in arrears,

Fastest lap: P. Revson, 1 min 0.66 sec (112.76 mph).

Round 10	LOS ANGELES TIMES GRAND PRIX	31st October, 1971

Riverside Raceway, California — 61 laps (201 miles)

1st, D. Hulme (McLaren M8F-Chevrolet 8.3-litre), 1 hour 37 min 36.0 sec (123.73 mph),
2nd, P. Revson (McLaren M8F-Chevrolet 8.3-litre), 1 hour 38 min 22.62 sec,
3rd, H. Ganley (BRM P167-Chevrolet 8.1-litre), 1 lap in arrears,
4th, S. Posey (McLaren M8E-Chevrolet 8-litre), 1 lap in arrears,
5th, C. Parsons (McLaren M8E-Chevrolet 8-litre), 2 laps in arrears,
6th, M. Minter (Porsche 917 4.5-litre), 2 laps in arrears.

Fastest lap: D. Hulme, 1 min 34.33 sec (125.94 mph).

CANADIAN-AMERICAN CHALLENGE CUP

	Points
1st, P. Revson	142
2nd, D. Hulme	132
3rd, J. Stewart	76
4th, J. Siffert*	68
5th, L. Motschenbacher	52
6th, M. Minter	37
7th, T. Adamowicz	34
8th, C. Parsons	30
9th, V. Elford	25
10th, H. Kazato	19

* Deceased.

14 Indianapolis 500 Miles Race

Indianapolis Speedway — 29th May, 1971

Circuit length: 2.5 miles

Race length: 500 miles (200 laps)

At the 1971 race the thirty-three qualifying cars consisted of six Eagles, four McLarens (three of them brand-new cars), three Kuzmas, two each of Colt, Coyote, Brabham, Gerhardt, King, Lola, McNamara, Mongoose and Vollstedt and one each of Hawk and Scorpion. Eighteen cars were fitted with Meyer-Drake-Offenhauser turbo-charged engines and fifteen with Ford turbo-charged engines. Fastest qualifier was Peter Revson with his new McLaren who lapped in 178.696 mph and he was joined on the front row of the grid by Mark Donohue, also with a McLaren (177.087 mph) and Bobbie Unser with an Eagle (175.816 mph). An odd aspect of the race was that the pace car crashed after pulling off the track and the driver sustained very serious injuries. The race was won by Al Unser for the second year in succession.

Results:

1st, A. Unser (Colt-Ford), 3 hours 10 min 11.56 sec (157.735 mph),
2nd, P. Revson (McLaren M16-Offenhauser), 200 laps,
3rd, A. J. Foyt (Coyote-Ford), 200 laps,
4th, J. Malloy (Eagle-Offenhauser), 200 laps,
5th, W. Vukovitch (Gerhardt-Offenhauser), 200 laps,
6th, D. Allison (Coyote-Ford), 199 laps,
7th, B. Tinglestad (Brabham-Offenhauser), 198 laps,
8th, D. Zimmerman (Vollstedt-Offenhauser), 189 laps,
9th, R. McCluskey (Kuzma-Kenyon-Ford), 188 laps,
10th, G. Bettenhausen (Gerhardt-Offenhauser), 178 laps,
11th, L. Ruby (Laycock-Ford), 178 laps (gearbox failure),
12th, R. Unser (Eagle-Offenhauser), 164 laps (accident),

13th, M. Mosley (Eagle-Offenhauser), 159 laps (accident),
14th, D. Simon (Vollstedt-Ford), 151 laps (still running),
15th, G. Follmer (King-Offenhauser), 147 laps (broken piston),
16th, C. Yarborough (Mongoose-Ford), 140 laps (broken valve)
17th, D. Hulme (McLaren M16-Offenhauser), 137 laps (water leak),
18th, J. Rutherford (Eagle-Offenhauser), 128 laps (still running),
19th, J. Leonard (Colt-Ford), 123 laps (engine failure),
20th, D. Hobbs (Lola-Ford), 107 laps (engine failure),
21st, R. Muther (Hawk-Offenhauser), 85 laps (accident),
22nd, R. Harkey (Gerhardt-Offenhauser), 77 laps (transmission failure),
23rd, B. Warren (Eagle-Offenhauser), 76 laps (broken u-joint),
24th, W. Dallenbach (Kuzma-Kenyon-Offenhauser), 69 laps (valve failure),
25th, M. Donohue (McLaren M16-Offenhauser), 66 laps (transmission failure),
26th, A. Pollard (Scorpion-Ford), 45 laps (valve failure),
27th, S. Sessions (Lola-Ford), 43 laps (engine failure),
28th, L. Dickson (King-Offenhauser), 33 laps (engine failure),
29th, G. Johncock (McLaren M15-Offenhauser), 11 laps (accident),
30th, M. Andretti (McNamara-Ford), 11 laps (accident),
31st, S. Krisiloff (McNamara-Ford), 10 laps (engine failure),
32nd, M. Kenyon (Kuzma-Kenyon-Ford), 10 laps (accident),
33rd, G. Snider (Eagle-Ford), 6 laps (engine failure).

Pastest lap: M. Donohue, 51.44 sec (174.961 mph – record).
Previous lap record: L. Ruby (Gene White Company Special), 168.67 mph (set in 1968 race).
1970 winner: A. Unser (Colt-Ford), 155.75 mph.

15 Tasman Racing Results

Round 1 LEVIN INTERNATIONAL RACE 2nd January, 1971

Levin, New Zealand 63 laps (75 miles)

1st, G. McRae (McLaren M10B-Chevrolet 5-litre), 50 min 31.2 sec (87.90 mph),
2nd, N. Allen (McLaren M10B-Chevrolet 5-litre), 50 min 45.1 sec,
3rd, C. Amon (March 701-Cosworth 2.5-litre), 51 min 2.0 sec,
4th, D. Oxton (Lotus 70-Ford 5-litre), 51 min 10.4 sec,
5th, J. Cannon (McLaren M10B-Chevrolet 5-litre), 51 min 14.4 sec,
6th, T. Pilette (McLaren M10B-Chevrolet 5-litre), 1 lap in arrears.

Fastest lap: G. McRae, 44.0 sec (96.00 mph).

Round 2 NEW ZEALAND GRAND PRIX 9th January, 1971

Pukekohe, New Zealand 58 laps (101.5 miles)

1st, N. Allen (McLaren M10B-Chevrolet 5-litre), 56 min 27.0 sec (107.90 mph),
2nd, F. Matich (McLaren M10B-Holden 5-litre), 56 min 27.4 sec,
3rd, G. McRae (McLaren M10B-Chevrolet 5-litre), 56 min 34.7 sec,
4th, M. Eyerly (Surtees TS8-Chevrolet 5-litre), 56 min 59.7 sec,
5th, J. Cannon (McLaren M10B-Chevrolet 5-litre), 57 min 29.6 sec,
6th, G. Lawrence (Ferrari Dino 2.4-litre), 1 lap in arrears.

Fastest lap: F. Matich, 56.7 sec.

Round 3 LADY WIGRAM TROPHY RACE 16th January, 197

Christchurch, New Zealand 44 laps (101.2 miles)

1st, G. McRae (McLaren M10B-Chevrolet 5-litre), 57 min 51.8 sec (104.94 mph),
2nd, F. Matich (McLaren M10B-Holden 5-litre), 58 min 19.0 sec,
3rd, G. Lawrence (Ferrari Dino 2.4-litre), 1 lap in arrears,

4th, F. Gardner (Lola T192-Chevrolet 5-litre), 1 lap in arrears,
5th, C. Amon (March 701-Cosworth 2.5-litre), 1 lap in arrears,
6th, M. Guthrie (Lola T192-Chevrolet 5-litre), 2 laps in arrears.

Fastest lap: G. McRae, 1 min 17.3 sec.

Round 4 TERETONGA INTERNATIONAL RACE 24th January, 1971

Teretonga Park, New Zealand 62 laps (99 miles)

1st, N. Allen (McLaren M10B-Chevrolet 5-litre), 1 hour 0 min 57.4 sec (98.00 mph),
2nd, F. Matich (McLaren M10B-Holden 5-litre), 1 hour 1 min 17.4 sec,
3rd, T. Pilette (McLaren M10B-Chevrolet 5-litre), 1 hour 1 min 35.8 sec,
4th, K. Bartlett (Mildren-Chevrolet 5-litre), 1 hour 1 min 58.8 sec,
5th, M. Guthrie (Lola T192-Chevrolet 5-litre), 2 laps in arrears,
6th, L. Goeghegan (Lotus 69-Waggott 2-litre), 3 laps in arrears

Fastest lap: N. Allen, 57.1 sec (100.45 mph).

Round 5 ROTHMANS INTERNATIONAL 100 RACE 14th February, 1971

Warwick Farm, Australia 45 laps (101.25 miles)

1st, F. Gardner (Lola T192-Chevrolet 5-litre), 1 hour 5 min 18.1 sec (93.10 mph),
2nd, C. Amon (Lotus 70-Ford 5-litre), 1 hour 5 min 28.8 sec,
3rd, K. Bartlett (Mildren-Chevrolet 5-litre), 1 hour 6 min 3.8 sec,
4th, N. Allen (McLaren M10B-Chevrolet 5-litre), 1 hour 6 min 14.4 sec,
5th, T. Pilette (McLaren M10B-Chevrolet 5-litre,) 1 hour 6 min 24.8 sec,
6th, R. Muir (Mildren-Waggott 2-litre), 1 hour 6 min 26.6 sec.

Fastest lap: F. Gardner, 1 min 25.1 sec (95.10 mph).

Round 6 GOLDEN 100 RACE 21st February, 1971

Sandown Park, Melbourne, Australia 56 laps (109 miles)

1st, G. McRae (McLaren M10B-Chevrolet 5-litre), 1 hour 0 min 29.7 sec (107.11 mph),
2nd, T. Pilette (McLaren M10B-Chevrolet 5-litre), 1 hour 0 min 32.9 sec,

3rd, F. Matich (McLaren M10B-Holden 5-litre), 1 hour 0 min 33.4 sec,
4th, C. Amon (Lotus 70-Ford 5-litre), 1 lap in arrears,
5th, K. Holland (McLaren M10B-Chevrolet 5-litre), 1 lap in arrears,
6th, G. Lawrence (Ferrari Dino 2.4-litre), 1 lap in arrears.

Fastest lap: N. Allen (McLaren M10B-Chevrolet 5-litre), 63.3 sec (109.65 mph).

Round 7 ROTHMANS INTERNATIONAL 100 RACE 28th February, 1971

Surfers' Paradise, Brisbane 50 laps (100 miles)

1st, F. Matich (McLaren M10B-Holden 5-litre), 57 min 55.5 sec (103.59 mph),
2nd, F. Gardner (Lola T192-Chevrolet 5-litre), 58 min 5.1 sec,
3rd, G. McRae (McLaren M10B-Chevrolet 5-litre), 59 min 3.3 sec,
4th, G. Lawrence (Ferrari Dino 2.4-litre), 1 lap in arrears,
5th, R. Muir (Mildren-Waggot 2-litre), 1 lap in arrears,
6th, M. Guthrie (Lola T192-Chevrolet 5-litre), 1 lap in arrears.

TASMAN CHAMPIONSHIP

Points are awarded on the basis of 9 6, 4, 3, 2 and 1 point for the first six places (the same as for the Formula 1 Drivers' Championship).

	Points
1st, G. McRae	35
2nd, F. Matich	31
3rd, N. Allen	27
4th, F. Gardner	18
5th, C. Amon	15
6th, T. Pilette	13